Working Together for Children

Also available from Continuum

Good Practice in the Early Years, Janet Kay
Learning Through Play, Jacqueline Duncan and Madelaine Lockwood
Observing Children and Young People, Carole Sharman, Wendy Cross and Diana Vennis
Protecting Children, Janet Kay
Psychology and the Teacher, Denis Child
Teaching 3–8, Mark O'Hara

Working Together for Children

A Critical Introduction to Multi-Agency Working

Gary Walker

continuum

Continuum International Publishing Group

The Tower Building	80 Maiden Lane, Suite 704
11 York Road	New York
London SE1 7NX	NY 10038

www.continuumbooks.com

© Gary Walker 2008

British Library Cataloguing-in-Publication Data
A catalogue record for this book is available from the British Library.

ISBN: 978-0-8264-9817-5 (paperback)

Library of Congress Cataloging-in-Publication Data
Walker, Gary (Gary D.)
Working together for children : a critical introduction to
multi-agency working / Gary Walker.
    p. cm.
Includes bibliographical references.

ISBN-13: 978-0-8264-9817-5 (pbk.)
ISBN-10: 0-8264-9817-5 (pbk.)

1. Child welfare–England–Handbooks, manuals, etc. 2. Family services–England–
Handbooks, manuals, etc. 3. Interagency coordination–England–Handbooks, manuals, etc.
4. Social service–Teamwork–England–Handbooks, manuals, etc. I. Title.

HV751.E5W35 2008
362.7—dc22

                          2008012052

Typeset by Newgen Imaging Systems Pvt Ltd, Chennai, India
Printed and bound in Great Britain by Cromwell Press, Wiltshire

This book is dedicated to my wife, Julie, and two children Josh and Rosie, for their support and understanding. They have demonstrated nothing but the best features of 'working together'. Mention should also go to our dog, Maddie, who kept my feet warm during the long hours at the computer.

Contents

Acknowledgements

Thanks are due to the following: to Jo Allcock and Kirsty Schaper from Continuum, for their faith in me, and their very helpful suggestions and advice; to Leeds Metropolitan University who enabled me to weave the writing of the book into my regular work; to my colleagues in the Childhood and Early Years team for their unstinting encouragement; and to my students for discussing and challenging ideas. I am grateful to the Office of Public Sector Information and to Hodder & Stoughton Publishers for permission to use material. Needless to say, I take full responsibility for the content of the book, and – while I have tried to produce a scholarly work – for any errors contained within it.

Introduction

Parameters of the book

There is an old adage that everyone has at least one good book in them. Looking back at my career, it seems inevitable that my offering would cover the subject of multi-agency work for children: I have worked, for children aged from birth to 17, within the private and voluntary sectors, a local authority special school, local authority social services departments, health authority settings and a local education authority. These experiences have provided me with a breadth and depth of understanding which informs, and hopefully enriches, this book. Whether the book is judged to be 'good' is the prerogative of others; I have tried to produce a useful and honest account which aims to increase the readers' understanding of the complexities of multi-agency work.

Multi-agency working, for the intended benefit of children of families, is of course not new. Teams of professionals from a variety of agencies and backgrounds have long been engaged in assessing, supporting and protecting children in a variety of circumstances. This includes children 'in need' as defined, in England and Wales, by Section 17 of the Children Act 1989, who may be disabled or who may require services in order to achieve or maintain a reasonable standard of health or development. It also includes children in need of protection from harm. What is relatively new is the emphasis, particularly in the Department for Education and Skills' publication *Every Child Matters* (DfES, 2003) which applies to England, on the prime importance of multi-agency working with families. (The Department for Education and Skills was renamed the Department for Children, Schools and Families in late 2007.) Some of the key elements of *Every Child Matters* are:

- Professionals will be expected to work in multidisciplinary teams based in and around schools and children's centres. They will be expected to provide a rapid response to the concern of frontline teachers, childcare workers and others in universal services.
- Local authorities will be expected to work closely with public, private and voluntary organizations.
- In the longer term, services will become integrated under a Director of Children's Services in each area, as part of Children's Trusts.
- To reflect this new practice, inspections of services will be integrated to judge how well services work together for the benefit of children in a particular area.

In order to facilitate this, Children's Trusts will be expected to provide joint training for relevant staff in order to ensure consistency of approach, and to learn about each other's roles and responsibilities. However, this major shift in practice – from an essentially 'silo' based way of working to a fully integrated model, may well prove to be more complex and problematic than envisaged. In order to operate effectively in the new arena of multi-agency integration, professionals need to understand this complexity, and the attendant issues.

The aim of this book, therefore, is to provide, in a single volume, factual, descriptive and analytical material on the systems and processes of multi-agency work with children and families as they exist and are developing. Readers should be able to get much relevant information about multi-agency work, and evaluation of it, from this single volume. The book is an introductory text, and as such is not a detailed review of research or available literature in the area of multi-agency work. I have had to make choices regarding the selection of material to include in the book, for which I take full responsibility. For instance, multi-agency work associated with supporting children with Special Educational Needs (SEN) within an educational setting is not covered in any detail.

I have used the term 'children' to include all children and young people up to the age of 18, except where I am specifically referring to older children, when the term 'young people' is used. I acknowledge that the experiences of 'children' and 'young people' are qualitatively different; however, in order to avoid constant repetition of the clumsy phrase 'children and young people' I have generally used 'children' to refer to both.

Although (for the sake of keeping the book to a manageable size) the focus is on multi-agency systems in England, where appropriate, references are made to differences in approach in the other three countries of the United Kingdom. Detailed discussion of these is not possible but readers are given references to follow up if they wish. To this end, the volume edited by Clark and Waller (2007) compares the policies and practices in education and care across the United Kingdom and is therefore useful and relevant to a consideration of multi-agency practice. Furthermore, the general principles and critical issues that arise out of a focus on England are applicable to a much wider, even an international, setting.

Outline of the book

The book is divided into three parts. Part I – Frameworks and principles – concerns general issues related to multi-agency work. The aim here is to provide the reader with detailed information, and critique of, some key areas. Therefore, Chapter 1 begins by asking 'What is multi-agency work?' The history, and current definitions, of multi-agency work are discussed. This includes consideration of why multi-agency work is necessary. The chapter then considers in detail the aims and functions of the different agencies or job roles that might be involved in multi-agency work.

Chapter 2 then considers 'Frameworks for practice'. Within this, the key legislation and guidance documents will be examined. The chapter also considers issues around partnership, the barriers to effective multi-agency working, and moral and ethical issues that might arise in such work.

Chapter 3 examines 'Multi-agency assessment' in detail, explaining and critiquing the national guidance. This includes the Common Assessment Framework for children potentially or actually in need of support, as well as assessments where children may be at risk of significant harm. Effective assessment of children's needs lies at the heart of good multi-agency practice, and therefore full coverage of this is appropriate.

Part II of the book – Multi-agency work in specific contexts – focuses on five areas in detail, and forms the central practice-based planks of the volume. Hence, Chapter 4 discusses 'Safeguarding children' and offers an analysis of the current systems and processes, based around the role of social services, and social workers in particular, in engaging other professionals in protecting children.

Chapter 5 considers the role of the schools and early years settings in safeguarding children. Current systems and guidance are scrutinized. Of course, there are significant differences in the way schools might try to achieve the aim of protecting children compared to early years settings, and these are addressed. Nevertheless, many principles and approaches are similar across the two settings, and these are considered together.

Chapter 6 concerns multi-agency working as related to children in care. As a result of their experiences and potential isolation from support networks, these are among the most vulnerable children with whom professionals may work. Therefore a full understanding of the current systems and processes is necessary in order to maximize effectiveness of the services which aim to support these children.

Chapter 7 considers information sharing as it relates to multi-agency working. This is an area than can cause professionals confusion and uncertainty. Current legislation and guidance is discussed in an attempt to clarify some of the issues involved.

Chapter 8 examines issues in working with parents, especially in child protection cases. Parents should, of course, be considered a key player in multi-agency work, and there is much emphasis, in official guidance, on developing partnerships with parents. This chapter considers the practical implications of such an aspiration.

Part III of the book – Looking to the future – is concerned chiefly with the *Every Child Matters* agenda in England which forms the basis of Chapter 9. Reference is made to similar programmes in Wales, Scotland and Northern Ireland. This vision for future working with children and families is considered and evaluated, and resulting issues and tensions discussed.

The conclusion to the book draws together key emerging themes and learning points from across the book, as a way of summarizing the many commonalities, complexities and contradictions that surface when different agencies work together for children.

Learning tools used in the book

Reflection on practice will be a theme running throughout the book. To assist readers with this, there are two types of boxes used to contain material in addition to the main body of the text. The first are information boxes, giving further factual details of particular areas related to multi-agency work. These are marked with the following symbol:

The second type of box is those containing reflective exercises. These boxes are marked with the following symbol:

These have fictitious case studies, vignettes or statements. Where details of children are given, an ethnic origin is always mentioned. This is to highlight the importance of noting and considering any additional needs which might arise from the ethnic background of the child; if ethnicity was not cited, readers may make assumptions about this. Each case study or vignette is followed by questions for readers to consider. These questions are designed to stimulate reflection on the issues raised in the text, and to highlight the complexity of multi-agency work. The Appendix of the book provides suggestions for readers to consider in trying to answer the questions. While they cannot always provide definitive answers, these suggestions will hopefully stimulate further thinking and understanding of some of the issues associated with multi-agency work.

Part One
FRAMEWORKS AND PRINCIPLES

What is multi-agency work?   1

Chapter Outline

Introduction

This chapter will begin by tracking the history of multi-agency work from medieval times to the present day, using key legislation and social changes as focal points. Following this, full consideration will be given to what multi-agency working actually is, and why it is considered important to the achievement of good outcomes for families. Three models of multi-agency work will then be discussed. Finally, the functions of some of the key agencies involved in multi-agency work are described, as are the generic multi-agency responsibilities of all services engaged in such work.

The history of multi-agency work

The historical context of multi-agency work with children and families needs to be fully understood in order to appreciate how the development of this approach impinges on current philosophy and practice. Accordingly, the very beginnings of structured work with families can be traced back to medieval times. Webb and Webb (1963) give a detailed and informative account of the history of relief for the poor in England and Wales, while Byrne and Padfield (1985) provide an illuminating summary of the sequence and context of events from before the fourteenth century. This history is complex and convoluted, and therefore a summary will suffice here in order to give an overview of the key factors at play. Limited space prevents a full exploration of the differences in this history between the four countries of the United Kingdom, but short references are made to these where appropriate.

The first point to be made is that it is impossible to separate structured work with families from poverty. If suffering did not exist, it would be unnecessary for others to feel the need to relieve it in some way. In early medieval times, assistance with, and relief from, poverty was provided by the church, the parish itself or from relatives. The first Poor Law legislation of 1388 applied to England and Wales, and was made in response to a particular social situation that had arisen as a result of a high death rate following the Black Death plague epidemic in the 1340s. Adult male labour was in short supply and as a result wages rose steeply. Initial legislation aimed at forcing all able-bodied men to work and keep wages at their old levels had mixed success, as many labourers simply moved around looking to settle in an area where the wages were still high and where the labour laws were not strictly enforced.

 Information: The first Poor Law

The legislation of 1388 is titled the Statute of Cambridge and only later came to be regarded as the first Poor Law. This introduced restrictions on the movements of all labourers and beggars. Local officials – Justices of the Peace – were responsible for overseeing the relief from poverty of what were termed the 'impotent poor' in their own parish. This included those who were unable to work due to their age or infirmity.

A lack of enforcement, or variation in enforcement between parishes, limited the impact of this new legislation. Further legislation during the reign of Queen Elizabeth I, in 1597 and 1601 respectively, unified these varied local practices and strengthened the role of the 'Overseers of the Poor' as Justices of the Peace came to be called. Hence this new legislation had the effect of forcing each parish to look after its own poor, and of penalizing able-bodied beggars. The Overseers of the Poor administered the collection of funds from local inhabitants, first as voluntary contributions – alms – and then as compulsory rates. The assumption was that if someone was physically capable of working, there was no excuse for them not working, and therefore no free help or support was available. This did not mean that beggars and other able-bodied paupers had to pay cash for support. What it meant was that relief was separated into two kinds: outdoor relief and indoor relief. Outdoor relief was typically given to able-bodied paupers in the form of food, clothing or even money, but only in return for work. The term 'outdoor' refers to the fact that these people were effectively supported in the community. Indoor relief involved bringing those unable to work or support themselves – the 'impotent poor' into what were called almshouses. Here we see the first real structured work with families, including children, based around a set of principles. Scotland launched its own Poor Law system in 1579 and similar developments to that in England and Wales followed until the middle of the nineteenth century (Mitchison, 2000). The Poor Laws were not extended to Ireland until 1838, and were even harsher than in England and Wales (O'Connor, 1993).

The situation described above continued in England and Wales, with some additions and developments, until the nineteenth century. However the system was still parish based, with variations between parishes being evident. A new crisis then emerged. Between 1784 and 1818 the cost of funding the relief of the poor rose fourfold and the existing system came to be seen as unworkable. Furthermore, there was concern that landowners were shouldering much of this financial burden. The poor themselves were also discontented and in some areas there were serious protests and even rioting. Therefore, in 1832 the British government decided to appoint a Royal Commission to review the whole poor relief system. As a result of this, the Poor Law Amendment Act of 1834 was introduced. This was termed the New Poor Law, and it had a quite dramatic effect. It introduced a standardized and rigorously enforced system across the country. The central structure of this Act was the workhouse. Under the New Poor Law outdoor relief was restricted to the aged, sick or disabled. Able-bodied individuals and their family would only be supported within the workhouse. Furthermore, conditions within the workhouses were deliberately worse than those found outside in order to deter entry and to induce the poor to work.

 Information: The New Poor Law

A central part of the Poor Law Amendment Act of 1834 or New Poor Law as it came to be known, was the concept of 'lesser eligibility' – in other words lower standards of living within the workhouse which made it less eligible to go inside the workhouse than stay on the outside and tend for oneself. The underlying notion of the Act was that of fostering independence and self reliance, and of reinforcing the inherent value of work. It cemented the notion of the deserving versus the non-deserving poor, where the deserving poor (the aged, sick or disabled) were seen as being unable to help the fact that they could not work. The non-deserving poor, on the other hand, were those able-bodied people not in work, and the assumption was they could work, and that they were lazy for not so doing.

Unsurprisingly, many despised the New Poor Law because it divided families in the workhouse (men and women were separated). Furthermore it humiliated those inside as idle, and they lost the right to vote (until 1918). The psychological effect of this legislation was huge as poverty came to be seen as the fault of the individual, the poor were viewed as 'less eligible' people, and poverty was to be relieved rather than prevented. One can see remnants of this mindset in current United Kingdom social policy, particularly as related to welfare benefits, where subsistence payments are kept deliberately low in order to induce claimants to find work. Take Jobseeker's Allowance as an example. In 2007, the rate of payment for this benefit was £59.15 per week for a single adult over the age of 25. The median gross weekly pay for full-time employees in the United Kingdom in April 2007 was £457 (Daniels, 2007). Clearly, some claimants of Jobseeker's Allowance may be eligible for further benefits, but without entering into a complex debate on the benefits system, the central point is borne out – generally speaking benefit levels reflect the view that living on benefits should be at least uncomfortable in order to induce those claiming them to find work.

Continuing with the theme of linking this history to modern practice, in order to avoid the worst consequences of the New Poor Law, many self-help organizations were set up to offer help and charity to those who needed it. These were very successful, and they remained independent of any government control or interference. Their number continued to grow, and in 1869 there were so many that the Charity Organization Society was set up to coordinate their work. This introduced

- systematic methods to help families
- individual, disciplined, organized and consistent casework
- record keeping of work with families
- criteria on which decisions about entitlement were made
- monitoring of progress of the work.

The first national group of workers that could be linked to modern day social workers were probation workers, which were established in the late 1800s. Their role was to 'advise, assist and befriend' first time young offenders. It is interesting to note that the precise language here is still present in the Children Act 1989, Section 35 dealing with Supervision Orders, which states that while a supervision order is in force it shall be the duty of the supervisor to advise, assist and befriend the supervised child deemed to be at risk of significant harm.

By 1895, medical social workers, called almoners, began to apply casework principles to medical patients, and the status of such professions grew. For the next 40 or so years, the idea emerged that 'social work' should be a benefit to all, not a charity to a targeted few. Therefore, the concept of individualism gave way to collectivism, and many liberal reforms were passed by Parliament. Despite this, social work continued mainly in probation and hospital settings, although there was some formal training available for social workers. At the same time, there continued the steady development of voluntary groups, and some of the giants still with us today emerged, including the National Society for the Prevention of Cruelty to Children (NSPCC), and Dr Barnardo's, or Barnardo's as it is now called.

The Second World War, as well as resulting in the obvious personal and social horrors, revealed the weaknesses in social provision that still existed. The process of evacuation of children in particular showed city dwellers to be poor, dirty, and ill-provided; many soldiers were undernourished and undereducated, and there was a shortage of housing due to bombing.

After the War, therefore, there was a real impetus to improve the state of the nation, and the Welfare State was born. This covered the following areas:

- Social Security (benefits)
- Health Services
- Education
- Housing
- Personal Social Services for
  - physically disabled people
  - elderly people
  - mentally ill people
  - deprived children.

Social Workers were seen as valuable workers to help those in distress or shock after the war, because they could link the support available to those who needed it. Here we see the real cementing of a basic concept of multi-agency working which had begun in the late nineteenth century – a worker from one agency or group contacting another service or group in order to invoke effective support for families.

By the 1950s, most local authorities had social workers. In 1968, the Seebohm Report recommended that the separate groups of social workers that existed should become generic (general). This would allow social workers to bring a more comprehensive approach to family problems. This in turn led to the Local Authority Social Services Act 1970, which created social service departments for children and adults under a single director, and ultimately led to the birth of the modern social work 'profession'. And of course, because social workers practiced generically, they could bring to bear their skill and expertise in linking with other agencies in order to support families.

In January 1973, a 7-year-old girl named Maria Colwell was killed by her stepfather in Brighton, England, despite there having been intervention in the family from social services. The inquiry and moral panic that followed led to a number of policy changes in England (Parton, 1985). Chief among these was an emphasis on multi-agency teamwork, manifested by the establishment of the modern system for responding to concerns about children, still in force largely unaltered today. Hence, multi-agency case conferences (now called Initial Child Protection Conferences) were introduced along with formal reviews (now known as Child Protection Review Conferences) as key decision-making apparatus. The intention was to ensure childcare planning was informed by accurate information, clear decision making, informed medical and legal advice, and authoritative intervention (ibid).

In spite of this, there continued to be deaths of children with whom a variety of agencies were involved, and about whom serious concerns had been raised. These include, and this list is not exhaustive, Jasmine Beckford (1984), Tyra Henry (1984), Heidi Koseda (1984), Kimberley Carlile (1986), Doreen Mason (1987), Leanne White (1992), Rikki Neave (1994), Chelsea Brown (1999), Victoria Climbié (2000), Lauren Wright (2000), Ainlee Labonte (2002).

The findings of the subsequent inquiries into these deaths led to further minor changes to the child protection system or guidance being issued from central government (the origins and appearance of the landmark piece of legislation – the Children Act 1989 – will be discussed in Chapter 2). However, what is interesting about this tragic history is that only selected cases go on to lead to major changes in child protection policy or legislation. It is therefore tempting to argue that these child deaths act as a convenient 'hook' upon which the government hangs an ideological imperative which they were already considering implementing. Hence, the inquiry into the death of Victoria Climbié chaired by Lord Laming (2003) led ultimately to arguably the most radical programme of change in children's services yet seen – the *Every Child Matters* agenda (DfES, 2003). This will be discussed in detail in Chapter 9. What is worth noting here, however, is that this wholesale change not only to how child protection is conceptualized, but also to how children and families are supported more generally, was implemented despite Lord Laming stating in his inquiry report that 'the legislative framework for protecting children is basically sound' (Laming, 2003, p. 6). Instead, it seems, the government chose to emphasize another of Laming's comments, indeed on the same page, that it 'is not possible to separate the protection of children from wider support to families' (ibid.).

(?) Reflections: Child death trends

It is worth reflecting upon the fact that the number of child deaths at the hands of their parents or carers (with or without multi-agency support) has remained more or less constant over a number of years, in spite of a series of changes to systems and procedures. Creighton and Tissier (2003) report that since 1975 child homicides has averaged out at seventy-nine a year – one to two children per week.

1. What reasons can you think of for the number of child deaths at the hands of parents or carers being constant in spite of a series of improvements to the child surveillance and child protection system?

One of the key changes to most social work departments since the 1970s is that they have now moved away from a generic approach. Instead front-line services are arranged into different areas – one for adults, one for children, and within these perhaps even more specialist teams dealing with disability, referral and assessment of families, or longer term support. Nevertheless, the rationale and impetus for multi-agency working remains strong. Practitioners from all agencies who work with children and families are expected to cooperate to achieve better outcomes for their clients. The extent to which these workers always share a common understanding of what constitutes 'better outcomes' will form part of the discussion in future chapters of this book.

What is multi-agency work?

There are various definitions of multi-agency work available. Of these, two have been chosen. The first is that multi-agency work is 'a range of different services which have some overlapping or shared interests and objectives, brought together to work collaboratively towards some common purposes' (Wigfall and Moss, 2001, p. 71). The second, containing a striking image, is that multi-agency work is about 'Bringing various professions together to understand a particular problem or experience . . . In this sense they afford different perspectives on issues at hand, just as one sees different facets of a crystal by turning it' (Clark, 1993, p. 220).

What these have in common is the idea of different workers from different agencies joining together with a shared aim of understanding, and then trying to solve or alleviate a problem. It is important to distinguish multi-agency work from either multidisciplinary or multi-professional work. Multi-agency work necessarily involves the collaboration of workers from different agencies, say Social Services, Health and Education. On the other hand, multidisciplinary or multi-professional work (the two terms are used interchangeably here) *may* involve the collaboration of workers from different agencies, but does not necessarily do so. For instance, as Wilson and Pirrie (2000) point out, the working relationship, in a school, between a nursery teacher, nursery nurse, learning support assistant and classroom assistant would be multidisciplinary – they are from different disciplines, but are all housed within the single agency of education; indeed they all work in the same school. Another example may include the collaboration of a General Practitioner, Health Visitor and a hospital Consultant – they represent different professionals but within the single agency of Health.

There is a further distinction to be made – that between inter-agency and multi-agency work. Wilson and Pirrie (2000) engage in a helpful discussion about the terminology here (actually in relation to multidisciplinary work but the issues are the same) and argue that the choice of prefix can be determined by three factors – the number of workers involved, the territory involved, and the extent to which new ways of working are created. Thus inter-agency work may only involve two professionals from different agencies while multi-agency work involves three or more. Furthermore, this work, if it is to be fully multi-agency in nature, would have to involve the workers entering into each other's territory or space (physically as well as culturally) and then creating or reproducing together a new and common understanding or pattern of working. Interestingly, however, the latest version of the national guidance for England on *Working Together to Safeguard Children* (DfES, 2006i) seems to use the two prefixes interchangeably, although also uses both terms in the same sentence implying some difference without expanding on what this might be. For instance, in a passage related to training the document states: 'Training for inter and multi-agency work means training which will equip people to work effectively with those from other agencies to safeguard and promote the welfare of children' (ibid., p. 65).

For the purposes of this book, the term multi-agency work is going to be used throughout, to mean at least two workers from different agencies who carry out essentially different roles and who are engaged in joint work to address the needs of children.

Why multi-agency work?

This may seem like a strange question to ask, but it is worth reflecting in some detail on the rationale for, and potential benefits of, multi-agency work. The starting point is that multi-agency work is a statutory requirement upon all agencies and all professionals who work within them. Section 17 of the Children Act 1989 confers a duty on the whole local authority to safeguard and promote the welfare of children within their area who are in need. Section 22(3) of the same Act places a duty on the local authority to safeguard and promote the welfare of children within their area who are in care. Clearly the local authority includes a number of agencies, and therefore implicit in this duty is the need for them to work together to achieve this aim. There is, however, a more direct duty placed upon agencies in Section 27 of the Children Act 1989. Under the terms of this section, if approached, agencies must respond positively to requests for help from another agency, as long as the request is in keeping with their role.

(?) Reflections: Case study – Amy

A social worker contacts a primary school because they are undertaking a full assessment of Amy, a white British girl aged 6. Appropriate parental consent has been gained. They ask the school to provide the following information:

The child's educational progress.
The child's social functioning in school (friendships, relationships with peers, staff etc.).
The school's perceptions of the child – parent relationship, based on what the school have observed of this.
The family's financial circumstances – household income and outgoings, any debts they may have etc.

1 Based on Section 27 of the Children Act 1989, which of the assessment elements do you think the school is obliged to provide?
2 Which do you think they would have a right to question or refuse to do?
3 If the school does refuse to carry out any of these requests, how might they go about doing this without harming the relationship with the social worker?

This requirement to respond to requests for help has been strengthened by the introduction of the Children Act 2004. Section 10 states that agencies must make arrangements to promote cooperation between one another to improve the well-being of children. This is a clear addition to the requirements of Section 27 of the Children Act 1989. Now, instead of, as it were, waiting around to be asked to help, agencies must proactively work with each other to see how they can forge links and create systems of working that actively and demonstrably support children and families. This is a much more robust requirement – for agencies to be actively engaged with each other for the benefit of families.

Of course, one would hope that workers do not engage in multi-agency work simply because they are told they must do so. It is much more desirable for them to see and understand the potential benefits to the children and families of so doing. There are compelling reasons related to good practice as to why professionals should engage in multi-agency work. These can be summarized as follows:

- To coordinate the work of those involved. For instance, if a social worker and health visitor are both involved in supporting a parent with a young child, coordination may ensure that they visit the family on alternate weeks and do not, say, both arrive at the house at the same time (unless by arrangement).
- Multi-agency work can lead to sharing of resources. A social worker may plan to engage in some direct work with a child as part of an assessment, and has the time and other materials necessary, but not an appropriate venue. The child's school may offer the use of a room within school to carry out this work.
- Multi-agency work can lead to joint funding of projects. Under the *Every Child Matters* vision, this would become a requirement. However, creative and flexible responses to complex circumstances can currently sometimes be solved by a number of different agencies offering funding.
- Multi-agency work should lead to better outcomes for children, as their holistic needs are addressed. If there are several agencies involved, the child's educational, health, and social care needs (to name just three key areas) should be properly assessed and met.

Models of multi-agency work

Three broad models of multi-agency work have been identified within a document published by the Department for Education and Skills, which was renamed the Department for Children, Schools and Families in late 2007 (DfES, 2006f). This document sets out a description of each model, together with a list of possible benefits and challenges. Each model has an increasing level of integration. They are reproduced here with minimal changes to the original.

Multi-agency panel

The key feature of a multi-agency panel is that practitioners remain employed by their home agencies, agreeing to meet as a panel on a regular basis to discuss children who would benefit from multi-agency input.

Key characteristics
- There is a good mix of agencies represented on the panel, for example, education, health, social care and youth.

- Panel members remain based in and employed by their home agencies. They continue to 'identify' as members of these agencies, rather than as workers in a multi-agency initiative.
- Practitioners are likely to focus on individual support for the child or family, though some may undertake group or whole settings work.
- They are likely to carry out joint assessment and information sharing. Some practitioners may continue to use their home agency systems.

Key benefits and opportunities

- No recruitment is necessary, as practitioners remain employed by their home agency.
- Practitioners remain fully involved in what is happening in their home agency, and have access to its training and development opportunities.
- Practitioners have the opportunity to work together regularly and get experience of different working styles and remits.
- Where panels work effectively, structures and processes are in place to allocate a lead professional role, giving them the authority to carry out their role, and share information as appropriate.
- There is no need to find a permanent base or infrastructure.

Key challenges

- A lack of frequent contact can make it hard to develop good partnership working which is focused on outcomes for the child rather than the contribution of individual agencies.
- There may be a tendency for representatives to identify with their home agency rather than their role with the multi-agency panel.
- Panel members may not be given enough time to carry out their casework responsibilities with the panel, particularly if these are in addition to statutory or other duties carried out in the home agency.
- Case planning meetings can take up a significant amount of time.

Multi-agency team

The key feature of a multi-agency team is that practitioners are recruited into it (temporarily or permanently), making it a more formal arrangement than a multi-agency panel. Practitioners share a sense of team identity and are generally line managed by a team leader, though they may maintain links with their home agencies through supervision and training.

Key characteristics

- There is a dedicated team leader.
- There can be a good mix of staff from different agencies, including education, health, social care, youth justice and youth work.
- The people who work in the team are more likely to think of themselves as team members.
- The team can engage in work at a range of levels – not just with individual children, but also small-group, family and whole-school work.
- The team is likely to share a base, though some staff may continue to work from their home agencies.
- There are regular team meetings to discuss case working as well as administrative issues.

Key benefits and opportunities

- There is the opportunity to develop a good sense of team identity.
- Co-working is at the heart of the team's approach, which should allow for the sharing of skills and knowledge.
- Communication should be straightforward.
- Joint training should be easy to facilitate.
- There are opportunities to carry out preventive and early intervention work in whole-school and early years settings, as well as small-group and individual casework.

Key challenges

- Recruitment may be time-consuming or problematic.
- Time and resource needs to be set aside for team building and development.
- Where teams are not based together, this can present challenges for team working and communication.
- Good relationships with schools and other providers are vital to ensure success of the work of the team.
- There is a need to set aside sufficient time for meetings and other team contact time.

Integrated service

The key feature of an integrated service is that it acts as a service hub for the community by bringing together a range of services, usually under one roof, whose practitioners then work in a multi-agency way to deliver integrated support to children and families.

Key characteristics

- It is likely to be made up of a range of services that share a common location and a common philosophy, vision and agreed principles for working with children and families.
- It is a visible 'service hub' for the community, with a perception by users of cohesive and comprehensive services.
- It is usually delivered from a school or early years setting.
- There is a commitment by partner providers to fund and facilitate integrated services.
- Staff work in a coordinated way to address the needs of children and families using the service. This is likely to include some degree of joint training and joint working.
- The services on offer may include:
  - o access to childcare and education
  - o specialist advice and guidance to children and families on a range of matters
  - o outreach support to local families.

Key benefits and opportunities

- There is an opportunity to address a full range of issues for children in a non-stigmatizing universal setting.
- There could then be knock-on benefits for educational standards.
- There is greater co-working and cross-fertilization of skills between agencies.
- There are opportunities for joint training.

- A shared base enhances communication between the different services.
- Members are still linked in to what is going on in their home agency.
- Members are likely to have access to training and personal development in their home agency.

Key challenges

- This model requires fresh thinking around the concept of the school or early years setting and their purpose in the community.
- There is a question of how to bring a range of partners and the whole school community on board through 'collaborative leadership'.
- Developing a sense of joint purpose so that practitioners identify more with the new service than their role in their home agency may be problematic.
- There may well be an issue of managing differences in pay and conditions for staff doing joint work at varying levels of pay.

It is clear from these descriptions where the preference of the Department for Children, Schools and Families lies. Although they do acknowledge some potential difficulties, the number and nature of benefits associated with the integrated service leaves little doubt that, as far as the Department for Children, Schools and Families is concerned, the integrated service is the superior model. Some of the claims, however, not just for this model, but for the others too, appear rather bold and unproven. Take two examples. First, in multi-agency teams, the claim is that 'practitioners share a sense of team identity'. Second, integrated services will apparently deliver 'knock-on benefits for educational standards'. Some of the underlying complexities, tensions and barriers to effective multi-agency work that might militate against these outcomes are mentioned only in passing, and even these are superseded by a series of claims as to the benefits of multi-agency working, in particular of the integrated services model. While it is incontrovertible that there are benefits to children and families of such as a way of working, the chapters that follow will explore in detail the intricate, labyrinthine and at times downright difficult nature of multi-agency work, which needs to be balanced against the advantages that flow from it.

Who might be involved in multi-agency work?

What follows is not an exhaustive list of every agency or professional that might work with a family. Included are some of the key and most common agencies, along with a description of their main responsibilities. This section is introductory, designed to present an overview of the agencies involved. Many of the issues and activities referred to here will be discussed in detail in later chapters. The key references for each subsection are placed besides each heading.

An important distinction needs to be made between universal and targeted services. Universal services are offered to every child or family, while targeted ones are only offered or delivered to a specific group of children or families who fulfil certain criteria. Furthermore, the order in which these services are presented does not represent or imply a hierarchy.

Education (DfEE, 2000; DfES, 2007c; DfES and QCA, 2004; Whitney, 1993)

Schools

Schools are a universal service, although some parents can choose not to send their children to school, as long as they provide efficient education for their children at home or elsewhere. The compulsory age for a child to start full-time education in England, Wales and Scotland is at the beginning of the school term after the child's fifth birthday. In Northern Ireland it is as low as 4, depending on the date on which the child was born. Children in all four countries are expected to receive education until the age of 16. For children below statutory school age, children's centres or other early years settings are available. The principal role of both schools and children's centres is to provide education and care by implementing the national curricula and guidance for all children, from birth to at least 16. Within schools, there can be a variety of job roles: teachers, teaching assistants, nursery nurses, lunch-time supervisors, caretakers and learning mentors. Learning mentors are non-teaching staff who provide a bridge across academic and pastoral support areas within schools with the aim of ensuring that pupils and students engage more effectively in learning and achieve appropriately (DfES, 2007d).

Education services

Within any local authority, there is likely to be a range of specialist education services. These are targeted services, which provide expert support, usually to teachers or directly to children within schools on a variety of matters to support particular groups of children. These could include children with physical disability, dyslexia, dyspraxia (impairment of movement), autistic spectrum disorder, hearing impairment and visual impairment. In addition, educational psychologists have a responsibility for assessing children who have been identified as possibly having Special Educational Needs, and then supporting the education of these children. The education welfare service has a responsibility for supporting the school attendance of pupils who are of statutory school age.

Children's social services (DfES, 2005b)

Social workers

The job role that is perhaps most closely associated with social services is that of the social worker. They provide a targeted service based on need. They might be organized in various ways, into teams with different specialities across local authorities. Nevertheless, they all have a responsibility to provide or at least coordinate the provision of, similar services as follows:

- Assessment for, and provision of, support services to children 'in need'.
- The protection of children where necessary.

Support services to children 'in need'

These are children who, broadly speaking, without the extra services may not achieve or maintain a reasonable standard of health or development. This is often referred to as family support work. This work is conducted with full agreement and consent of the parents or carers, and is carried out on an entirely voluntary footing – parents can cancel the support services at any time. If this happens, social services should make a decision as to whether the withdrawal of services may leave the child at risk of significant harm. If not, they could continue to encourage the parent or carer to accept support. If the child may be at risk of significant harm, they should then instigate formal child protection procedures. Work supporting children 'in need' could cover a variety of circumstances and subsequent support services:

- Respite packages for disabled children.
- Support, and coordination of support from other agencies, for children
  - who are experiencing or are at risk of experiencing low-level neglect or emotional harm, or other forms of harm which do not meet the threshold for formal child protection intervention. This could include the child being beyond the control of parents or carers.
  - who care for parents or carers who may be disabled or physically or mentally ill.
  - who have suffered the bereavement of a parent or significant person in their life.

Protection of children

This involves carrying out different levels of assessment, seeking court orders where necessary and, where children cannot safely stay at home, arranging for them to be brought into care, which may be a placement with a relative or foster carer, or within a residential unit. Once children are in care, social services then have a responsibility to lead the ongoing oversight of their welfare, although as we have already seen, the whole local authority has a duty under Section 22(3) of the Children Act 1989 to safeguard and promote the welfare of children within their area who are in care. Work to protect children is clearly not something with which parents or carers can choose to engage. If parents refuse to cooperate with a social worker's enquiries, the social worker will need to make a decision as to whether the quality of the 'evidence' they possess at that point requires them to impose themselves on the family in order to make a fully informed opinion about the level of any actual or potential harm to a child. There are various legal routes that the social worker could embark upon at this point.

Family support workers

As well as social workers, most local authorities employ family support workers, who offer targeted support according to an assessed need. These workers are usually not qualified as social workers, and they can provide a variety of support services to children and families. Job titles may vary from Family Aide, to Outreach Worker or even Resource Worker, and their functions can be similarly varied. Some will work directly with parents of children 'in need', developing parenting skills. Others will work more directly with the child – befriending them and providing enriching experiences. Others, indeed, may do both. Usually, a qualified social worker will have overall responsibility for the work, and family support workers operate closely with them.

Health (Amicus/Community Practitioners' and Health Visitors' Association, 2006; David, 1996; DH and DfES, 2002; Haslam, 2006; NHS Careers, 2006; Royal College of Midwives, 2006)

Midwives

Midwives offer a universal service to every expectant mother. According to *The Concise Oxford Dictionary of Current English* (1976), the word 'midwife' means 'with woman'. This gives a good indication of the general role of the midwife – supporting expectant mothers (and fathers where appropriate) during pregnancy, throughout labour and the postnatal period up to about two weeks. As well as the obvious role of delivering babies, the midwife helps mothers to make informed choices about the services and options available to them, carries out clinical examinations, and provides health and parent education.

Health visitors

Health visitors offer a universal service to every family with children under the age of 5. They offer support and advice to parents on a range of issues such as feeding, sleeping, teething, immunization programmes, parenting classes, managing difficult behaviour and any special needs a child may have. Health visitors can provide information on local support groups and childcare options, or direct parents to more specialist help in response to such matters as serious illness, bereavement, domestic violence, family conflicts, disability or settling into a new culture if the family has have recently arrived from abroad.

School nurses

Offering another universal service to all children of statutory school age, school nurses fulfil such functions as health screening, implementing immunization programmes, providing health education, tackling bullying and promoting children's emotional well-being.

They also support teachers in delivering aspects of the curriculum, such as Personal, Social and Health Education, and Citizenship.

Taken together, midwives, health visitors and school nurses offer a universal health monitoring and support service to every child from before birth up to at least the age of 16.

General Practitioners

General Practitioners, or GPs as they are usually referred to, offer universal medical help as and when required to all children and families. They can prescribe medication to treat illnesses and conditions or refer children on for more specialist treatment as necessary. They are based in surgeries in the community but make home visits as required.

Mental health workers for adults

There are a variety of workers who can offer intervention to parents or carers as a targeted service to those who need it. This could include Psychiatrists, Community Psychiatric Nurses, Psychologists, Counsellors or other Therapists. Some may be employed by a voluntary organization. Broadly speaking they can be divided into two groups – those supporting adults with some form of mental illness (Psychiatrists and Community Psychiatric Nurses) and those helping adults with a psychological problem or a barrier to personal growth (Psychologists, Counsellors or Therapists).

Mental health workers for children

Similarly, there are a variety of workers who can offer intervention to children as a targeted service to those who need it. As with adults, they can be divided into two groups – those supporting children with some form of mental illness (Child Psychiatrists and Community Psychiatric Nurses) and those helping children with a psychological problem or a barrier to personal growth (Child Psychologists, Counsellors or Therapists, such as Play Therapists, Music Therapists or Art Therapists).

Police (Her Majesty's Inspectorate of Constabulary, 1999)

The police potentially respond to any situation, and therefore can be said to perform a universal duty. In general terms, their function is to protect the public, including of course, children. They gather evidence if a criminal offence is suspected to have occurred, and refer evidence to the Crown Prosecution Service. A decision is then made as to whether a case will be taken forward to court.

In relation to children, the work of the police is usually associated with child protection. The scope of this is broad and includes:

- investigating offences against children
- youth justice commitments (safeguarding the welfare and rights of child victims, witnesses and offenders)

- care issues (responding to emergency situations and assisting local authorities)
- working with schools on truancy, bullying and exclusions
- policing local concerns (including child pornography and abuse of children through the internet and child prostitution).

Police forces have dedicated child protection units (CPU) that carry out much, but not all, of the above work. For instance, young offenders are more likely to come into contact with mainstream uniformed police or those working within Youth Offending Teams. Uniformed community police officers often work closely with schools. Police working within child protection units are generally non-uniformed and specially trained officers, who nevertheless have full powers of arrest.

Youth Offending Teams (Youth Justice Board, 2006)

Youth Offending Teams (YOT) are made up of representatives from the police, probation service, social services, health, education, drugs and alcohol misuse and housing officers. They offer a targeted service to those young people who are, or may be, engaged in some level of offending behaviour. They respond to the needs of these young people in a comprehensive way. They identify the needs of each young person through a national assessment which highlights the specific problems that make the young person offend as well as measuring the risk they pose to others. This enables the YOT to identify suitable programmes to address the needs of the young person with the intention of preventing further offending.

The probation service (National Probation Service for England and Wales, 2005)

The aims of the probation service are to protect the public, reduce reoffending, punish offenders appropriately in the community, ensure that offenders are aware of the effects of crimes on victims and communities, and to rehabilitate offenders. Targeted at adult men and women who have committed offences, the probation service supervises offenders in the community who are subject to a court order, or who have been released on licence from prison. Probation staff also write pre-sentence reports, where requested by the court, for offenders who have been convicted in court. These describe the circumstances of the crime, factors involved and the risk the offender poses to the public. The court considers this report before passing sentence.

Housing (DfES, 2005c; ODPM, 2004)

Housing departments are responsible for making sure that the best use is made of all housing in their areas. Broadly, they offer a service targeted at those who do not privately own or rent housing. Since the 1988 Housing Act, housing associations have moved from complementing the work of local authorities to becoming the main providers of new social housing. Local authorities are responsible for allocating tenancies in their own housing stock and in a large proportion of housing association homes. The law requires authorities to allocate tenancies only to people included on a housing register (or waiting list) and in accordance with a published allocation scheme. It is open to authorities to decide who does or does not qualify. However, the allocation scheme must give priority to certain specified households, for example:

- those in unsatisfactory, insecure or temporary accommodation
- those who need housing on medical or welfare grounds, which includes pregnant women and families with dependent children or people
- low income or non-working households
- homeless people with a priority need for accommodation.

Where people applying for assistance have become homeless through no fault of their own, and fall within a 'priority need' group, the housing authority must help them to obtain suitable accommodation. The 'priority need' group includes families with dependent children, pregnant women, people who are vulnerable in some way (e.g. old age, disability or mental illness) and those made homeless by an emergency (such as flood or fire).

Some local authorities – those judged to be performing efficiently – have been allowed to set up Arms Length Management Organizations (ALMO). These are organizations which are effectively private companies, with the local authority as the sole shareholder, set up to manage and improve all or part of a local authority's housing stock. Under this arrangement, ownership of the housing stock remains with the local authority and the local authority remains the legal landlord. Tenants remain secure tenants of the authority and there is no change in their rights, such as the right to buy, right to repair and right to manage. However, as its name implies, an arms length body has a significant degree of independence from its local authority in the way in which it manages the housing stock. Those local authorities who choose to set up ALMOs are given a financial incentive.

The voluntary and community sector (DfES, 2005a)

Through the provision of targeted resources, the voluntary and community sector has an important role in shaping and delivering services to children and families. They do this by complementing statutory services. Their work could include:

- carrying out independent assessments of families
- providing direct support or funding to children and families.

The sector includes organizations that vary enormously in size, from small local groups staffed exclusively by volunteers, to large national charities that are household names.

However, all of them are independent of government and all are self-governing. Furthermore, their primary purpose is to promote social, environmental or cultural objectives in order to benefit society as a whole, or particular groups within it. They are not established for financial gain, and they reinvest any surpluses to further their primary objectives. The benefits of such organizations are that they can often provide localized services (which only families living in a certain area or postcode can access), and they can be seen by families as less stigmatizing than local authority social services.

Parents or carers (DH, 1995)

Although not part of a formal agency, of course, it is crucial not to neglect the role of parents or carers. The complex issues involved in working with parents will be discussed in full in Chapter 8. Generally, parents or carers should be encouraged to take part in the decision making of any agency or agencies at whatever level considered necessary. However, here it is appropriate to mention the term 'parental responsibility'. This is a legal term introduced in Section 2 of the Children Act 1989 and is defined as 'all the rights, duties, powers, responsibilities and authority' that go with being a parent. This means that parents who have parental responsibility have a duty to care for and protect their children, and that they have a right to make decisions regarding their children's future. It is worth noting that parents who have it never lose parental responsibility, even if their children are taken into care and made subject to a Care Order. In this circumstance, parents technically share parental responsibility with the local authority.

All parents do not, however, automatically have parental responsibility for their children. At the time of the inception of the Children Act 1989 and up to 1 December 2003, those who had parental responsibility were:

- all mothers
- fathers who were married to the mother at the time of the child's birth, or who later married the child's mother
- parents (female and male) who adopt a child or children.

This meant that, technically, unmarried fathers did not have parental responsibility, in the legal sense of the term. Through Section 111 of the Adoption and Children Act 2002, the law changed on 1 December 2003. This added a new group of parents to those above who have parental responsibility: fathers registered on the birth certificate as the father. Stepfathers do not have parental responsibility, unless they acquire it. They can do so by applying to the courts for a parental responsibility order to be made in their favour.

Unmarried fathers can therefore acquire parental responsibility by either:

- Reregistering the birth of a child born before December 2003, adding the father's details.
- Making a parental responsibility agreement with the child's mother, as long as she agrees with the father having parental responsibility. This agreement must be witnessed by the court to be valid.

- Applying to the court for a parental responsibility order. This is usually a last resort, where the father is unable to add their name to the birth certificate and the child's mother refuses to make an agreement with the father.

There is no connection between parental responsibility and child maintenance, or child support. All parents (either by birth or by adoption) have a duty to financially support their child, whether or not they have parental responsibility. Parental responsibility is also unconnected to any right a parent has over contact with the child, or regarding children living with a particular parent (Advice Services Alliance, 2005).

General functions of agencies in multi-agency work (DfES, 2006i)

So far, only the core functions of each agency or service have been described. However, they all share common responsibilities in terms of multi-agency working. These shared roles are many and varied, and might vary across individual agencies. They include:

- **To monitor children's development and welfare where necessary.** This would involve services gathering information to enable them to safeguard the child's welfare by responding appropriately in a multi-agency arena where necessary. This might include seeking parental consent to make a referral for support from another agency, or making a formal referral to social services regarding a child protection concern.
- **To share information with other agencies as required.** This might be reactive (responding to a request for appropriate information) or proactive (sharing information as necessary and, where needed, with appropriate consent having been gained).
- **To liaise with parents or carers.** Workers within services should discuss most initial concerns about individual children with parents or carers. There may well then be ongoing dialogue between parents and agency staff.
- **To refer to other agencies or services as required.** Professionals may gain parental consent to make a referral for support services for particular children. These support services could include health, education, social services or those provided by the voluntary sector. Services may also need to make child protection referrals to social services if they have some evidence the child may be at risk of significant harm. In these circumstances, workers within the referring agency have to make a judgement as to whether it is appropriate to either seek parental consent for the referral, or inform the parent that the referral is being made, or neither. If this last option is deemed appropriate, the agency will make the referral to social services without the parents' knowledge.
- **To take part in decision making.** Where there are a number agencies involved in a piece of work with a family, then all involved have a responsibility to take an active part in decision making. This could include telephone conversations as well as taking part in planning or other similar meetings.
- **To take part in assessments.** Where another agency is leading an assessment of a child, then services have a duty to take part appropriately in that assessment. This will usually involve the provision of information relating to the child that is relevant to the service's core functions. For example, for schools and early years settings, this would be likely to include the child's educational

performance and progress, but may also include observations of child–parent interactions at the beginning or end of the school day, or of the extent to which parents or carers engage with the school, including attendance at such events as parents' evenings.

- **To advocate for the child, parent or carer where necessary.** Clearly, workers within services often build positive and supportive relationships with parents or carers. They may therefore have a role in acting as an advocate for them. This could range from relatively simple actions such as allowing parents to use the office telephone to make lengthy calls to a benefits agency in an effort to resolve an issue of finance, to helping parents write a letter of complaint to another service (and perhaps using the office computer for this), to supporting a parent over a particular aspect of the child's care or welfare. For example, a school or early years setting, or health visitor, may feel it appropriate to support a parent in securing respite care from social services for a child with special needs, because the professional concerned believes that it is in the child's and the parents' best interests that this service is provided. A further element of the advocacy role is that services should be prepared to challenge one another where necessary, if they believe the best interests of the child may be compromised by a particular decision.

(?) Reflections: Case study – Jenny

Jenny is 11 years old, white British, and is in Year 6 at school. She has been in foster care for about a year, after sexual abuse by her father came to light. She is on a Care Order, and has contact with her mother about once every 2 months. She cannot live with her mother because her mother has not fully accepted the extent of the abuse, and continues to see Jenny's father.

Jenny has been maintained in her present primary school via social services transport. It is January. Social services have decided that they want Jenny to move to a new school at Easter to be nearer the foster placement, as the transport is proving too costly. The school is deeply unhappy with this, as Jenny is settled in school. Her Standard Assessment Task tests (SATs) are due to take place in May. Jenny would be moving to a high school near the foster placement in September.

1 How do you think school should respond to this scenario?
2 What arguments could the school bring to bear if they decided to challenge social services on this decision?
3 How can school act as an advocate for Jenny, and maintain a positive relationship with social services?

Conclusions

Modern multi-agency work, where a number of professionals from different service disciplines work for the common good of a child, has a long history which reaches back to the fourteenth century. The roles of the various agencies involved, and of key professionals within them, have been considered in this chapter. Multi-agency work is potentially full of complexity, tensions and pitfalls. It is an analysis of these matters that forms the main content of the chapters that follow. Multi-agency work takes place within a fundamentally important framework of legislation and guidance, and therefore it is to this that the book now turns.

2 Frameworks for practice

Introduction

In line with the book as a whole, this chapter will focus on legislation in England and Wales. The major legislation here that remains the key guiding force in work with children and families is the Children Act 1989, and this will be discussed in detail, in relation to multi-agency work, as will the accompanying guidance on *Working Together to Safeguard Children*. Scotland is covered by the Children (Scotland) Act 1995, while Northern Ireland has the Children (Northern Ireland) Order 1995. The Children Act 2004, again as it relates to multi-agency work, will also be examined. For these significant pieces of legislation and guidance, the political contexts and drivers will be discussed. In addition, consideration will be given to what factors might contribute to effective partnership, and what barriers might prevent successful partnerships from forming.

The Children Act 1989

The Children Act 1989 came into force in October 1991 (the date of the Act itself refers to the year in which it was written) and this date gives a significant clue as to the origins of the Act. Written almost exactly midway through the rule of the Conservative government, first under

Margaret Thatcher and later John Major, it very much reflects the values and philosophy of the 'New Right' as they came to be called.

 Information: The political context of the Children Act 1989

Burden (1998) explains that the political philosophy of the Conservative government during the 1980s, also known as Neo-Liberalism, perceived the welfare state as damaging the operation of the market system, and the state in general as capable of violating individual rights if it is not limited in its function.

The events leading to the development of the Children Act 1989 are worth charting in some detail. Pragnell (2002) argues that the government were already planning changes to legislation concerning children well before the precipitous events that may be interpreted as having led to the development of the Act. In the summer of 1987, a scandal emerged in Cleveland, an industrial area in the northeast of England. Pragnell (2002) provides a detailed account of the complex events surrounding the Cleveland incident. In the first half of 1987, the number of referrals to Cleveland Social Services for all forms of child abuse was 505 referrals compared with 288 referrals in the equivalent period in the previous year. The reason for this appeared to be chiefly that two consultant paediatricians at a Middlesbrough hospital were diagnosing child sexual abuse based on an unproven medical diagnosis termed the anal dilatation test. Furthermore, as a result of this, social workers began removing the children from their families on what was then termed Place of Safety Orders, often in unannounced 'raids' on the family home where children were literally taken from their beds and placed in care.

A real practical crisis arose when all the care placements were allocated, and as a result a special ward had to be set up at the hospital to accommodate the children who continued to be diagnosed as having been sexually abused. Initially, public sympathy and concern, as well as that of the media, was in favour of the social workers and paediatricians. However, a turning point came in late May of 1987, when a group of parents approached a local newspaper, and began telling their versions of events. This differed considerably from that given by paediatricians and social workers. The media turned to support the parents, and the social workers came under intense public scrutiny. The government also took a deep interest, and a public inquiry was established, led by Justice Elizabeth Butler-Sloss, an eminent judge.

The inquiry examined the cases of 121 children where sexual abuse had been alleged. Of these, the Courts subsequently dismissed the proceedings involving 96 of the children. In other words, in over 80 per cent of the cases, the Courts were satisfied that the allegations were false. One of the major findings of the Butler-Sloss inquiry was that children had been removed too readily by social workers who had failed to seek supportive evidence in relation to that presented by the paediatricians and who had not carried out comprehensive assessments of the children and their families. A famous quotation from Butler-Sloss was that 'the child is a person and not an object of concern'. It was believed that social workers did not pay sufficient attention to what children were telling them, and therefore that the interests of children and their parents, were being ignored.

The key theme here is that the right to privacy of families was seen to be too easily invaded by what were perceived to be overzealous social workers. In other words, the state, in the form of social workers, was seen to ride roughshod over the rights of children and parents. This chimed neatly with a key political philosophy of the ruling Conservative government, namely that the state should have a reduced role in people's lives.

 Information: The impact of the Cleveland inquiry on the emergency protection of children

One direct consequence of the Cleveland inquiry was a delay in publishing the Children Act 1989, and the subsequent introduction of a new order – the Emergency Protection Order – to replace the Place of Safety Order used extensively in Cleveland. The key difference between the two is that the former lasts just 8 days and can be challenged in the courts by parents after 72 hours. The latter could not be challenged for 28 days. The Children Act 1989 also required that in care proceedings, courts should seek to reach decisions as quickly as possible, as many of the children in Cleveland were left in the limbo of Interim Care Orders, lasting in some cases up to 2 years. Once again, we see here a key underpinning political ideology of the Conservative government: intervention by the state, if required, should be for the minimum period necessary.

General principles

This ideology is reflected in the general principles that drive the Children Act 1989. There are eight of them as follows, all of which coincidentally can be configured to begin with the letter 'P'.

Paramountcy of the child

Where decisions are made, what is understood to be best for the child should determine the course of action that is followed.

Parental responsibility

This has already been discussed in Chapter 1, where parental responsibility was seen to be defined as 'all the rights, duties, powers, responsibilities and authority' that go with being a parent. The fact that unmarried fathers did not automatically have parental responsibility is further testimony to the implementation of a piece of social policy by a government designed to encourage marriage which it believed to be the foundation of successful family life.

Prevention

Agencies should work in a preventative manner with families, identifying and responding to problems early by offering appropriate support. Statutory state intervention should be a last resort. Here there is an immediate tension. This position presumes that families – parents and children – will always welcome intervention and will accept and utilize the support on offer. It is a model that reinforces families as passive recipients of services. Several questions arise from this. What should workers do if families refuse help? Clearly, if there is no significant harm (this concept will be unpicked at a later stage) to the child, they have no choice but to encourage or cajole the parents into accepting help, try a different supportive approach, or withdraw. The Children Act 1989 is quite clear – parents have the right to raise their children as they wish, as long as they do not abuse them. With this in mind, the judgement by the workers whether or not to initiate statutory intervention may become influenced by this driving philosophy, and therefore children may be left in harmful situations longer than necessary. Furthermore, if there is something called 'significant harm' it suggests that there is also non-significant 'harm' to children, which is acceptable, if parents refuse voluntary intervention. This could well create a moral dilemma for the worker – they can clearly see a child suffering harm (for instance low-level neglect) that has not yet reached the threshold of 'significant', yet they have no power to intervene unless the parent is agreeable. Of course, the communication skills of the worker, their creativity and tenacity in these situations may well win a reluctant parent over; however, the fundamental position is that the worker may well have to leave a child in a harmful situation without the support of additional services.

Protection

Where intervention between agencies and families finds evidence of risk to children from abuse or neglect, the former should act swiftly to protect the children involved. Clearly, there is a fine balance to be achieved here – on the one hand, agencies should work in an unobtrusive way, only intervening when necessary; on the other hand they should act quickly when it is necessary. While it is true that clear, evidence-based judgements made by well-trained and supported staff will aide this decision-making process, it cannot be denied that there is a tension at play here, which can be characterized as 'Don't go in unless necessary, but when it is, go in hard.'

Partnership

This refers to an expectation that, in order to support and protect children effectively, agencies should work in partnership with one another, with parents and with children themselves. Thus, multi-agency work is here further enshrined in the fundamental principles of the Children Act 1989. Agencies should facilitate a positive relationship between each other, and between themselves and parents. This concept of partnership raises many complex and pressing issues, which will be fully analysed later in this chapter (in relation to multi-agency work) and later in the book (in relation to partnership with parents). Finally, children should, too, have a voice, and be consulted by professionals at every stage of a given process. This is a principle that, sadly, appears to be implemented too infrequently. For example, Freeman (2002) explores what he sees as the pitiful lack of rights of children to be consulted regarding a whole range of significant matters.

Participation

This is closely allied to partnership, in that once agencies, parents and children are linked up effectively, the next phase is then to ensure that all are afforded the opportunity to participate fully in the processes. Thus agencies and parents should be enabled to take a full part in the decision-making processes from assessment, to planning, to review. Parents should be fully informed of the intentions of agencies as these are developed – they should not hear any 'surprises' from agencies at public meetings. Generally speaking, decisions should not be made behind parents' backs without their knowledge or input. The exception is where parental presence or involvement is likely to be seriously disruptive or against the interests of the child. Children, too, should be encouraged to take part in decision making, so long as this is appropriate to their age and understanding, and is in their interests.

Planning

Multi-agency or even single agency work should be effectively and clearly planned. Here we see a further clear consequence of the Cleveland inquiry – the perception here was that once children were removed from parental care, there was little systematic planning of what should happen next. Consequently, children were seen to remain in care for long periods with no long-term solution being implemented. Therefore, it became a key principle of the Children Act 1989 to ensure that there was timely, child-centred planning based on sound assessment and evidence based practice.

Permanency

Linked to the notion of planning, the final underlying principle insists that children have the right to grow up in a permanent family environment. Where possible, and where it is safe, this should be the birth family. Where this is neither possible nor safe, a permanent alternative family environment (in other words, long-term fostering or adoption) should be found as soon as possible. The underpinning intention is that children should not be waiting for long periods in short or medium term placements, or in non-family environments. While this may be a laudable intention, it has proved very difficult to fulfil. There is a shortage of good quality, permanent fostering or adoptive placements and carers (British Association for Adoption and Fostering, 2007). Furthermore, some children, mainly as a result of their life experiences, cannot easily cope with the intensity of a family environment and actually tend to thrive better in the emotionally more diluted atmosphere of group living (Waterhouse,

1989). For these children, insisting on the full acting out of this principle could have painful and disastrously disruptive results, as they would be likely to experience a series of unsuccessful family placements.

In addition to these underpinning principles, and as has already been shown in Chapter 1, Section 27 of the Children Act is very explicit about the duty of agencies to cooperate with one another.

 Information: The philosophy of the Children Act 1989

The basic tenet of the Children Act 1989 can be summarized, but hopefully not caricatured, by the phrase 'private is good, state is bad'. In the government guidance accompanying the publication of the Children Act 1989 it is interesting that very early on the point is made, in a section headed 'Protection from "Protection"' that 'potent powers, if misdirected, may themselves cause harm to a child by enabling the state to intervene in his or his [sic] family's life when it should not' (An Introduction to the Children Act 1989, p. 6). In other words, the state should only intervene if and when it can demonstrate that there are grounds to do so, and that it is in the best interests of the child. If it cannot do so, it should leave well alone and allow families to parent children without interference.

Working Together to Safeguard Children

The duty to cooperate is further cemented in the national guidance document titled *Working Together to Safeguard Children* (DfES, 2006i). This is practice guidance to accompany the Children Acts 1989 and 2004. Dealing more specifically with child protection matters, it sets out the duties and responsibilities of all agencies in safeguarding children. All agencies are expected to follow this guidance. The 2006 edition is the fourth version of this guidance, and it reflects the broad *Every Child Matters* agenda of supporting children and families (DfES, 2003). It is worth charting the history of the *Working Together* guidance documents, as this provides further evidence of the link between government ideology and social policy for children and families.

The first version of *Working Together* dates back to 1988, and reflects the Cleveland inquiry already discussed in this chapter. This slim volume deals mainly with sexual abuse.

The second version is dated 1991 and was published to coincide with the inception of the Children Act 1989. The full title of this document was *Working Together Under the Children Act 1989: A Guide to Arrangements for Inter-Agency Co-operation for the Protection of Children from Abuse.*

The third version was published in 1999, following the coming to power of the New Labour government in 1997. The full title of this version of the document was *Working Together to Safeguard Children: A Guide to Inter-Agency Working to Safeguard and Promote the Welfare of Children.* The fourth (2006) version shares this title.

The reason for providing details of the subtitles of these various versions of the guidance is to point to a clear shift from version one to version four. This shift is away from narrow protection based on the ideology of minimal state intervention of the 1988 and 1991 versions, towards a broader approach to promoting children's welfare. Here, state intervention can be welcome if it is supportive. Some circumstances for this are laid down in what are called 'sources of stress' (DfES, 2006i, p. 158) on families:

- social exclusion
- domestic violence
- substance abuse by parents
- mental illness in parents
- parental learning disability.

Here, appropriate support services can also be important elements in the *prevention* of abuse.

The shift then is clear: intervention from agencies has moved from being an unacceptable intrusion into private family space unless there was a clear crisis or child protection emergency, to being a helpful and at times necessary support to enable children to reach their full potential. This latter philosophy reflects the thinking of the New Labour government which contrasts with that of the previous New Right government. Furthermore, there is now an explicit acknowledgement that parenting itself is a difficult task, and that 'asking for help should be seen as a sign of responsibility rather than as a parenting failure' (ibid., p. 1). The relationship between the family and the state, therefore, appears to have come full circle – from perceived overintrusiveness that led to the 'scandal' of Cleveland, through minimal intervention unless absolutely necessary, to benign and supportive preventative intervention. The *Every Child Matters* programme extends this last position even further, and this will be examined in detail in Chapter 9.

The Children Act 2004

This section cannot deal with the full Children Act 2004, as this is a wide-ranging piece of legislation that gives legal grounding to the extensive *Every Child Matters* agenda. The focus here is on how multi-agency work is advanced within the Children Act 2004. The Act covers England and Wales, although it refers to the functions of a new position, the Children's Commissioner, in all four countries of the United Kingdom.

The first important point to make is that the Children Act 2004 exists in addition to, and not instead of the Children Act 1989. Bearing in mind that the 2004 Act buttresses the *Every Child Matters* programme of state intervention in family life, this raises some questions. Of course, workers should receive training on the new 2004 Act and on expectations upon them under the attendant *Every Child Matters* programme. However, one wonders how easy it will be for workers to quickly jettison the previous powerful messages of minimal intervention (albeit this has been softening since the introduction of the 1999 version of *Working*

Together to Safeguard Children). Workers are now expected to offer timely and early support, assessment, and services designed to promote positive parenting or supplement parenting where it is believed to be less conducive to good outcomes for children. Years of training and practice based on a cautious approach must now be replaced by proactive, visible and palpably beneficial support. Furthermore, some workers may feel or indeed find a conflict of interest between the 2004 and 1989 Acts. For instance, where a parent is refusing to accept help, under the 1989 Act the clear message to workers was that unless there was evidence of actual or potential significant harm to children, the worker had no choice but to withdraw (since parents had the right to raise children as they wished, as long as they did not abuse them), whereas under the 2004 Act there appears to be a clear expectation that workers will continue to try to engage the parent where the worker believes the child will benefit from the support on offer. The conflict here, therefore, is between the previously held belief that 'parents know best' and the current view that 'the state knows best'. At its worst, this state of affairs – where both the 2004 and the 1989 Act are concurrent – could lead to confusion and poor decision making among workers struggling to implement the rather conflicting philosophies and imperatives of both Acts.

Nevertheless, it is possible to draw out from the Children Act 2004 some clear and unambiguous departures from the 1989 Act:

- Now, agencies *must actively* make arrangements to promote cooperation between one another to improve the well-being of children. This means that instead of waiting to be approached by another agency for any assistance, agencies must work together in a preventative and pre-planned manner to try to ensure that their shared resources are put to best effect for the benefit of children and families.
- More multidisciplinary teams with a lead professional.
- The co-location of services in schools.
- The development of a common assessment framework to identify needs.
- The development of Children's Trusts in each area to integrate services under one plan.

These and other proposals will be discussed in detail in Chapter 9.

The language of partnership

A dominant theme in the preceding legal framework surrounding multi-agency work is that of partnership. This is a complex concept, which all agencies are expected to embrace and work towards. Four sequential levels of partnership have been identified within a government guidance document on the subject (DH, 1995)

Level 1 – providing information – is the most basic level of partnership and typically involves giving clear and accurate information and checking it is understood. For example, this could include a school contacting social services to make a referral regarding a child experiencing neglect.

Level 2 – involvement – is still predominately passive. It may involve, for example, receiving information or observing meetings without taking an active part in the process, especially decision making. To continue the example above, the social worker receiving the referral may then process this within the office, and arrange for a follow-up visit to the family or school.

Level 3 – participation – is seen as active involvement, for instance contributing to discussions and decision making at meetings or in other arenas. Should Social Services arrange an Initial Child Protection Conference in respect of the neglected child in the above example, then those agencies, and the parents, attending, could well be operating at this level of participation, as they would be expected to contribute to the decision as to whether or not the child needs to be subject of a formal child protection plan, according to the criteria laid down.

Level 4 – full partnership. The guidance document presents a detailed list of characteristics that comprise a full partnership between agencies:

- Shared values – that partners share fundamental values, for example, that the priority of any joint work is the welfare of the child.
- A shared task or goal – that partners have a common understanding and agreement of what the work is attempting to achieve.
- All parties contribute resources and/or skills – there is the opportunity for all concerned to provide positive input into the work.
- Trust between partners – all agencies concerned have confidence in the ability of the other parties.
- Negotiation of plans – areas of work, priorities, details of tasks to be undertaken are decided together, and no agency is left out of these discussions.
- Decisions are made together – the direction of the work, any changes or new priorities are jointly discussed and negotiated. Once again, no agency is isolated from these decisions.
- Mutual confidence that each partner will deliver – where agreement has been reached on which agency will perform certain tasks, all parties are confident that this work will actually take place.
- Equality or near equality between partners – all agencies are able to contribute, and these contributions are valued by all. Contributions are not 'weighted' so that certain agencies have more prestige or kudos than others.
- Choice in entering the partnership – all parties should join the endeavour out of a genuine desire to support the children and families concerned, and not because they may have been co-opted or coerced into the work.
- A formalized arrangement for agreed working – the plans, and subsequent work, should be written and formally shared and agreed. Formal written minutes of meetings should be shared and agreed. It should be explicit as to which individual or agency has any 'final say', particularly where any disagreement exists between parties.
- Open sharing of information – parties should not keep any relevant information back. If any professional is unsure on the protocol for sharing information, they should be able to ask.
- Mechanisms for monitoring, reviewing and ending the partnership – the progress of the shared work should be formally and jointly monitored and reviewed. It should be explicit when, or to what extent, the initial goals have been achieved. A joint and, once again, formal decision should be made to end the partnership for a particular piece of work. This avoids the work drifting to a close with little or no clarity in respect of how successful it has been.
- Dealing with power issues – the guidance acknowledges that it is possible that some agencies may attempt – consciously or otherwise – to use or exert power or influence over others. A true partnership would not only accept this, but also deal with the resultant issues in an open yet robust manner.

The guidance makes a final point regarding effective partnerships, which is that partnership is not, nor should become, an end in itself. Parties concerned should not congratulate themselves for, or measure their success by, achieving a high level of effective partnership. The objective of the partnership is the protection and welfare of the child, and only if this is clearly achieved or enhanced, should the professionals involved gauge the work as a success.

Writing some 16 years before the publication of the government guidance on partnership, and even before the Children Act 1989, Stainton Rogers (1989) highlights further principles of good multi-agency work. Her chapter, which as we shall go on to discuss, also considers some fundamental difficulties with multi-agency work, now appears ahead of its time, and since many of the issues she raises remain relevant, can also be described as enduring and insightful. She claims that the following are characteristics of good partnerships.

Characteristics of good partnerships

Clearly agreed and defined functions

All parties have explicitly agreed roles and all concerned are clear what these are, both for themselves and for others. No agency should therefore be wondering, for example, what the Health Visitor does when she visits the family every fortnight. The focus of the work should be shared, and be clear to all.

Tasks with agreed boundaries

When the focus of any work for each agency is agreed, it should be clear where one agency's responsibility ends and where another's begins. Good partnership should mean that no two (or more) agencies are inadvertently duplicating work or overstepping professional boundaries.

Well-organized and established communication

All agencies involved in work with children and families should know precisely how to contact their partners. This includes knowledge of formal referral channels and mechanisms as well as how to contact individuals during ongoing work. The system for leaving and receiving messages should be clear and explained to all.

Well-developed local relationships

Professionals engaged in joint work should have the opportunity to meet and build relationships other than at times of crisis or intense work. Local support groups, training events or other arenas should be available to foster the development of effective local relationships. If these are established, it is much more likely that other actions will flow from it – for example, referrals to another agency for support, less formal queries, attendance at planning or other meetings.

Overcome ignorance and prejudice about each other

A key factor in effective partnership work is mutual respect for what the others bring to the process. This may involve each party leaving behind whatever prejudices they may have about others who are involved. These prejudices may have developed as a result of rumour or unfair or stereotypical portrayals of a profession, or through an isolated experience. For instance, social workers may be seen as gullible, woolly minded vegetarians who are always late for appointments; teachers may be viewed as lucky (and difficult to get hold of at certain times) because they finish work at 3.30 p.m. and have long holidays; nurses may be viewed as over-worked 'angels' who are constantly kind and patient. Described thus, each of these is a laugh-able caricature; nevertheless if even a vestige of these parodies exists, it can damage true partnership. This is because the process involved is a subtle one. If a teacher, for instance, does harbour unarticulated beliefs that social workers are well-meaning but disorganized, then should an otherwise efficient and well-prepared social worker happen to be late for a particular meeting, it is possible that the teacher will have their original beliefs confirmed, without these being balanced out by the weightier experiences of the social worker as rigor-ous and punctual. In the same vein, should a particular nurse not express total selfless and enduring devotion to their task, then a social worker who might happen to believe that nurses should possess such characteristics may feel resentful that the nurse is not acting according to their stereotype, or worse, that the nurse is somehow a failure for not displaying constant and unfailing kindness to all.

Defining common goals

As the government guidance on partnership stated, effective multi-agency work involves all parties concerned taking time to agree what the aims are of any work undertaken. In this way, all professionals involved are clear about what is trying to be achieved.

Using common language

Good partnerships avoid the use of jargon between each other, especially if this is not explained or commonly understood. Technical words, abbreviations or other agency specific vocabulary should either be avoided or clearly explained. If a professional does happen to use a phrase or word that others do not understand, then an effective working partnership would enable an individual to ask what this means. For instance, if a teacher states in a meeting that a child 'is in Year 3 and last year achieved Level 1 in Key Stage 1 SATs for English and Maths, and is therefore now having differentiated sessions with the SENCO' then others in the meet-ing who may not understand what the meaning or implications of this are, should feel com-fortable in asking about this. The use of technical language is particularly unhelpful if it is used to convey power or authority over others in the meeting. If, for example, a doctor or consultant reported that the child had 'a jagged spiral fracture of the ulna' it would be helpful if they went on to simplify this as 'a broken bone in the lower arm' and then commented on likely or possible causes, in the light of any explanations given. If the initial version was in letter form, and read out at a meeting, then there would be no recourse to question or clarify the precise nature or implications of the injury, thus compounding the difficulty in attempting to reach a common understanding of the risk to this particular child.

Respecting different skills

This is similar to the concept of equality between partners discussed as part of the government guidance. Effective multi-agency work recognizes and respects the contribution of all concerned, and does not have a hierarchy. Thus, the contribution of an eminent doctor or headteacher should not outweigh the input of a health visitor or classroom assistant, especially if the latter are more likely to have detailed, day-to-day knowledge of the children and family. It may be that the classroom assistant may need support in expressing their views, and an effective partnership should enable this to happen.

Ensure all know what the local arrangements are

Effective partnership involves clarity regarding precisely how local systems work for such things as making referrals, securing appointments for paediatric assessments of children, sending and receiving minutes of meetings and other information, and contacting individuals in the network.

Set against this positive exposition of the concept of 'partnership', some researchers have questioned the use of the term. For instance, Daines, Lyon and Parsloe (1990) argue, as a result of their research into four discrete projects over 2 years, that 'partnership' is unachievable, and that the word would be better replaced with the term 'participation', which provides sufficient challenge for agencies to achieve. For their purposes, 'partnership' had to include three elements: mutual support, alliance (working together, sharing the load) and control (having a voice, having some power in the service). They found little evidence, in their research, of such 'partnership' but many examples of 'participation'.

Barriers to effective multi-agency work

Continuing the theme of putting forward alternatives to the positive nature and benefits of good multi-agency work, Stainton Rogers (1989) also addresses (again, in a manner that puts her way ahead of her time, as these remain relevant and pressing matters) the potential barriers to effective multi-agency work. They are presented here with some interpretation of my own, including the addition of practical examples of each to help the reader contextualize them.

Different core functions of agencies which may clash and compete

For instance, as Stainton Rogers explains, the main job of the police in any joint enquiry with social services is to seek evidence of a possible criminal offence to help any future prosecution. Social workers, on the other hand, are concerned with the welfare of the child, and in assessing the needs of the child in the family environment. At times, these different functions may not sit easily beside one another. For example, part of evidence gathering may involve the police officer and social worker interviewing the child who may become distressed during the interview, although police officers are trained in accordance with national guidance on interviewing child witnesses which covers how to assist children in distress (HO and DH, 1992). Nevertheless, the social worker may feel uncomfortable, from a purely child-centred perspective, being part of this process.

Different values, cultures and practices between agencies

This can include agencies having different generalized perspectives and views from one another. For instance, some may link all abuse to the actions of individual 'abusers' while others may take a broader view, arguing that poverty and social exclusion are equally 'abusive' to children, and therefore that these social ills should be tackled. Furthermore, agencies are structured in vastly different ways. In the police force, for instance, the practice and culture is for officers to call their superiors 'Sir' or 'Ma'am' whereas in social work, first names are usually used. In many health settings, especially hospitals, consultants are held in very high esteem and are likely to be referred to as 'Mr' or 'Mrs' or perhaps 'Doctor'. These differences may not appear to matter in the detail of any joint work, and yet they are present, in the fabric of the work. Still further, individual people within and between agencies are likely to hold differing views on such matters as how harm and abuse is defined and understood, how any 'abusers' should be dealt with, and what are the desirable outcomes of any joint work. These differences, if not addressed, discussed and resolved, are likely to have a significant impact on the efficacy of the work.

Lack of clarity in boundaries

If workers are unclear about their own role, and that of others, then this could lead to them duplicating the work of others, or giving advice that might conflict with that from a different worker. For example, if a health visitor and social worker are jointly involved in supporting a family, but neither fully understands what the other party actually does when they visit the family, this could mean that the health visitor pursues social care support strategies such as respite care, or that the social worker might give healthcare advice on the children. Both of these might be well-meaning, but they are also likely to be ill-coordinated and incomplete.

Clearly, there is a link here with the need for good and effective communication between the parties involved to try and avoid such overlaps.

Lack of clarity in lines of authority and decision making

The benefits of multi-agency work, where various professional perspectives are brought to bear can be undermined if it is unclear precisely how the agencies involved arrive at major decisions about the work. Of all the agencies involved, if it is not clear, from the very beginning, which has the ultimate authority to override decisions or arbitrate where there are conflicting opinions, the result can be confusion, loss of motivation and potentially disastrous consequences for children.

Historical or current jealousies or rivalries between agencies

Sometimes, agencies have a history of fraught relationships. This could be caused by a fundamental difference in outlook on a particular issue or a clash of personality between key individuals within the agencies. It might also be caused by a sense of jealousy if one agency is perceived to be performing generally 'better' than another. In this instance, individuals within the agency perceived or judged to be performing less well may resent the 'better' agency. This could manifest itself in several ways. Workers within the 'inferior' agency may (unconsciously or otherwise) strive to outwit or outperform the 'better' agency in an effort to demonstrate either that their agency is as good or better, or that the 'better' agency is not as good as perceived. It might also be possible that workers within the 'inferior' agency may deliberately attempt to undermine the work of the 'better' agency in order to show them as ineffective. A further reason for the origin of rivalry between agencies may be that an agency has had a poor experience of an individual within another agency. They may then label all workers within the same agency in the same way, and begin to behave according to the label which they have ascribed to the agency as a whole. An example here may help. A teacher in a school contacts Social Services at lunch-time by telephone with concerns about a child. The teacher cannot get through to a duty social worker until the third attempt because the line is busy. When she does speak to a social worker, the teacher feels the social worker is generally defensive and unhelpful, although the social worker does agree to speak to a manager about the case and ring the teacher back. By 4.30 p.m. the teacher has not received a return call, so rings the social worker back, to be told that a decision was made not to take the matter any further, and asking the teacher to arrange for the school to continue to monitor the child. The decision by Social Services may well be the correct one, but the teacher feels unhappy with the process here, in particular the difficulty in getting hold of a social worker, then their general attitude, then the fact that the teacher had to ring the social worker back to hear the outcome. The teacher comes to the conclusion that it is a waste of time ringing Social Services with concerns in the future unless they are very serious as the response is likely to be similar to that which she experienced. The reason why these issues are important is that they prevent agencies from focusing on the work, and more significantly, on the child concerned. If energy and time is spent on one-upmanship rather than on working collaboratively, then valuable resources are lost to the child.

Different and conflicting social policy or legislation

Laws and social policy governing and affecting the lives of families and children are plentiful and complex. At times these may clash with one another, causing at the very least confusion, and at worst a debilitating state where different agencies can justify their action (or inaction) on the basis of legislation. Take one example: the government, in its *Every Child Matters* vision, demands that children be put at the centre of all social action. There appears to be something of a clash between this laudable proclamation and the government's own terms of reference for a review of child support policy (that is, financial support for children where parents have separated). As Green (2006) points out, these terms of reference place parental responsibility above the interests of children, and do not mention child poverty at all. The imperative of these terms of reference for a revised child support policy still appears to be extra revenue for the Treasury rather than improving the quality of life of children. Therefore a direct contradiction exists here, between the government rhetoric of every child being precious and the subsequent demands upon all agencies to deliver better outcomes for children, and the hard social policy of the government itself on child support which does very little to alleviate hardship for children. A second example is more closely related to multi-agency work. Take a single mother with three children living in a small, two-bedroom flat, whose children are subject to a formal child protection plan as a result of neglect. The assessment shows that part of the context here is overcrowding and the lack of a safe outside play area for the children. The social worker therefore supports an application for rehousing to a three-bedroom house with a garden. Housing law allocates accommodation on the basis of 'reasonable preference' (Shelter, 2005, p. 1) and councils have systems to prioritize applications, usually on a points basis. Matters which they consider include *homelessness*, the conditions in which the family is living, any medical conditions, the need to avoid hardship, and risk of violence and threat. The family described above, therefore, may have some priority if they are adjudged by the council to be officially overcrowded, and may gain additional points if it is accepted they need to move from the flat to a house to avoid further hardship. However, councils cannot take into account per se the fact that the children are subject to a formal child protection plan, or that according to the Children Act 1989, the best interests of the child should always be prioritized. Councils have to assess applications for accommodation on housing need alone, and while there may be some discretion to include additional priority points for certain circumstances, there does appear to be a clash here between, on the one hand, the palpable needs and interests of the children, and, on the other hand, the detail of housing law. This could result in a considerable wait by the family to be rehoused, a fact which could jeopardize the welfare of the children.

Lack of clarity about why agencies are involved

Where there are a number of agencies working together, it is imperative that they are all very clear about why they are all involved, what work they are undertaking, and what they are hoping to achieve. If this clarity is absent, it could lead to confusion as to what particular agencies or individuals are doing. Assumptions, perhaps incorrect, could then be made, as to what the work involves. This could lead to resentment if one agency perceives themselves as working harder than another, or if an agency does not understand or approve of the manner in which another agency is carrying out their work. For instance, if a social worker announces they are going to engage in some direct work with the children in a particular family, they have a responsibility, without betraying the confidences of the children by divulging unnecessary detail, to outline what the objectives of this work are, what it will involve, over what approximate timescale will it take place and so on. Failure to do so may lead others to conclude that the social worker is engaging in rather nebulous social interactions with the children while the other agencies do the 'real' work.

These tensions between agencies are discussed at a macro level by Morrison (1991). He describes, in the context of how agencies might perceive the prospects for change in clients, four distinct perceptions and attitudes agencies might hold about collaboration:

- **Paternalism**. Here, the agency collaborates only if they approve of it, and even then does so on its terms. Collaboration is seen not as an obligation, but as a benefit the agency gives to others – the benefit of its expertise, for which recipients should be grateful. The agency may find it hard to see other agencies having equal expertise or valid skills. Paternalistic agencies do not believe they need other agencies.
- **Strategic adversarial**. Collaboration is approached with wariness, as the agency sees it involving more losses than gains. In addition, the agency may believe that other agencies will exploit the collaboration for their own ends. This could lead to a siege mentality. Collaboration is likely to become conflictual, with time spent negotiating the terms of engagement, checking what others are doing and so on. It is collaboration essentially based on mistrust. The clients themselves can become marginal to the process.
- **Play fair**. Here, agencies believe that clients need and have the right to an effective multi-agency service. The agency tries to ensure that everyone is clear about their role and responsibilities. The agency appreciates and respects the different roles of other agencies. The agency involves clients in this process, which could potentially lead to conflict with other agencies if, say, information is withheld from parents during child protection work.
- **Developmental**. This is similar to 'play fair' but broader. Collaboration is seen as a dynamic process to motivate staff and clients to change. Multi-agency work is seen as organic, alive and changing, including such things as taking risks, learning from mistakes or pooling resources.

The key point in discussing these four approaches is to take note of the fact that unless these differences in the expectations, practices and attitudes between agencies are acknowledged and worked through, they are likely to interfere negatively on the quality of the work with children and families.

As if to illustrate the enduring nature of these barriers, Joughin and Law (2005) report on similar findings in their work. They highlight three key barriers to effective multi-agency work:

- poor communication
- lack of information sharing
- conflicting professional and agency cultures.

They go on to say that possible solutions to these problems include the use of a 'hybrid' professional with experience of different agencies, and joint training of agencies to overcome the differences. While these are interesting suggestions, they raise additional questions regarding the availability and precise role of individuals with experience of working for more than one agency, and about whether training is treated as something as a panacea to solve a multitude of problems. The idea that centuries of cultural identity and values within agencies can be eradicated via a day or so of joint training is perhaps naive and unrealistic. That is not to say that joint training cannot be useful and effective; however, there is a need to be cautious about the claims that can be made for it, especially as so much may depend on the quality of the training on offer.

Allied to the notion of barriers to effective multi-agency work, is the problem of how agencies, or individuals within them, respond to a range of moral and ethical issues which may arise. Hence, it is necessary to consider how any individual may respond to the following:

- Particular individuals in the network having or using power or status. For example, a senior manager or worker from a particular agency, who is perhaps removed from the day-to-day running of the case, may wish to exert their opinions as to how best to proceed. This may clash with the view of those who know the situation better.
- Structural issues in another agency, for example, staff shortages or delays which are impacting on the efficacy of the work.
- Another agency not delivering promises which they have made. A Health Visitor may have agreed to visit a family fortnightly to monitor the development of a child. However, it emerges that after 6 weeks no visit has yet been made.
- Another agency doing something which others believe is wrong or against the child's interests. Social Services may be adamant that maintaining children at home while being subject to a formal child protection plan is the correct approach in a particular case, whereas others may strongly believe the children are at risk of serious harm and should be removed immediately.
- Unreasonable demands from another agency. Individuals may find they are being asked, by another agency, to perform duties and tasks which are outside their remit, and which place pressure upon them.
- Another agency using different legislation, as discussed above, to justify their actions, or inaction.

In all of these scenarios, the difficulty is how to challenge the other agency in a manner that maintains a positive relationship with them. Often, by the very nature of the issues involved, very strong emotions are elicited by the actions described above. Particularly as many of them tap into an individual's own morality and value base, they can easily become flash points which then serve to deepen divisions and differences between agencies. This reinforces the importance, perhaps, of the need for multi-agency work to be guided by a very clear line of authority which can adjudicate in such instances, remove the personal element from any differences in opinion, action or emphasis, and move the work forward in a way that maintains the focus on the child.

(?) **Reflections: Case study – Jack**

Social Services have called an Initial Child Protection Conference to discuss a physical injury to Jack, who is 5 years old, white British and in Year 1 at a local primary school. The injury is believed to have happened while Jack was in the care of his parents. The following agencies attend: Social Services, School, Health Visitor, Police and Parents. All agencies have written a report which they summarize at the conference. Without notice or prior warning, the headteacher also produces a hardback book and begins to list a number of 'misdemeanours' or concerns hitherto not mentioned to anyone else. These include Jack being late on a number of occasions, arriving somewhat dirty and dishevelled, and the parents sometimes collecting him slightly late from school. The parents and other agencies are taken aback, and this produces some discussion. The headteacher suggests that the injury is the latest in a long line of concerns which he has not, however, shared with anyone else. A letter from the family's GP is also read out. He is unable to attend the meeting. He reports routine visits to him by members of the family, and ends by saying he cannot believe the parents would deliberately harm their son, because they are such pleasant people.

1 Look at the section of this chapter titled 'The language of partnership'. At what level of partnership do you think the agencies involved in this work are operating? Remember that different agencies can be at different levels. Try to give reasons to support your answer.

2 Can you identify any elements from the list for Level 4 – full partnership – in this scenario?

3 From the list of 'barriers to effective multi-agency work' discussed in this chapter choose those you think are present in this scenario. Try to be as specific as you can.

Conclusions

From 1991 through to 2004 and beyond, professionals working with children and families have had to adjust to changing legislation arising from different political ideologies of successive governments. The Conservative government's approach of the 1980s and 1990s was predicated on the notion of non-intervention in family life, while the Labour government of the late 1990s reversed this sharply by planning a huge programme of intervention in family life, centred around more integrated multi-agency working. This has the potential to cause confusion and difficulty for all, as workers and families try to adjust to these changing expectations. Throughout all of this, there appear to be some constant elements which have been shown to enhance the quality of multi-agency work. On the other hand, barriers which can detract from effective partnerships also remain, and these can have the effect of deflecting attention away from the needs of the child. The central importance of keeping the child at the heart of the work is highlighted in the chapter that now follows which focuses on multi-agency assessment.

Multi-agency assessment

Chapter Outline

Introduction

Assessment of children's needs, and the extent to which those needs are being met by the child's parents or carers, has traditionally been one of the cornerstones of social work practice. Whether the family situation was one where the child may be classed as being 'in need' as defined by Section 17 of the Children Act 1989, or may be at risk of significant harm, a crucial aspect of the social worker's role was to carry out an assessment in order to determine the level of need or risk, and thereafter to help determine what the appropriate response might be.

Other agencies, of course, also conduct assessments in accordance with their specific functions. For instance, in England and Wales, professionals working within education have a responsibility to lead the assessment of children who may require a Statement of Special Educational Needs (SEN), although other agencies are usually consulted as part of the process. National Health Service Trusts or local councils employ Occupational Therapists who also have a clear role in assessing the needs of children with a variety of physical and/or psychiatric conditions with the aim of preventing disability and promoting independence (NHS Careers, 2006).

This chapter will explore two distinct forms of multi-agency assessment. First, the assessment required in England under the document titled *Framework for the Assessment of Children in Need and Their Families* (DH, DfEE and HO, 2000) will be described and critically evaluated. Wales has its own very similar version that is set within the context of that country (National Assembly for Wales and Home Office, 2001). In Scotland, no national system for multi-agency assessment was mooted until 2005 when the publication *Getting It Right for Every Child: Proposals for Action* appeared (Scottish Executive, 2005a). In Northern Ireland, since 2003, the four Children and Young People's Committees have agreed a 'whole child and family support model' which includes a common approach to assessing children (see McTernan and Godfrey, 2006).

Second, the assessment required by the relatively recent Common Assessment Framework (DfES, 2006b) will be discussed. This only applies to England, although Wales begun piloting a very similar system, under the Welsh Assembly Government's 'Rights to Action' programme, from September 2007 with a view to full implementation by the end of 2008. A single assessment record and plan is proposed for Scotland, contained within the document mentioned in the paragraph above (Scottish Executive, 2005a). In Northern Ireland, a single assessment framework for children's services is seen as a key element of fundamental reforms announced by Health Minister Paul Goggins in January 2007 following an unsatisfactory inspection report into child protection services (DHSSPS, 2007b).

 Information: Children with special educational needs across the UK

In England and Wales, Section 323 of the Education Act 1996 determines that local authorities have a statutory responsibility to conduct assessments of children who 'probably need' a Statement of SEN to enable them to receive special educational provision to meet their specific needs. This assessment is carried out under the auspices of the SEN Code of Practice (DfES, 2001). In Scotland, the Education (Scotland) Act 1980 confers upon local authorities a similar responsibility; in Northern Ireland, under the Education (Northern Ireland) Order 1996 as amended by the Special Educational Needs and Disability (Northern Ireland) Order 2005, the statutory responsibility for securing provision for pupils with special educational needs rests with the Education and Library Boards and Boards of Governors of mainstream schools.

Framework for the assessment of children in need and their families

This document, and the assessment model that flows from it, is refreshing in that it is explicit about the potential dangers of allowing large numbers of children to live and develop with significant unmet needs. Right at the beginning, it states that over 4 million children in England (in the year 2000) live in families with less than half the average household income; in other words, they live in poverty. Furthermore, the poorest neighbourhoods have become 'more run down, more prone to crime and more cut off from the labour market' (DH, DfEE and HO, 2000, p. 2). The *Framework for the Assessment of Children in Need and Their Families* is presented as one tool among several 'major strategies' (ibid.) implemented by the government to tackle these problems. The aim of these combined strategies is to encourage and promote preventive work and early intervention to help reduce the scale and difficulty of the problems described above, and to tackle them before they become entrenched. Thus, the early assessment and consequent meeting of the needs of children should help reduce the number of children who are described as 'vulnerable' (ibid.). These are 'those disadvantaged children who would benefit from extra help from public agencies in order to make the best of their life chances' (ibid.). In other words, children living in poverty are seen as being vulnerable to social exclusion, which the document suggests includes becoming involved in offending, being unemployed and ultimately being a threat to the social order.

It is with this context in mind that the details of the framework for assessment will be discussed. As we have seen, usage of the framework for assessment is envisaged as being potentially relevant to a large number of children living in circumstances which may lead them being 'in need' of services from the local authority. The starting point for any assessment is the initial referral to social services, which could come from any source – a professional, a member of the public or the family themselves. The children referred will undoubtedly have a variety of needs. Some of these will be alleviated or met by quick, short-term intervention involving advice or the provision of services. Others, however, will require a more detailed assessment as their needs appear to be complex, or their situation serious, for example, children in need of protection. Such an assessment will involve other agencies so that, once the relevant information is gathered and processed, appropriate plans and interventions can be provided.

For children 'in need', the assessment will be carried out on a completely voluntary basis with the child living at home. However, for children in need of protection, action needs to be swift in order to determine the extent of any harm suffered or likely to be suffered by the child, and if so, what the appropriate response may be. A detailed exploration of the system used for this work will be carried out in Chapter 4. Suffice to say here that where a child is in need of protection, immediate action should be taken to protect them, and only once this has been achieved, should a longer, more detailed assessment of the family's circumstances be undertaken. This could happen with the child still living at home, living with relatives or friends, or being in care. If the child has been taken into care, the main function of the assessment may well be to determine whether there is a realistic prospect of rehabilitation between the child and the parents, in a timescale to suit the child's needs, and in a manner which keeps the child safe. Technically the assessment here is still voluntary on the part of the parents, but if they refuse to cooperate the stakes are very high, and refusal to take part is more likely to result in the child remaining in care on a permanent basis, as current and future risk to them cannot be fully determined.

Principles of assessment

Whether the assessment is conducted in respect of a child 'in need' or in need of protection, the social worker takes the lead in coordinating the completion of the assessment.

Furthermore, the framework for assessment document presents certain underlying principles which should underpin all such assessments.

Assessments should be child centred

This means that the child should be the main focus of the assessment. Social workers (and any other professionals involved) should guard against being distracted by other issues, such as 'a high level of conflict between adult family members, or depression being experienced by a parent or acute housing problems' (DH, DfEE and HO, 2000, p. 10). The social worker should also ensure they undertake direct work with the child during the assessment, with the express aim of 'ascertaining their wishes and feelings, and understanding the meaning of their experiences to them' (ibid.). This is clearly a laudable aim and central to both enhancing the quality of life of children in need, but also to protecting children in need of protection. It is not without its difficulties, however. The workers involved need a high level of training, skill, confidence, support and supervision to separate out the child's distinct needs and experiences from those of the parents.

Assessments should be rooted in child development

Social workers should use their knowledge of child development to inform their assessment and judgements. This includes such matters as understanding that children (including those with learning disabilities or who are disabled) have different rates of progress, that at different life stages there are different imperatives in child development and different milestones that one would expect to see reached, and that the development of a particular child is a complex interplay between their experiences, their genetic inheritance or temperament, any health problems or impairment they may have, their culture, and the physical and emotional environment in which they are living. As with the first point, social workers need a good level of supervision to help them process the information they receive in order to make objective decisions.

Assessment should take an ecological approach

This means that the assessment should take account of the wider context in which the child is living – their family, their community, their culture. The child should not be seen as an isolated individual but rather the links between, and influences of, the various aspects of the child's life should be explored and understood. This is not a new approach and the psychologist Bronfenbrenner (1979) has proposed a model which integrates the personal, familial, cultural and structural layers of a child's life. Once again, while the logic of this approach is compelling, there is something of a paradox and contradiction between social workers being told on the one hand that they must focus on the child and not be distracted by other factors, and on the other hand being told that taking account of wider factors is crucial to enhance understanding of the child's situation. This reinforces once more the fact that assessment is a high-level skill, requiring an understanding and maintenance of the delicate balance between focusing on the child and exploring the impact of wider factors upon that child.

Assessments should ensure equality of opportunity

Social workers need to respect differences in bringing up children due to family structures, religion, culture and ethnic origins. Furthermore, children with specific social needs arising out of disability or a health condition should have these needs assessed and met. Helpfully, the document states that 'ensuring equality of opportunity does not mean that all children are treated the same' (DH, DfEE and HO, 2000, p. 12) but rather that it does mean 'working sensitively and knowledgeably with diversity to identify the particular issues for a child and his/her family, taking account of experiences and family context' (ibid.). The government has produced practice guidance to accompany the framework for assessment specifically on working with disabled and black children (DH, 2000a). Achieving this aim requires a well-trained workforce simultaneously cognizant of the need to embrace cultural differences to map their relevance to the child's specific needs, and at times, to stand back from these in order to process them and separate out the child's specific needs from those of the culture in which they are immersed. For example, cultural or religious factors need to be acknowledged but not be accepted as explanations for abusive behaviour towards a child. This example serves as a reminder that 'professionals should guard against myths and stereotypes – both positive and negative – of black and minority ethnic families' (DfES, 2006i, p. 191). To maintain a careful, evidence-based assessment in these circumstances – where one could add a further ingredient of a fear of being accused of racist practice if cultural factors are ignored – is no easy task. For white workers in particular, the visceral anxiety involved may, as Ahmad (1989) has noted, serve to reinforce 'blackness' as a problem, and therefore impinge negatively on practice.

Assessments should involve working with children and their families

An underlying assumption of the framework for assessment is that the majority of parents want to do the best for their children, and that, in these circumstances, partnership between professionals and families is the key to a successful outcome. Therefore, an assessment is something that should be done *with* rather than *to* a family. Chapter 8 will discuss in depth the issues involved in working with parents. At this point, it is important to acknowledge that there may well be differences in how professionals can, do or should engage with different families.

Assessments should build on strengths as well as identify difficulties

This means that the assessment should be balanced, identifying both the positive and negative influences. While it is important that assessments do not gloss over any difficulties, and that the impact of these on the child are fully understood, the strengths in any given situation should also not be ignored or played down. Once more, this serves to illustrate the tightrope that workers have to negotiate in order to arrive at sound judgements during and following an assessment: balancing strengths and weaknesses of the family, but not over-playing either element, and at the same time keeping a constant focus on the child. The role of supervision here is once again crucial in assisting the worker to achieve this delicate and intricate task.

Assessments should be inter-agency in approach

Although social services have the lead responsibility for their conduct, assessments are, or at least should be, by their very nature multi-agency in character. The reason for this is that all children are very likely to have had contact with the universal services outlined in Chapter 1, and that, therefore, these services will have information to offer an assessment. A further reason is that these agencies may also be required, in some cases, to provide more specialist assessments, and it is therefore best that they have been involved from the very beginning of the assessment process. As well as these clear advantages, the inherent difficulties of the multi-agency nature of assessments should not be underestimated, and these will be addressed towards the end of this chapter.

Assessments should be a continuing process, not a single event

This has two main elements to it. First, sound assessments cannot be completed in a single visit due to their complexity (especially when the multi-agency work is factored in). Second, a form of assessment should continue through any intervention, so that plans and developments are continually discussed and reviewed. Certainly key decision-making meetings should be informed by an up-to-date assessment of the child's circumstances. On the other hand, as the document explains, this does not mean that assessments should be 'over intrusive, repeated unnecessarily or continued without any clear purpose or outcome' (ibid., p. 15). Once again, we see here the potential for contradiction and misunderstanding by professionals – on the one hand assessment should be continual, on the other hand it should not be intrusive – and once more there is the need for workers to tread the tightrope between the two and hope to maintain a steady, acceptable course.

Assessments should ensure that action and services are provided in parallel with the assessment

The document correctly recognizes that while assessments are spoken of as a discrete process, they do and should happen alongside other helpful activities with the family. If there are obvious and speedy services which can be provided, the workers should not wait until the outcome of the assessment to provide these. In the case of children at risk of significant harm, then clearly immediate steps may need to be taken to protect them; waiting for the outcome of a multi-agency assessment could be disastrous. There should, therefore, always be consideration of what services or intervention are needed to support the family during and after the process of assessment.

Assessments should be grounded in evidence

This means that assessments should make use of the expertise and bodies of knowledge of the various professionals involved in them. Furthermore, social workers (and their managers) should ensure that assessments are grounded in the most up-to-date knowledge. In addition, they should record information systematically, distinguish between sources of information (e.g. direct observation, other agency records or interviews with family members), learn from the views of family members, review progress and evaluate their own practice in order to continually develop their own skill levels. The key message here is that workers should use real, tangible knowledge based on hard evidence to inform their decisions, rather than rely on speculation, optimism or intuition. This, too, however, could prove difficult to achieve. Take one example to illustrate: if a child was being subject to emotional abuse by his or her parents, one of the factors to balance would be potentially conflicting information regarding what would be the best plan for that child. Maintaining an attachment with family members is known to be a key factor for sound development (see Smith, Cowie and Blades, 2003) so it could be argued that every effort should be made to enable the child to continue to live at home. However, if the emotional harm they are suffering is assessed as being significant, then the child should be protected from it, as there is also clear evidence that children who live in an emotional climate which erodes their personality are likely to be severely adversely affected by this (see Hagele, 2005). If the child is therefore removed from the parents and placed in care, this is also a potentially damaging experience – not only because the stability and continuity of the care by the parents is fractured, but also because, generally speaking, children in care fare less well than children living at home with their parents (see DfEE and DH, 2000). The workers involved in such a case would therefore have to evaluate at least two equally weighty but conflicting pieces of evidence about child development: on the one hand that living at home is generally best; on the other hand that exposure to significant emotional harm could potentially have a long-lasting negative impact on the child. In some cases of significant harm – physical or sexual abuse, for example – the decision is straight-forward and it is clear the child should be removed. It would also be wrong to assume that all children in care fare badly. However, certain decisions, where the harm is perhaps more insidious and nebulous, may be more difficult to make in the context of different expert opinions about what would be in the long-term interests of the child.

The structure of the assessment

Assessments consist of gathering information and coming to a deep understanding of three key areas, or domains. Each of these domains is then further subdivided into dimensions. The social worker is responsible for gathering information on all of these areas.

Domain 1: The developmental needs of the child
Dimensions

- **Health:** this is widely construed and includes growth and development as well as physical and mental well-being.
- **Education:** this too, should be interpreted broadly, and should cover all areas of a child's cognitive development, including play, from birth onwards.
- **Emotional and behavioural development:** the appropriateness of the responses, demonstrated by a child in terms of feelings and actions, to parents or carers, and, as the child grows older, to others beyond the family.
- **Identity:** the child's growing sense of self as a separate and valued person.
- **Family and social relationships:** the development of empathy and the capacity to place oneself in someone else's shoes. It includes such issues as the stability and warmth of the relationship between the child and parents or carers.
- **Social presentation:** the child's growing understanding of the way in which their appearance, behaviour, and any impairment are perceived by the outside world and the impression that these may create.
- **Self-care skills:** the acquisition by the child of practical, emotional and communication skills associated with increasing independence.

Domain 2: The capacity of the parents to meet the needs of the child
Dimensions

- **Basic care:** the extent to which the parents or carers provide for the child's physical needs, and appropriate medical and dental care.
- **Ensuring safety:** the extent to which parents or carers ensure the child is adequately protected from harm or danger.
- **Emotional warmth:** the extent to which parents or carers ensure the child's emotional needs are met, and that the child is provided with a sense of being specially valued.
- **Stimulation:** the promotion of the child's learning and intellectual development through encouragement and cognitive stimulation and the promotion of social opportunities.
- **Guidance and boundaries:** the parent's ability to provide appropriate boundaries and to enable the child to regulate their own emotions and behaviour.
- **Stability:** the provision of a sufficiently stable family environment to enable a child to develop and maintain a secure attachment to parents or carers in order to ensure optimal development.

Domain 3: Wider family and environmental factors
Dimensions

- **Family history and functioning:** this includes both genetic and psychosocial factors.
- **Wider family:** this should be interpreted broadly to include the role not only of blood relatives but also significant associates of the family.

- **Housing:** the quality of the accommodation in which the child lives.
- **Employment:** the nature and impact of work in the family.
- **Income:** the availability of income over time.
- **The family's social integration:** the exploration of the wider context of the local neighbourhood and community and its impact on the child and parents.
- **Community resources:** the facilities and services in a particular neighbourhood, including universal services of primary health care, day care and schools, places of worship, transport, shops and leisure activities.

Clearly, the social worker alone is highly unlikely to have access to all of the above information. Certainly, the parents or carers should be involved in providing some of the details. However, in order for the assessment to be full and meaningful, several agencies should also contribute to it. For example, schools or early years settings should provide information for the 'education' dimension or perhaps on some dimensions of the parenting capacity domain too. A health visitor, in addition to furnishing details for the 'health' dimension may also have insight into the parenting capacity domain. The local Housing Authority could be contacted in respect of any rent arrears or other relevant matters where the family is living in local authority rented accommodation. In engaging these other professionals, the social worker will need to be cognizant of the issues surrounding the gaining of consent from family members for the sharing of information, details of which are explored in Chapter 7.

The lengthy list of domains and dimensions is very likely to yield a large amount of detailed and rich information. The social worker will therefore need to ensure that this information is dealt with in a structured manner. The framework for assessment document reminds us of the importance of a number of issues related to this. It specifies that it is important that:

- information is gathered and recorded systematically and precisely. If this does not happen, there is scope for information to become lost, confused or misrepresented.
- information gathered is checked with parents and the child where appropriate. Clearly this refers mostly to factual information regarding the family and their circumstances. Opinions or interpretations of information should be openly shared with family members but the social worker would not be expected to have them approved before including them in the final report. Nevertheless, it is important that family members have an opportunity to check the veracity of data and certain claims within the assessment report before it is shared with a wider audience. Older children should be included in this exercise at a level which is appropriate to their age and understanding.
- differences in views are recorded. Particularly where the social worker has a view, based on the available evidence, about a particular aspect of the family, and where the parents disagree with this view, this should be recorded in the assessment report. Clear reasons for the difference in opinions should also be logged.
- clear strengths and difficulties are identified. In the assessment report, the social worker should, perhaps in summary form, list the clearly identifiable strengths and weaknesses of the family situation which contribute to the overall conclusion of the assessment. This is important in presenting both to the family and to other relevant professionals a balanced view of the issues which have been considered, and which impinge upon the child.

- vulnerabilities and protective factors in the child's world are examined. This means that the mass of information needs to be properly and carefully processed. The social worker should be asking a fundamental question – 'What does all this information mean?' This should lead systematically to a focus on the child, which is the subject of the final point here.
- the impact of what is happening to the child is identified. The whole point and fulcrum of the assessment should be the child, and how their needs are or are not being met, how capable are the parents of meeting their needs both now and into the future, and how the wider family and environmental factors impinge upon the welfare of the child. The assessment report should include very clear information and conclusions regarding the daily experiences of the child, so that one fundamental question is addressed and answered – 'What is life like for that child living in that household?'

What factors might impede sound assessment?

The *Framework for Assessment* guidance document sets out what the ideal approach to, and standard of, assessment should be. However, this ideal can be compromised by a number of factors which have been explored in a further publication from the Department of Health (DH, 2000b) whose very title emphases the child-centred imperative of assessments. It is called *The Child's World: Assessing Children in Need* and this reflects the need for assessments to explore, and reach clear conclusions about, how the child experiences their world and how these experiences impact on their well-being and safety.

The publication highlights many factors that could distract professionals from focusing on the child during the course of an assessment, grouped into four categories: factors about the child, about the worker, about the family and about the agency. It is important that these are not presented and understood as criticisms, weaknesses or faults of the child, the family or the worker. Rather, they are real, whether tangible, conscious or subconscious and reflect the complex array and interplay of issues at work when professionals engage with human beings under stress, in difficulty or in crisis. These distracting factors require articulating, acknowledging and addressing if children are to be kept at the focus of the assessment. Responsibility for this lies not only with the professional undertaking the assessment, but also with their supervisor, to ensure that sufficient focus is given to the *process* during assessments as well as to any outcomes. If the former is ignored, it can make the latter shallow and dangerously meaningless.

In keeping with the theme of the book, this chapter will only focus on those factors associated with agencies. Readers are urged to consult the original publication for the full list under the other three categories.

Factors about the agency which could distract from focusing on the child include:

- **Changes happening, for example, reorganization.** Where an agency is going through a structural change, this can cause anxiety and stress to the worker. They may be concerned, for example, about whether their job is safe, who their new manager may be, where they may be based if moving offices, or who their new colleagues may be. These preoccupations may prevent the worker from fully focusing on the needs of the child whom they may happen to be assessing at the time.

- **Poor inter-agency communication.** Where some of the barriers already discussed in Chapter 2 are present, it can be difficult for the worker to maintain focus on the child. They may be distracted by the problems with other agencies, or simply fail to have all the necessary information on which to make an informed decision regarding the welfare of the child.
- **New legislation or policy introduced.** The agency may be coping with the introduction of a major initiative which impacts on all workers. This may require a large training schedule. Where the initiative has a significant impact on practice, this can lead to anxiety among workers about 'getting it right', which in turn can lead to them being concerned about this, perhaps at the expense of focusing on the needs of any child they happen to be assessing at the time.
- **Cut-backs in resources.** Where agencies have to make substantial savings, and therefore reduce expenditure, the worker may well be worried about the impact of this upon them. They may be concerned about their job security, or about having to take on more work if colleagues retire or are made redundant. Once again, these preoccupations may prevent them from fully focusing on the needs of the child during any assessments undertaken at the time.
- **Staff shortages.** If the agency is short-staffed for whatever reason, this could have a knock-on effect upon remaining individual workers. They may be placed, or feel, under huge pressure or moral obligation to fulfil the work of their absent colleagues, or they may be anxious about the levels of incomplete work. It is likely that staff shortages will lead to stress among workers, which itself may prevent them from functioning as fully as possible.
- **High use of agency staff.** Where permanent members of staff are unavailable for whatever reason, agencies may use short-term, temporary staff employed through social work agencies to plug any gaps. While this is helpful at one level (there are bodies present to complete work), it can also cause difficulties. The permanent staff may be required to mentor them or generally support them in office procedures and so on. If there is a high turnover of agency staff, the permanent workers have to familiarize themselves with new colleagues on a regular basis. They may also be concerned about the quality of work undertaken by agency staff, if they feel that they are inexperienced or that their training is out of date. In this context, maintaining a clear focus on the child may be problematic.
- **Functional divisions, for example, between child protection and disability services.** Where an agency has separated out different functions it can cause barriers. On the one hand, of course, it is positive that there are specialist workers say in disability who can be called upon where the worker may be assessing the needs of a disabled child. However, the process can be slow, as the commitments of the specialist worker may be at odds with those of the worker undertaking the assessment. There may also be subtle differences in how the families are perceived and approached by the different workers, thus potentially causing confusion or even a split, which parents could use to demonstrate that, for instance, the worker undertaking the assessment is being harsh or unfair.

Having considered each of these many factors individually, it is important to bear in mind that it is very likely that any particular worker may well be faced with a combination of these at any one time, thus potentially exaggerating their impact upon their ability to fully focus on the needs of the child. For instance, if an inexperienced and poorly supervised worker, working in the context of staff shortages, is assessing a deaf child whose parents are hostile and suspicious, then there is a real possibility that the needs of the child may become lost in this maelstrom. In these circumstances, one real danger is that workers begin to make assumptions about the family, and about the needs of the child, and how these are or are not being met. What is so dangerous about assumptions is that they limit further exploration. If a worker makes an assumption about a family or a child, they have the 'answer' and therefore do not need to seek it elsewhere. In this way, children can be left in situations which are potentially dangerous for them.

The Common Assessment Framework (CAF)

According to the Department for Education and Skills, renamed the Department for Children, Schools and Families in late 2007, the Common Assessment Framework (CAF) is a 'key part of delivering frontline services that are integrated and focused around the needs of children and young people' (DfES, 2007b, p. 1). The government appears to have high hopes for the CAF as a standardized approach to conducting an assessment of a child's additional needs and deciding how those needs should be met. The intention is that it will be used by all practitioners across children's services in England by the end of 2008.

As described in the practitioner's guide to the CAF, it is designed to be used for children with additional needs. These are defined as children who, in the judgement of the practitioners, 'will not progress towards the five *Every Child Matters* priority outcomes' (DfES, 2006b, p. 10) without additional services. The five outcomes referred to here are:

- Being healthy
- Staying safe
- Enjoying and achieving
- Making a positive contribution
- Achieving economic well-being.

The *Every Child Matters* programme will be discussed in detail in Chapter 9.

 Information: Distinguishing children 'in need' from children with 'additional needs'

Children requiring a full assessment under the *Framework for Assessment* guidance are those who may be 'in need' as defined by Section 17 of the Children Act 1989, including those in need of protection. The approximate number of children involved in England and Wales here is 300,000 to 400,000. The Common Assessment Framework (CAF) is intended for those children with 'additional needs', especially those who may not realize the five broad outcomes mentioned in *Every Child Matters*. It therefore covers a wider range of children. Interestingly, the guidance document for practitioners regarding the CAF does not put a figure on this, although it is surely reasonable to suppose that those children described as 'vulnerable' by the *Framework for Assessment* guidance are very likely to have additional needs. This is approximately one-third of all children. Since the CAF is potentially relevant for children aged up to 19 years and the population of children under the age of 20 in England and Wales is 13 million, this amounts to approximately 4.3 million children (Office for National Statistics, 2004).

One of the reasons for this much broader sweep of children for assessment, made explicit in the practitioner's guide, is the early identification of problems and subsequent provision of appropriate services in order to prevent crises being reached. Other benefits of the CAF put forward include a quicker and better service provision, less repetition and duplication for families (as only one worker gathers all relevant information), more effective communication between agencies (due to the common language used), and more efficient use of worker's time (as they can build on existing information).

In contrast with the assessment for children in need, it is not the social worker who undertakes the CAF. Rather, practitioners in universal services such as early years settings, schools and health settings are expected to carry them out. The rationale for this is that staff in these services are best equipped to identify possible needs in their early stages. The police are also identified as having an important role in identifying children with additional needs and arranging for common assessments. While all services should train some staff in how to complete the CAF, the aim is that everyone working with children should be aware of the sorts of situations that indicate the need for a common assessment.

The process of the CAF

The CAF consists of the following elements:

- A simple pre-assessment checklist to help practitioners decide who would benefit from a common assessment.
- A three-step process (prepare, discuss, deliver) for undertaking a common assessment.
- A standard form to help practitioners record, and, where appropriate, share with others, the findings from the assessment.

In line with the *Framework for Assessment*, the CAF involves assessing the needs of the child across three domains: the child's development, parenting capacity, and wider family and environmental factors. Each of these is further subdivided into dimensions more or less precisely in line with those in the *Framework for Assessment*. The process which then follows involves three distinct steps:

- **Step 1: Preparation.** This involves the worker recognizing potential needs and engaging in an initial discussion with the child, parents or carers as appropriate. The worker may liaise with their manager, colleagues or others, possibly those already involved with the child. One of the aims of this information sharing would be to find out whether a common assessment already exists. A decision is then made whether or not to undertake a common assessment. This can only be done with the agreement of the child and/or family as appropriate. It is entirely voluntary on the part of the family. If there are concerns regarding the child's welfare, the worker would follow local safeguarding children procedures.
- **Step 2: Discussion.** This involves completing the assessment with the child and family, along with a statement confirming their consent. The aim of the discussion and assessment is to better understand the child and family's strengths and needs, along with what services may be of help.

- **Step 3: Delivery.** The first step here is for the worker and family to agree what each can deliver. Secondly, there should be consideration of what may be needed from other services. Thirdly, these other services are contacted, and additional support agreed as appropriate. Where integrated support is required, a lead professional is appointed. It is important to emphasize that workers cannot promise a service from another agency without consulting that agency.

The role of the lead professional mentioned above requires further discussion. Briefly their role is to coordinate the actions identified in the assessment, and be a single point of contact for families being supported by more than one service (ibid.). They have a responsibility to support the family in making choices and in navigating their way through the support systems available. They should ensure that the family receives appropriate and timely services which are well planned and reviewed.

The idea is that the lead professional role helps to ensure that professional involvement is rationalized, coordinated and communicated effectively such that, ultimately, the children and families experience better support than if there were no lead professional appointed. The Department for Education Skills (2005d, p. 1) states that 'evidence from practice suggests that the lead professional role is a key element of effective frontline delivery of integrated children's services'. This is supported to a degree by research into a very similar role, that of key worker for families who have disabled children (Greco *et al.*, 2005). However, this study also found that outcomes varied between and within areas, and that the factors associated with better outcomes included effective management of the service, a clear definition and understanding of the key worker role, and provision of training and supervision for key workers. These findings very much support the notion in order to build and maintain effective services to families, workers involved in the delivery of these need to be well managed, trained and supported. This clearly takes time, money and effective use of resources, and the use of a lead professional or similar role should never be seen as a cheap 'short-cut' option.

Evaluation of the CAF

Twelve local areas formally trialled the CAF and the role of the lead professional during 2005 and 2006. The University of East Anglia (Brandon *et al.*, 2006) was commissioned to evaluate these trials. This study involved a total of 114 practitioner, manager and senior manager respondents in interviews, workshops, diary recordings, telephone interviews and telephone surveys. It raises some serious questions about the process and casts something of a shadow over the claims made for the CAF by the government. While there was general enthusiasm for the CAF and the role of Lead Professional, there were real challenges presented by it, such as the generation of additional work. Furthermore, some services found it difficult to fully understand what a holistic assessment entails, and how to work in partnership with families. Most pointedly perhaps, in the light of the barriers to effective multi-agency work encountered in Chapter 2, 'anxiety and frustration was generated by lack of clarity about how the work was to be done, lack of support, threshold differences and lack of join up between agencies and sectors' (ibid., p. 6). It seems that this research reaffirms the message that merely 'making' different agencies work together does not automatically result in seamless, unproblematic high-quality work: many of the traditional barriers to effective multi-agency work seem to remain.

In relation to the role of the lead professional, results suggested that less than half felt well supported, although the majority of individuals were comfortable in the role. In particular, lead professionals found the high level of responsibility and the chairing of meetings daunting. Within this, there was little knowledge of what to do if disagreements arose. The researchers also found a reluctance to share equitably the responsibility for taking on the lead professional role, such that those who appeared confident in this role were left to take on the lion's share. Finally, ongoing support and multi-agency training is seen to be essential to promoting effective work.

The Department for Education and Skills appears to have rushed through the CAF rather hastily. The research referred to above reports that a common response from participants was 'It's still too early to say' (ibid., p. 77). Furthermore, it is interesting that the research brief from the Department for Education and Skills to the researchers did not include eliciting the views of children and families as to the benefits of the process. The authors of the report refer to this as a 'major omission' (ibid.) and it seems especially so in light of the apparent focus the government has placed on listening to children and families. One can draw several conclusions from this, including that the Department for Education and Skills wanted a quick and limited evaluation with which to support the rhetoric of the CAF; another conclusion could be that they were somewhat apprehensive of what children and families might say about the process.

Additional questions regarding the whole CAF process remain. The much broader sweep for assessments of families compared to the *Framework for Assessment* brings into focus a potentially major practical problem of how agencies offer a quality service to what could be 4.3 million children. It could be argued that this is a deliberate and rather clever move by the government to pass responsibility for improved outcomes for children to local level, while they themselves appear reluctant to fully tackle, for instance, the problem of child poverty which remains a major contributor to poor outcomes for children. Furthermore, there is something of a contradiction at the heart of this process – if the completion of the CAF by families is entirely voluntary, and if other agencies can refuse to offer any additional services requested, then a key premise of the CAF can be questioned: early identification and prevention of deterioration can be seriously compromised by families declining to take part and/or by agencies declining to offer help and support. Not that compulsory imposition of services upon families is desirable; rather the CAF appears to have certain inherent and fundamental difficulties in trying to meet its aim, particularly when one considers the very real and entrenched problems associated with multi-agency working that appear to surface with its use.

(?) Reflections: Case study – the McLoughlin family

Read the following case study which contains an assessment. Consider the questions which then follow.

McLoughlin family composition (all white British)

Laura (Age 26)	Mother
Mark (Age 6)	Son
Stella (Age 4)	Daughter
Christopher (Age 18 months)	Son

The family lived in a small, poorly furnished local authority flat with no safe play area outside. The area of town was not well served by public services. Family income was via state benefits. One night, at around 2.00 a.m., a member of the public found Mark wandering around the street. He had got out of the flat after the three children were left alone. The police were called and they forced entry to the flat. The children were physically unharmed, but the flat was in a very dirty and insanitary state. The children's bed clothes were soiled with urine and faeces, and the toilet and bath were similarly infested. There was almost no food in the house. The children were taken into police protection, and Social Services were contacted. A social worker was assigned to the case. The children were made subject to a legal order and initially placed in foster care. They then went to stay with their father who lived nearby. The social worker's key tasks were twofold: conducting an assessment of the family, and coordinating and implementing a multi-agency plan to support the family. This involved offering practical support to the father, Thomas, as well as supporting Laura emotionally and practically to improve her situation, with a view to the children returning to her care. A large part of this was supporting Laura in addressing her emotional needs, helping her to understand how the situation that led to the children's removal had arisen, and what needed to be done to put things right. This was counselling-type work which discovered that Laura's acute depression in the preceding months had been sparked by a miscarriage which she kept secret from everyone. She also began to drink heavily. During this malaise, the toilet broke, and she did not have the energy to contact Housing to get it fixed – the family began using the bath as a toilet. This added to the stress and sense of overwhelming helplessness and ended up with the total neglect of the children's physical and emotional welfare. During this work, it emerged that Laura was a capable parent who had temporarily failed to meet the needs of her children. She showed a great deal of determination and resilience in working towards having her children returned to her care. The assessment identified other needs which led to the following multi-agency responses:

- Securing full-time nursery places for Stella and Christopher to provide opportunities for play and stimulation.
- Securing and funding a place at the after-school club for Mark to allow him to socialize with peers, as he took some caring responsibilities for the younger children during his mother's period of depression.
- Ensuring Laura had all the benefits she was entitled to.
- A positive response to an application for rehousing.
- Direct work with, and observations of, the children (individually and together) to determine their wishes and feelings.
- Practical assistance for the children to attend health appointments.

The outcome was that after 4 months, a multi-agency decision was made that it was in the interests of the children to be returned to Laura's care. The father supported this decision. Initially the children returned to live with her in the flat (now restored to a good state of hygiene) but soon after the family were offered, and accepted, a three-bedroom house with a garden and much closer to local amenities. The children made good progress and after a further 12 months, social services involvement was no longer required.

1 Which assessment framework do you think the social worker used here – the *Framework for Assessment* or the Common Assessment Framework?
2 How were the children's needs addressed?
3 How was Laura's parenting capacity assessed?
4 What were the significant wider family and environmental factors that impinged on this case? How were they addressed, and how did this contribute to the successful outcome?

Conclusions

This chapter has discussed two distinct types of assessment. The first, under the *Framework for the Assessment of Children in Need and Their Families* is led by a social worker, and is appropriate where it appears a child is 'in need' of extra services, or in need of protection from harm. The second, under the Common Assessment Framework, can be led by a trained professional from any discipline, and is appropriate when children have additional needs, potentially a very large group of children. A significant issue here is how professionals make the distinction between a child being 'in need' and a child having additional needs: there is the potential here for uncertainty. Furthermore, there is a question as to whether full resources are available to meet the needs of all the children who may be identified as having additional needs. A significant moral dilemma may arise if large numbers of children and parents are led to believe support is available, and yet that support is then not forthcoming. One consequence of this is that assessments and resources might become focused on those children who professionals decide need safeguarding. As this is such a key area, it forms the subject of the next chapter.

Part Two
MULTI-AGENCY WORK IN SPECIFIC CONTEXTS

Safeguarding children   4

Introduction

This chapter will consider current systems and processes, based around the role of social services, and social workers in particular, in engaging other professionals in protecting children. It will cover implications for multi-agency working flowing from the formal definitions of abuse which all professionals are expected to use, and from the system in place for the referral of, and subsequent response to, serious concerns about children. The chapter will not consider matters related to family court proceedings, the ultimate destination for those small numbers of cases which cannot be successfully resolved while maintaining the child within their family. As the focus is on legislation and guidance produced by the then Department for Education and Skills (renamed the Department for Children, Schools and Families in late 2007) as it applies to England, readers are referred to the following documents covering safeguarding children in the other three countries of the United Kingdom:

Wales: The Welsh Assembly Government (2007a) document Safeguarding Children: Working Together under the Children Act 2004.

Scotland: The Scottish Executive (2004) publication Protecting Children and Young People: Framework for Standards.

Northern Ireland: The Department of Health, Social Services and Public Safety (DHSSPS, 2003) document Co-operating to Safeguard Children.

Each of these contains similar guidance to that contained within the English version.

What is safeguarding children?

The first consideration is that of a change of language, in line with the shift away from a restricted approach of 'child protection' towards a much broader agenda of 'safeguarding and promoting the welfare of children' as discussed in Chapter 2. This is worth unpacking a little further. The term child protection or protecting children was commonplace among professionals until around 2003. Then, along with the *Every Child Matters* programme (DfES, 2003) there came a central government emphasis on changing the language to reflect what they believed should be a much broader approach than intervening only when there was acute risk of serious harm. This new approach linked in with the notion of prevention: rather than waiting for the crisis, as it were, it was deemed much better to get in early and stop the crisis from happening in the first place; hence the new terminology of 'safeguarding children' and 'promoting their welfare'. One tangible example of the imposition of this new approach was that one key existing multi-agency structure for coordinating child protection activity at local level – Area Child Protection Committees – were replaced by a new body – Local Safeguarding Children Boards, with wider powers and responsibilities.

 Information: What is safeguarding and promoting the welfare of children?

The national guidance *Working Together to Safeguard Children* (DfES, 2006i) provides some answers to this question, stating that it means:

- protecting children from maltreatment
- preventing impairment of children's health or development
- ensuring that children are growing up in circumstances consistent with the provision of safe and effective care
- professionals undertaking their role to enable children to have optimum life chances and to enter adulthood successfully.

Child protection is therefore seen as one part of safeguarding and promoting the welfare of children. The guidance goes on to say that children need protecting when:

- they are suffering, or likely to suffer, 'significant harm' and the harm is attributable to a lack of adequate parental care or control. There are no absolute criteria for judging what 'significant' harm is, but in doing so, consideration should be given to the:
  o severity of any ill-treatment
  o degree and extent of harm
  o duration of harm
  o frequency of harm.

While the focus on prevention and a broader approach to child welfare is generally to be welcomed it does carry a potential danger. To subsume 'child protection' within a wide interpretation of 'safeguarding' and to reduce it to only one of four elements of 'safeguarding' – protection from maltreatment – is to risk losing a focus on child protection. Professionals, when faced with complex family problems which may or do include child abuse, may focus on the other three elements of 'safeguarding' in the belief that these together override the one element concerned with 'protection'. If they feel encouraged to take a 'safeguarding' approach rather than a narrower 'protection' approach, they will have to make decisions, for instance, about how to separate any harm they encounter from 'impairment of health or development' (which is not serious enough to warrant statutory intervention) or about what constitutes care that is not 'safe and effective', or indeed whether the harm is merely preventing children having 'optimum life chances . . . to enter adulthood successfully' or is more significant, and therefore requiring of immediate protective action. Clearly, experienced professionals generally make judgements based on sound evidence and processing of that evidence; however, if there is a further layer of processing involved, and an expectation to approach families in a broad preventative manner, this could blur the judgements regarding 'significant' harm, particularly where any harm is unsupported by dramatic physical evidence such as a serious injury.

Definitions of abuse

To assist professionals in reaching decisions as to what constitutes 'significant' harm, the national guidance *Working Together to Safeguard Children* (DfES, 2006i) provides what amounts to definitions of abuse under four categories. All agencies are expected to be familiar with these categories and definitions, and use them to classify harm to children. As these are the only categories in use, any form of abuse should be able to be catered for by them. They are reproduced here verbatim from the national guidance:

Physical abuse may involve hitting, shaking, throwing, poisoning, burning or scalding, drowning, suffocating, or otherwise causing physical harm to a child. Physical harm may also be caused when a parent or carer fabricates the symptoms of, or deliberately induces illness in a child.

Sexual abuse involves forcing or enticing a child or young person to take part in sexual activities, including prostitution, whether or not the child is aware of what is happening. The activities may involve physical contact, including penetrative (e.g. rape or buggery or oral sex) or non-penetrative acts. They may include non-contact activities, such as involving children in looking at, or in the production of, pornographic material or watching sexual activities, or encouraging children to behave in sexually inappropriate ways.

Emotional abuse is the persistent emotional maltreatment of a child such as to cause severe and persistent adverse effects on the child's emotional development. It may involve conveying to children that they are worthless or unloved, inadequate, or valued only insofar as they meet the needs of another person. It may feature age or developmentally inappropriate expectations being imposed on children. These may include interactions that are beyond the child's developmental capability, as well as overprotection and limitation of exploration and learning, or preventing the child participating in normal social interaction. It may involve seeing or hearing the ill-treatment of another. It may involve serious bullying causing children frequently to feel frightened or in danger, or the exploitation or corruption of children. Some level of emotional abuse is involved in all types of maltreatment of a child, though it may occur alone.

Neglect is the persistent failure to meet a child's basic physical and/or psychological needs, likely to result in the serious impairment of the child's health or development. Neglect may occur during pregnancy as a result of maternal substance abuse. Once a child is born, neglect may involve a parent or carer failing to provide adequate food and clothing, shelter including exclusion from home or abandonment, failing to protect a child from physical and emotional harm or danger, failure to ensure adequate supervision including the use of inadequate care-takers, or the failure to ensure access to appropriate medical care or treatment. It may also include neglect of, or unresponsiveness to, a child's basic emotional needs.

A point worth making immediately is that, clearly, the received definitions of what constitutes child abuse change over time. This is based upon our developing awareness of what is harmful to children and upon the way children and childhood are socially constructed within society. For instance, in Victorian England it was commonplace, even encouraged, for very young children to be set to work in dangerous occupations such as mining, reflecting what Williams (1961) calls the 'dominant social character' (p. 60) of the time which believed in the value of work. Furthermore, working children from poor families were seen to contribute to the financial stability of the family and to general economic growth (see Kirby, 2003). The four definitions given above have indeed changed twice since they were first introduced in 1991. Generally they have expanded to include a wider range of activities. Some examples may be helpful here. For sexual abuse, the words 'including prostitution' are added to the 2006 version. This reflects a change in the way children who are engaged in prostitution are now dealt with: a move away from treating them as 'prostitutes' who broke the law by soliciting and therefore in need of a punitive response, towards treating them as 'victims of abuse' in need of protection. A further example is provided in the definition of emotional abuse. An addition to the 2006 version, that emotional abuse 'may involve seeing or hearing the ill-treatment of another' is clearly a response to evidence that children living in households where there is domestic violence suffer significant emotional harm (see, for example, Mullender and Morley, 1994). The final example is with regard to neglect. Additions include that neglect 'may occur during pregnancy as a result of maternal substance abuse' or from a 'failure to ensure adequate supervision including the use of inadequate care-takers'. Here we have neglect pertaining to unborn babies, as well as to the complex area of babysitting. This will be further discussed later.

Multi-agency working and interpretations of the definitions of abuse

Professionals will bring to their work, and to the judgements they make within it, a range of views, perceptions and experiences which are very likely to influence their interpretations of situations and evidence they encounter, and their opinions regarding the thresholds for 'significant' harm under each definition.

Physical abuse

While every sensible minded person is likely to agree that many of the examples of abuse towards children given in this definition – throwing, poisoning, burning, scalding, drowning, suffocating – are unacceptable and need immediate action, there is a real problem with the first example given – hitting. In all four countries of the United Kingdom, it is not against the law for a parent to hit their child. In England and Wales, the Children Act 2004 retained for parents the right to use 'reasonable chastisement' against their children, and in 2007 the government reinforced this position by again ruling out plans to make smacking of children illegal (BBC News, 2007c). While parents can hit their own children, they cannot hit somebody else's child – however slight, this would be likely to constitute an assault. Furthermore, of course, a parent cannot hit another adult – this is also likely to constitute an assault. Therefore, the situation is that a child is unprotected by the law, in terms of being hit, if it happens to be their parent who is doing the hitting. The reason for this appears to be a view that children are the 'private property' of parents (rather than, say, the responsibility of the community or the society as whole) and as such, parents have certain inalienable rights over their children, including the right to hit them. Apart from the contradictory position of this law – the smallest, potentially most vulnerable members of society have the least protection against hitting if the perpetrator of the hitting is their parent – it also raises a question of what the word 'reasonable' means. There is no definition in law of this word: it is left up to professionals, alone and together where necessary, to interpret it and apply this interpretation to practical situations which they face. Immediately, therefore, we are propelled into a scenario where a professional, perhaps visiting a family alone, has to decide that the hit they have seen, or been told about, or suspect, is 'reasonable' according to their personal views, their experience and their understanding of what constitutes 'significant' harm. They may consider such questions as 'How hard does the hit have to be to count as abuse?' 'Is it more about the frequency of the hitting than about how hard it is?' 'If a parent hits their child occasionally (even quite hard) but otherwise is warm and supportive towards them, is this better than the child never being hit, but also not receiving very much warmth and support?'

Sexual abuse

Once again, at first glance it appears that the list of activities and examples given in the definition need addressing immediately if they came to light. That is not to say, however, that there are not tensions here as well. This is particularly likely to be so when professionals try to apply the definition to young people engaged in sexual activity. Here, the moral dilemmas can be acute. The law, at one level, is clear – there are legal ages of consent. However, many young people engage in sexual activity when younger than the legal ages of consent.

 Information: The age of consent in the United Kingdom

The age of consent for both heterosexual and homosexual intercourse in England, Wales and Scotland is 16; in Northern Ireland it is 17. More specific laws protect children under the age of 13 in England, Wales and Scotland, and 14 in Northern Ireland, who cannot legally give their consent to any form of sexual activity, and there is a maximum sentence of life imprisonment for certain acts. The law is not intended to prosecute two young people of a similar age engaging in mutually agreed teenage sexual activity.

Where this occurs, the ages, maturity, levels of consent or coercion of the two youngsters involved should be considered before a response is made. Decisions will need to be made as how similar the ages need to be to be acceptable, and how mutual was the sexual activity. Professionals may need to consider at what point an age gap might become unacceptable? What if the girl was 15 (under the official age of consent) but the man was 18? Is this acceptable? Would it depend on a whole set of additional circumstances such as the maturity of the girl, or the exact relationship between the two people, for instance, if the man was in a position of authority over the girl? If we do say that it is acceptable, what if we increase the age of the man? At what point would it become unacceptable? 19? 21? 25? What would be the reasons for any decision based on the age difference? What if we flip the genders around? What if the boy was 15 and the woman was 18? 19? 25? Is there a difference in how professionals should respond to such instances for boys compared to girls? If so, what might lie behind this difference? Should there be a difference in how same gender relationships are viewed? If so, what might be the reasons for this? For professionals working with young people on a daily basis, for example, in secondary schools, these questions may surface in some form when they are faced with situations involving young people and sexual activity.

Physical and sexual abuse can occur, and should be responded to, following a single incident. The other two categories – emotional abuse and neglect – must by definition occur more than once over a period of time. This brings its own difficulties for professionals struggling to act appropriately when faced with concerns, and these are discussed in the paragraphs that follow.

Emotional abuse

This form of harm can perhaps be the most difficult to detect, quantify and deal with. Often the issues are related to the quality and texture of the relationship between the adult and the child, and there is significant scope here for interpretation, differing perceptions or varying standards of acceptability to be at play. Parents, if faced with a suggestion they may be emotionally abusing their child, can respond by arguing the child is merely being oversensitive; professionals are likely to have very different ideas about what level of emotional harm is acceptable in parenting or not, given that it is likely to be highly unusual for them to encounter any parent who does not show some level of negative emotion towards their child. At what point does this become abusive? Of course, the definition is clear that the harm must be persistent and severe; therefore, occasional bouts of temper or shouting at children would not count if they were balanced with love, affection and support. It is the general emotional climate which professionals should assess when concerned with emotional abuse. They should ask 'Is the child receiving a balance of care, love and encouragement, or a balance of indifference, negativity and of being undermined?' If the latter, it is likely to need attention under the definition of emotional abuse.

Nevertheless, there still exists, in aspects of the definition, the opportunity for serious doubts and questions to be raised. Take parents who apply significant pressure on their children to achieve academically or in a particular sport, necessitating lengthy daily routines of practice, perhaps against the child's wishes. Is this abusive, if it is persistent over time? Might there be a double standard at play here, with middle-class parents perceived to be trying to 'better' their children receiving a more favourable response compared with working-class parents who might expect young children to help with household chores and childcare while the parents are at work?

The phrase in the definition that emotional abuse may involve 'overprotection and limitation of exploration and learning, or preventing the child participating in normal social interaction' is equally troublesome. Might this mean that a professional may perceive that if a parent does not attend a toddler's group with their child, or send their child to a nursery, or allow them to play outside, that they are emotionally abusing them? There is an assumption here that the private family space is inherently limited and limiting, and that public space is always good. Of course, in its extreme form, limiting children's opportunities for interaction and play can be very damaging; yet to include the above phrase in a definition of emotional abuse potentially allows state intervention into family life where parents, perhaps with sound reason, have chosen not to engage their child fully in what the state has decided is good for them. Furthermore, within this phrase, what is 'normal' social interaction? Who does, or should decide, what is meant by 'normal'? Unless these questions are raised and a working solution found, the dangers are either that there develops a silent consensus among professionals around what 'normal' means, or that individual professionals impose their own interpretation of 'normal', which is likely only to obfuscate decisions about children.

The key point from these examples is that if professionals feel that the definition of emotional abuse allows them potentially to draw in a wide range of behaviours, it could lead to conflict between different agencies. Some referrals to social services from other agencies may be considered inappropriate by social workers. Tension may also arise if a professional in the field feels strongly that the behaviour they have witnessed, catered for by the definition, is abusive, and that the social worker, taking a different position, is not taking their concerns seriously enough. These differences are likely to be particularly acute when trying to interpret harm which by its very nature is more ethereal, imprecise and nebulous than physical or sexual abuse.

Neglect

Like emotional abuse, to count as abusive, neglect must be persistent and serious. It is clearly not neglectful, therefore, if a parent forgets to send their child to school with a packed lunch once only, or if, due to parental illness, the care of the child takes a slight downturn for a week or two. The reason for the need to ensure that only serious matters are dealt with is to avoid professionals imposing their own values onto families: thus, for example, it could not be considered neglectful for a child to attend school with a creased uniform, shirt hanging out and shoelaces undone. If, on the other hand, the same child went to school every day with no lunch, was always hungry, dirty, smelly, had persistent infections and so on, then there is very likely to be an issue of neglect which needs addressing. However, in between these two extremes there are many grey areas.

For example, take the phrase that neglect may result from 'failure to ensure adequate supervision including the use of inadequate care-takers'. In its extreme form it would clearly be neglectful for young children to be left unsupervised for long periods, or for young children to be left in the care of other children, or adults who were palpably irresponsible. However, this is a complex area. There is the somewhat contradictory position that although the law does not set a minimum age at which children can be left alone, it is an offence to leave a child alone when doing so puts them at risk (NSPCC, 2006). Parents, therefore, have to make a judgement about this, and the NSPCC has produced a list of factors for parents to consider. These include:

- the age of the child
- the child's level of maturity and understanding
- the place where the child will be left
- how long the child will be left alone, and how often
- whether or not there are any other children alone with the child.

Some interesting points arise out of this, identified by the NSPCC. They argue that a 16-year-old child left alone for an evening is likely to be acceptable to most, but to leave the same child alone for a week is likely to be unacceptable. However, this seems somewhat bizarre when children can leave home and live independently at the age of 16. The NSPCC also states that while most children play outdoors without supervision, this is seen as vital for their development.

The law on babysitting is equally vague. Once again, the law does not state an age at which young people can babysit, or indeed the youngest age at which a child should be left with a babysitter. However, where parents use babysitters under the age of 16, they remain legally responsible to ensure their child comes to no harm. Furthermore, under the Children and Young Persons Act, 1933 (still in force) parents can be prosecuted for wilful neglect if they leave a child unsupervised 'in a manner likely to cause unnecessary suffering or injury to health'. In light of this, the NSPCC recommends that no child under the age of 16 is used as a babysitter. Parents, therefore, are expected to make a judgement regarding the suitability of babysitters in terms of their maturity and levels of responsibility. This can be difficult as, for example, a 15-year-old can be more sensible and mature than a 16-year-old, making a decision based on age alone complicated. The implication of all of this for professionals who may encounter a wide variety of babysitters or indeed of situations where children are left alone is that they, too, will have to make a judgement, based on all the factors identified above, and on their knowledge of the parents and the particular child concerned. Equally likely to impinge on these decisions are the personal value systems and experience of the worker making the judgement. Where these clash with those of other professionals with whom they are sharing any concerns, this could lead to tensions between agencies.

In and among all of these questions, tensions and issues, what needs emphasizing is that, when making decisions about whether children are suffering, or likely to suffer 'significant' harm, professionals need to remember that they should take account of the four fundamental factors:

- the severity of any ill-treatment
- the degree and extent of harm
- the duration of harm
- the frequency of harm.

If these are processed in a methodical manner, using the experience and knowledge of the professionals, it should be more than possible to reach agreement with other professionals on what level of harm they are dealing with, and what the appropriate response to that might be.

The prevalence of abuse

Having discussed in some detail the categories and definitions of abuse, it is necessary to consider the prevalence of such abuse. As a snapshot, on 31 March 2007, there were

27,900 children on the child protection register in England (DfCSF, 2007c). The figures (in 2006) for the other three countries of the United Kingdom are:

Wales: 2,163
Scotland: 2,288
Northern Ireland: 1,639

These figures have remained more or less constant for some years. The child protection register is essentially a list held by each local authority of children who are deemed to be at risk of continuing significant harm and who require formal intervention, usually by a variety of services, via a child protection plan in order to decrease or eradicate this risk. The majority of these children will be living at home with their parents or carers.

 Information: Children on the child protection register

The total figure of 27,900 children on the register in England on 31 March 2007 can be broken down by category of abuse as follows:

Neglect	12,500
Physical abuse	3,500
Sexual abuse	2,000
Emotional abuse	7,100
More than one category	2,700 (It is possible for children to be registered under more than one of the above categories).

It is little surprise, perhaps, that of those children on the child protection register, neglect is the highest populated category as it is often linked to poverty, and as was noted in Chapter 3, around 3.8 million children live in official poverty. Making this link does not imply that all or most poor parents neglect their children; however, there is a correlation between neglect and poverty. This may be enhanced by an oversurveillance of working-class parents compared to, say, middle-class parents who may practise forms of neglect not linked so tangibly to poverty, for instance expecting their child to make their own way home and then stay unsupervised in the home until the parents return from work, or by substituting material goods for emotional support. Given the discussion above regarding emotional abuse, it is perhaps more surprising to see this as the second highest populated category; it suggests that professionals are able to separate healthy parent–child relationships from dysfunctional ones to the extent where they can agree on which are significantly harmful to children.

The total figure of 27,900 children on the child protection register may at first glance suggest that England has only a minor problem with child abuse. After all, this figure represents only 0.20 per cent of the child population of around 13 million, or 1 in every 466 children.

However, this creates a false sense of security for a number of reasons. First, the figure of 27,900 is a snapshot; it does not account for new all new registrations that take place each year. For instance, for the year ending March 2007, there were 33,300 additions to the child protection register (ibid.), a greater number than the total number in March of that year. That is because children are also leaving the register by way of deregistration. Second, there are around 60,000 children in care in England at any one time, and the majority of these children are living in care as a result of abuse. As with the child protection register, new children are entering the care system and leaving it throughout the year. Third, and perhaps most dramatically, the number of children suffering or at risk of serious harm may be significantly higher than those identified by child protection registers.

In 1996, a seminal report was published under the title of *Childhood Matters* which took a much broader approach to child abuse (National Commission of Inquiry into the Prevention of Child Abuse, 1996). They used a definition of abuse which contrasted with the narrow and technical definitions found in the national guidance, as follows: 'child abuse consists of anything which individuals, institutions or processes do or fail to do which directly or indirectly harms children or damages their prospects of a safe and healthy development into adulthood'. The commission took contributions from over 10,000 people including a range of professionals, members of the public, children and leading experts in the field. In a nutshell, they found that abuse appears to be significantly underreported, such that the real figures, they estimated, might be thus:

Children suffering severe physical punishment	150,000
Children experiencing sexual exploitation	100,000
Children living in low-warmth, high-criticism environments (Emotional abuse)	350,000
Children being bullied at school at least once a week	450,000
Children living with domestic violence	250,000

Clearly although there may some double counting here, in that the same child may be experiencing harm under more than one of these categories, these figures, if correct, put the potential number of children experiencing serious harm at 1.3 million. This is now not 1 child in every 466, but possibly 1 in 10. Can child abuse really be that prevalent? Two examples will serve as illustrations that the answer may well be a resounding 'Yes'. A national representative study of 2,869 young people aged 18 to 24 years showed that 21 per cent of girls and 11 per cent of boys have experienced child sexual abuse, defined as acts 'to which they had not consented or where "consensual" activity had occurred with someone 5 years or more older and the child was 12 years or less' (Cawson *et al.*, 2000). This is 1 in 5 girls and 1 in 10 boys. Secondly, figures from the Department of Health (DH, 2002) indicate that the true figure for children witnessing domestic violence is not 250,000, but at least 750,000, and this is an annual figure. This equates to approximately 1 child in every 17.

The *Childhood Matters* report is the first to point out that their figures are only estimates. However, the general point is well made and supported by subsequent studies – by employing a broader definition of harm, and by carrying out careful research, more children are potentially captured. That they are not being identified and placed on formal child protection registers may relate to issues already mentioned: a lack of resources to do anything other than take a targeted approach, oversurveillance of working-class families, and confusion and uncertainty as to what constitutes significant harm.

(?) Reflections: When is harm significant?

Read each of the following scenarios and then consider the question that follows.

1. A mother decides to punish her 4-year daughter for being cheeky by sending her to her room from 4.00 p.m. until the next morning with no food or interaction with her at all. This only happens once.
2. A father hits his 7-year-old son with a belt on his back for hitting his younger sister.
3. Two parents inject heroin into themselves in front of their three children aged 2, 5 and 8. The children are left to play alone for long periods while the parents are under the influence of drugs. The two older children often miss school because the parents are not awake to take them.
4. A single mother of three children aged 2, 4 and 7 lives on benefits in an overcrowded flat. The flat is untidy and sparsely furnished. She gives her children lots of affection and plays with them. Occasionally, she gets frustrated with the stresses and smacks them or shouts at them.
5. A girl aged 10 is scapegoated by her parents. Her two younger brothers get full meals, new toys and clothes. She is made to eat inferior meals alone, is called 'the enemy within' by her parents, is made to wear old and torn clothes, and has few toys.

   1 Which of these do you think amounts to 'significant harm', rather than just 'harm'? Try to give at least one reason for your decision.

The safeguarding children system

Where professionals, or indeed members of the public, do have concerns about actual, likely or potential significant harm to a child, the system for responding to this is laid out in the national guidance (DfES, 2006i).

The starting point is a referral to social services. This could be a telephone call, a personal visit, a facsimile or other electronic means of communication. A social worker responsible for dealing with these referrals would consider them, probably in conjunction with a line manager. They should decide on the next step within 1 working day. The first possible option is that they decide that no further action is needed, as there is no identifiable need. Where this is the case, social services should communicate this decision, and the reasons behind it, to the original referrer, particularly where that referrer is a professional rather than a member of the public.

The Initial Assessment

Where social services decide that there appears to be some level of need, they are required to commence an Initial Assessment. The purpose of such an assessment is to determine whether the child is in need, including in need of protection, which additional services might be required, and whether a fuller Core Assessment is also needed.

 Information: The Initial Assessment

This is led by the social worker and should be completed within 7 working days of having received the referral. It involves seeing and speaking to the child, the family and a range of relevant professionals, as well as studying records about the family. A paediatric assessment of the child, conducted by a trained and experienced doctor, usually based at a hospital, may also form part of this assessment.

The Initial Assessment can have three different outcomes. First, that there is no evidence of the child being 'in need' as defined by Section 17 of the Children Act, and therefore no further action is required. The case would be closed. Second, that the child is 'in need', and this need can be met by the provision of additional services not requiring a child protection response. Social services may well then take a lead in coordinating these additional services. Third, that the child is suspected to be suffering, or likely to suffer significant harm, and therefore in need of protection. If this is the case, enquiries under Section 47 of the Children Act 1989 are then initiated. Once again, these decisions, and the reasons for them, should be communicated back to the referrer (if they are a professional). If the professional disagrees with this decision, particularly for no further action, or perhaps if social services conclude that a child is 'in need' rather than 'in need of protection', there should then follow a discussion about the case, with the aim of reaching agreement as to the appropriate course of action. Nevertheless, there is the possibility at this stage that professionals may be left feeling angry, undervalued and unheard if they feel strongly that the situation they have referred is one of significant harm, and social services disagree. It is also possible that these feelings will colour their response to future difficulties they encounter, such that they may decide that next time around, when faced with similar circumstances, there is little point in making a referral.

Section 47 enquiries

Section 47 enquiries will begin where social services suspect a child is suffering, or likely to suffer, significant harm, and therefore may be in need of protection. A key aim of these enquiries is to determine, as soon as possible, whether immediate emergency action is required to protect the child. One of the key mechanisms for doing so is the Strategy Discussion. This takes place between the social worker (and possibly their line manager), the referrer if a professional (members of the public making referrals would not be party to these discussions), the police and other agencies where appropriate. The purpose of this discussion, which ideally should be face to face, but could also be held via a series of telephone calls, is to:

- share information
- agree the conduct and timing of any criminal investigation (where a crime is suspected to have taken place)
- determine whether a Core Assessment should be begun (this is a key means of carrying out Section 47 enquiries, as its main purpose is to determine whether action is required to safeguard and promote the welfare of the child)
- plan how Section 47 enquiries should be conducted. In a nutshell, this is about who will do what, by when, and for what purpose. This could include whether there is a need for the child to receive medical treatment
- agree what immediate action is required to protect the child
- decide what information to share with the family at this stage (the determinants for this decision are the risk of significant harm to the child and the risk of jeopardizing a police investigation)
- decide whether civil legal action is required to protect the child.

Where the need for immediate protective action is identified, then clearly this should take place. This can be very speedy – it is possible that the referral, the Initial Assessment, the Strategy Discussion, and the emergency action (which may result in the child being removed), can all take place within a day, sometimes within hours. This would usually involve some level of legal intervention, either by the social worker approaching the civil court, or by the police pursuing a criminal investigation, or both. Where a Core Assessment has been initiated, the immediate action should cut across this, and should not wait until the outcome of the assessment.

Section 47 enquiries, and information from the ongoing Core Assessment if one has commenced, can have one of three outcomes. The first is that the concerns are not substantiated. In other words, the situation may have looked like one of 'significant harm' but no evidence of this has been found. In these circumstances, the Core Assessment, if begun, should be completed and the family offered any services they may require under Section 17 of the Children Act 1989. Once it has begun, a Core Assessment should be completed within 35 working days.

The second is that the concerns are substantiated, but the child is not judged to be at continuing risk of significant harm. Here, there is evidence that the child has suffered significant harm, but there is agreement between agencies that an Initial Child Protection Conference or formal child protection plan is not required. Examples of such circumstances are provided in the national guidance (DfES, 2006i) and include where the parent has taken responsibility for the harm caused and is working with agencies to address this, where the family circumstances have changed, where the person responsible for the harm is no longer in contact with the child, or that the harm resulted from an isolated abusive incident, say from a stranger. This can be a difficult decision, and one which could lead to strong disagreements between agencies. Although the family should not be left bereft of support and services where required under

Section 17 of the Children Act 1989, there needs to be clarity regarding what the child's needs are, how these will be judged to be successfully met and who will take particular roles in ensuring this is the case. Where a professional strongly disagrees with the decision not to convene an Initial Child Protection Conference, they have the right to request one, and if this is supported by a senior manager in their organization, the guidance suggests that this should always be agreed. Where social services resist this pressure, the guidance goes on to say that every effort should be made to resolve these differences through discussion and explanation, or as a final arbiter, via the Local Safeguarding Children Board. There is here, then, the potential for serious tension and differences to emerge. Where a professional invokes the support of a manager to force through a decision to hold an Initial Child Protection Conference, the social worker is likely to feel disempowered and undermined, particularly as they will have to coordinate much of the work that goes along with this decision. Furthermore, where a decision goes up to the Local Safeguarding Children Board, whichever agency is on the 'losing' side may well also feel a sense of despair or anger which may well colour future relationships.

The third possible outcome of Section 47 enquiries is that the concerns are substantiated, and the child is judged to be at continuing risk of significant harm. Where immediate action is needed to protect the child, this should take place as soon as possible. The child may well be removed from the care of the parents. However, it is also possible for a child to be at continuing risk of significant harm and yet remain living at home. In these circumstances, an Initial Child Protection Conference must be convened within 15 working days of the date of the Strategy Discussion. This decision can also be controversial in that some agencies may feel that the child should be removed from the care of the parents as the risk of significant harm is too great. Once more, attempts would need to be made to settle these differences, but there is a chance that certain professionals will be left with a bad taste in their mouth which could sour future interactions.

 Information: Family group conferences

These are formal conferences that provide an alternative to the traditional Child Protection Conferences. They are based on the principles that families have a right to be fully involved in the process of helping their children, have great knowledge of the problems, have good ideas about what would help and have resources to provide help. Family Group Conferences are therefore a way of giving families the chance to get together to try to make the best plan possible for children. They can be used in a variety of circumstances, including where children need additional services (including where Section 47 enquiries have not substantiated concerns about significant harm) and where Section 47 enquiries lead to an Initial Child Protection Conference, but that conference agrees that a Family Group Conference is the appropriate means of formulating a plan for the child in question. Within Family Group Conferences, the detailed plan to support the child is drawn up by family members, not professionals. Family Group Conferences are chaired by a worker independent of social services, and are formal meetings, with proper reviewing and monitoring procedures. For more information, see Marsh and Crow (1998).

The Initial Child Protection Conference

The purpose of the Initial Child Protection Conference is to:

- share and analyse information in a multi-agency arena
- decide whether the child is at continuing risk of significant harm
- decide what actions are needed to safeguard and promote the welfare of the child, what the aims of any are, and how that action will take place.

Those invited to attend would normally include:

- the social worker and their line manager
- the child's parents
- professionals involved with the family, for example, the health visitor, midwife, school nurse, paediatrician, school or early years staff, the general practitioner, adult or child mental health practitioners, probation service staff
- professionals with expertise in the particular type of harm suffered by the child or in the child's condition where there is a disability or illness
- the police involved in the investigation
- other professionals may also be invited to attend, although consideration needs to be given to avoiding the meeting becoming so large it becomes unwieldy and intimidating, particularly to parents. The child would normally not attend, unless it is deemed to be in their interests to do so. Where professionals are unable to attend, they should send a written report.

The Conference is chaired by an employee of social services who is independent of the social worker involved. Most local authorities have a central team who perform such a function. Although independent of the case, since the chair works for the same organization as the social worker it is possible there can develop a perception, particularly if a professional from another agency disagrees with a decision of the Conference, that the chair is biased towards the social worker's position. Nevertheless, the function of the chair is to try to ensure the Conference maintains focus on the key question, which is:

- Is the child at continuing risk of significant harm? The test here is either that there is evidence to show the child *has suffered* ill-treatment or impairment of health or development as a result of abuse under one or more of the available four categories, and that professional judgement is that further ill-treatment or impairment is likely; or that professional judgement, supported by evidence, is that the child *is likely to suffer* ill-treatment or impairment of health or development, also as a result of physical, sexual or emotional abuse or neglect.

If the answer to this question is yes, the child will require a formal child protection plan to coordinate multi-agency support. The category of abuse the child has suffered should also be agreed and noted. The Conference should then also, among other responsibilities, formulate an outline child protection plan which includes appointing a key worker (the social worker), identifying members of the Core Group who will implement the plan, and agreeing in principle key areas of work needed with timescales.

It is interesting that nowhere in the 2006 version of the national guidance are the words 'registration' or 'child protection register' used. Previous versions, including the 1999 version (DH, HO and DfEE, 1999) make clear reference to the Conference agreeing to place the child's name on the child protection register where it is agreed a child protection plan is needed. The reasons for this change appear to relate to a wish to emphasize the active, focused and short-term nature of the intervention. A child's name being on a register seems to imply a passive labelling of a situation which could continue unchecked for a lengthy period. In contrast, a child being subject of a child protection plan suggests activity focused around their needs, where, in the words of the 2006 guidance, '. . . cases where children are at risk of significant harm should not be allowed to drift' (DfES, 2006i, p. 124). This may be a laudable aim – to emphasize short-term action – but the notion of the child protection register is so integral to multi-agency practice that the removal of this term may cause some confusion or distress. While professionals will still be able to contact their local authority to determine if a particular child is known, this will be couched in terms of the child being subject of a child protection plan under a particular category of harm, rather than the child's name being on the child protection register. It also adds to the confusion somewhat that the annual statistical reports on these matters produced by the very government which abolished the term 'child protection registers' still refer to registers in the title, as in the figures quoted earlier in this chapter (DfCSF, 2007c).

The Core Group and child protection plan

Once a child is made subject of a child protection plan, the key worker (the social worker) takes responsibility for coordinating this plan. They should ensure the Core Assessment is completed. They act as the central point of contact for the agencies involved. However, it is the Core Group as a whole who are responsible for implementing the child protection plan.

 Information: The Core Group

Core Group membership includes the social worker and their line manager, the parents, and a small group of professionals with direct involvement with the family, likely to include, as a minimum, school or early years staff, and the health visitor or school nurse. The first meeting of the Core Group should take place within 10 working days of the Initial Child Protection Conference. This meeting adds more detail to the outline child protection plan and decides on who will take responsibility for the various elements of it.

The overall aims of the child protection plan are rather obvious but include:

- ensuring the child is safe and preventing further harm
- promoting the child's welfare
- supporting the family, where it is safe to do so, to safeguard and promote the welfare of the child.

Within this, the plan should therefore set out:

- the specific needs of the child
- specific intended outcomes
- strategies and actions to achieve these outcomes
- contingency plan should circumstances change suddenly
- the roles and responsibilities of professionals and family members involved
- how progress will be reviewed.

As the work progresses, the Core Group should review the impact of the interventions on the child's welfare.

The Child Protection Review Conference

A key decision-making body in this process is the Child Protection Review Conference. This is a formal meeting which has the purpose of:

- reviewing progress against planned outcomes as identified in the child protection plan
- ensuring the child continues to be safeguarded from harm
- considering whether the child protection plan should continue in place or be changed.

The first Child Protection Review Conference should take place within 3 months of the Initial Child Protection Conference. Subsequent meetings should be held at least every 6 months as long as the child remains subject of a child protection plan. Attendance at this meeting should mirror that of the Initial Child Protection Conference; however, in practice there are likely to be a smaller number of professionals involved as reflected in the Core Group membership. As with the Initial Child Protection Conference, the key question for consideration in the Child Protection Review Conference is whether the child continues to be at continuing risk of significant harm. If the answer to this is 'Yes', the child should remain subject of a child protection plan; if 'No' they should cease to be subject to such a plan. In the latter case, services under Section 17 of the Children Act should still be offered to the family if appropriate. One of the key considerations among all of this is whether the child's needs can be met within the family in a timescale that is meaningful for the child. Putting it bluntly, professionals need to decide how long the child can wait for their parents to change. It would be absurd for a child to remain subject of a child protection plan, where they are deemed to be at continuing risk of significant harm, for a lengthy period of time, say a year or more. Either they cannot be at risk of such serious harm (in which case they should not be subject of a formal child protection plan) or if they are at risk of significant harm, they should not be exposed to that risk any longer. In this case, it may be that a decision needs to be made to remove the child from the care of the parents. These decisions, due to their complexity and strength of feeling they can elicit, have the potential to provide a further source of tension and conflict between agencies where different views are taken and held regarding the best course of action for the child.

Removal of children from parental care

Where, at any stage, a decision is taken by social services to seek a court order via the civil courts to protect a child, this is likely to have resonance for other agencies at a number of levels. The details of the various orders available are beyond the remit of this chapter; however, it is worth reiterating that a social worker has no power (except, as any member of the public has, in cases of immediate risk of serious injury or death to a child) to remove children from their parents without first obtaining an appropriate order from the courts. Only one agency has the power to remove children from parental care without first seeking a court order – the police. Under Section 46 of the Children Act 1989, they can, where they have reasonable cause to believe that a child would otherwise be likely to suffer significant harm, take the child into police protection for a maximum of 72 hours. They have a responsibility to inform social services immediately of this, and social workers then usually take the lead in deciding on the next course of action. The key word here is 'reasonable', as it is not defined. The police have to make a judgement as to what is 'reasonable cause' and this may clash with the view of social services, who then have a responsibility to pick up the case and decide on future steps. A classic example may be children left alone. As we have seen, the law is fuzzy and complex, and it could be that the police, alerted to a situation, decide to remove a number of siblings aged, say, 14, 11 and 5, who have been left alone, in the belief that they are at risk of significant harm. On picking up the case, social services may take the view that it was acceptable for these particular children to be left alone, and that if a blanket approach is taken that all children of similar ages should not be left alone, then many hundreds of children in the area would need to be similarly protected on a daily basis. The potential here for disagreement to surface between the two agencies is plain to see. Such differences, where there is interpretation of a family situation involving such terms as 'reasonable cause' and 'significant' harm, require careful and thorough debate if the agencies concerned are to reach a common understanding of the motives, focus and future plans of the lead agency – usually social services in cases where protecting children is central – and so enable effective multi-agency work to take place.

Conclusions

The conceptual shift from 'child protection' to 'safeguarding children' involves a key role for services in the prevention of harm, where protecting children becomes just one element of a wider approach. A major potential difficulty here is that the sharp, narrow focus on protection may be blurred as professionals consider the broader issues that impinge upon the child.

Furthermore, the definitions of abuse are open to interpretation by different workers, and this can lead to different positions being adopted by individuals. Where children are subject to formal child protection processes, multi-agency tensions can arise as professionals hold and maintain different views regarding what is in the best interests of a particular child. Unless these differences are shared, understood and distilled, they have the potential to become running sores which can cause long-term damage to multi-agency relationships.

The role of the school and early years setting in safeguarding children

5

Introduction

The unique position of schools, and increasingly of early years settings, which have intensive day-to-day contact with large numbers of children justifies a separate chapter to consider their contribution to multi-agency work, and to analyse the issues that result for the practitioners involved. The current systems and guidance are scrutinized and where the principles and approaches are similar across the two settings – schools and early years settings – they will be considered together. However, where there are significant differences between the two, these too will be addressed.

National guidance for schools and early years settings on safeguarding children in the United Kingdom

The national guidance in England titled *Safeguarding Children and Safer Recruitment in Education* (DfES, 2006e) covers the school sector (local authority and private Primary, Secondary and Special schools and pupil referral units, attended by excluded pupils), the responsibility of local authorities and the Further Education sector (colleges and so forth that provide education for students under the age of 18). In Wales, the Welsh Assembly Government (2007b) document *Safeguarding Children in Education* covers similar ground. For Scotland, a publication by the Scottish Executive (2005b) titled *Safe and Well: A Handbook for Staff, Schools and Education Authorities* provides well-presented and thorough guidance. In Northern Ireland, the Department of Education Northern Ireland (1999) document *Pastoral Care in Schools: Child Protection* is supplemented with various more recent documents providing updated guidance on more specific matters such as the vetting of staff.

Interestingly, the English guidance for schools does not cover early years settings, and within the introduction the document makes a distinction between guidance for organizations and for individuals. The latter are provided for within a separate publication (DfES, 2006h) titled *What to Do if You're Worried a Child Is Being Abused*, a document intended to be distributed and kept by individuals working with children within a variety of settings. More general guidance on the role of 'childcare services' (DfES, 2006i, p. 68) is to be found within the national guidance *Working Together to Safeguard Children*. Here, within chapter two of the document, two short paragraphs explain that 'childcare services' – early years settings – include family and children's centres, day nurseries, childminders, preschools, playgroups, and holiday and out-of-school schemes. Beyond the responsibilities of individuals, these paragraphs specify that all day care providers:

- caring for children under the age of 8 must be registered with Ofsted (the regulatory body whose full title is the Office for Standards in Education, Children's Services and Skills, which gives a flavour of the range of institutions for which it has responsibility)
- should have a written statement regarding safeguarding children based on the publication *What to Do if You're Worried a Child Is Being Abused* which includes staff responsibilities for reporting concerns, contact details of local agencies and procedures to be followed in the event of an allegation against an adult in the setting
- should have a designated person responsible for liaison with local agencies and Ofsted on child protection matters. Other staff should be able to implement procedures in the absence of this person. This last requirement implies that training will be needed, and training requirements for all staff, which includes those in schools and early years settings are laid out in a later chapter in *Working Together to Safeguard Children*.

Discussion on the national guidance for schools and early years settings

The general responsibilities of early years settings mirror those expected of schools, which is one reason why it seems curious that early years settings are not included in the national guidance *Safeguarding Children and Safer Recruitment in Education*. This seems especially odd when one considers the remit of Ofsted in overseeing not only schools, but early years providers in what appears to be a drive to introduce a hard-nosed, outcomes based approach to measuring the success of early years services along the lines upon which schools are currently ultimately assessed as successful or otherwise – attainment results. The key reason for questioning the lack of inclusion of early years services in the very full national guidance *Safeguarding Children and Safer Recruitment in Education* is that the level of contact and direct involvement with children in these settings is as high as, if not higher than, that of schools. Schools, to characterize them, have children for 6 hours a day for 5 days a week. Some children may stay on the premises, albeit with different adults in charge, for a further 3 hours or so, in after-school clubs. Early years settings can have children for up to 10 hours a day, 5 days a week. The question, therefore, is 'What makes schools different, in terms of safeguarding children, that they require separate guidance running to 120 pages compared to early years settings that are provided with 2 paragraphs plus general information contained with publications designed for any practitioner who comes into contact with children?' While part of the answer may lie in the way schools are governed by governing bodies, one wonders if another part of the answer also lies within what appears to be a consistent central government culture of the overregulation of schools compared to early years services.

Before a detailed discussion begins, and in order to avoid confusion, it may be worth summarizing the guidance once more concerning schools and early year settings:

Safeguarding Children and Safer Recruitment in Education – national guidance for all schools, local authorities and Further Education providers. This guidance does not apply to early years settings.
What to Do if You're Worried a Child Is Being Abused – national guidance for any *individual* working with children, including early years staff and school staff.
Working Together to Safeguard Children – national guidance setting out the responsibilities of all agencies, including schools and early years settings. The latter have two paragraphs dedicated to them within chapter two of this document.

Responsibilities of schools and early years settings

Let us consider now the first of the documents listed above – *Safeguarding Children and Safer Recruitment in Education*. Of the three bodies to whom it is aimed – schools, colleges and local authorities – the focus will be on the role of schools. Technically, it is the responsibility of the governing bodies of schools to ensure that each establishment has effective safeguarding children procedures, and that it adheres to them. Governing bodies should have no involvement with, or oversight of, individual cases; rather they take a strategic lead in ensuring compliance with the guidance. 'Furthermore, while each governing body should have a nominated governor for child protection who takes the lead on such matters, this person has no role in dealing with allegations against the headteacher - the lead for this is taken by the chair of governors or their deputy.' I have found out this is factually incorrect. Here there is a striking difference between schools and early years settings – while in both cases the local authority also has a responsibility to ensure compliance with the safeguarding children requirements, in the case of early years settings, as there is no governing body, it is the responsibility of the manager of the setting or service (for instance childminding) to ensure such compliance.

Child protection policy

In schools, the governing body should ensure a number of things. First, that there is a child protection policy in place. This is very close to the requirement on early years settings, under *Working Together to Safeguard Children* to have a 'written statement' (DfES, 2006i, p. 68). In both cases, reference is made to this policy being in line with local or national guidance. While standardization and a minimum quality level for these policies are to be welcomed, it is possible to locate, on government sponsored national websites, examples of model policies (see, for instance, Teachernet, 2007). The Welsh guidance for schools also contains a model policy. The potential difficulty with this approach, where these policies have a blank space for the school simply to insert their name at the top of an otherwise fully completed and 'correctly' worded policy, is that the existence of such a policy reflects a tick-box approach to child protection where the school can demonstrate that, on paper, they are fulfilling their responsibilities. Unless this policy has been devised with the input of all school staff, set in the context of the particular school (the catchment population, faith issues and so on) and properly distilled and shared among all staff, there is a danger it will have little value as an organic, useful document beyond that of satisfying the narrow expectations of the local authority or external bodies such as Ofsted. The process of devising a meaningful child protection policy is time-consuming, and the worry in the approach that encourages quick fix responses is that if the policy has not been 'lived' by the staff, it is unlikely to be owned by them, and ultimately children may be less protected compared with schools where the policy has had a longer, more consultative gestation period.

Safe recruitment

Governing bodies should make sure that the school operates safe recruitment procedures by carrying out appropriate checks on all staff and volunteers. This would certainly also apply to early years settings, and should be a necessary, but not a sufficient action. In other words, an emphasis on the importance of what are called CRB (Criminal Record Bureau) disclosures or other checks prior to the appointment of staff or volunteers, while absolutely essential and correct, carries with it a danger that, once appointed, assumptions will be made that everyone who has passed the checks are safe to work with children. As the guidance itself recognizes, 'many individuals who are unsuited to working with children will not have any previous convictions' (DfES, 2006e, p. 24). The guidance goes on to describe the need for continuing awareness within schools (and, one could add, early years settings) where a culture can be created which allows staff (and indeed parents or children) to raise concerns about the behaviour of workers, and which sets out clear expectations for all staff regarding the standards and boundaries of appropriate behaviour, understood and agreed by all. This could be taken further, and it could be argued that this culture also needs to allow and facilitate the development of an open and transparent culture in which any staff member is both alert to how certain of their own behaviours may be interpreted by others, and questions, where appropriate, the behaviour of others. An example here may help. If a staff member has the need to take an individual or small group of pupils into an unobserved area of the school, a truly open culture would expect that they would let a colleague know where they are going, for what purpose, with whom and for what length of time. Likewise, colleagues of any individual staff member should be able to openly question both the actions and motives of the staff member if they are at all unconvinced by their explanation – for instance, does the staff member really need to take a pupil into a locked room where they cannot be seen? Now, to return to the earlier point regarding child protection policies, if a school adopts an off the shelf, pre-written generalized child protection policy (as they appear encouraged to do), there is something of a contradiction here, as it can be questioned whether they will then take the time to develop a safe culture within school especially, as the national guidance implies, such a culture requires a long-term investment of induction, training and awareness raising. It is interesting, then, that despite the reference in the national guidance to the importance of developing such a culture, of the thirty-six pages (across two chapters) devoted to recruitment, selection and vetting checks, barely one page is given over to discussing how schools can go about developing a safe culture.

Allegations against staff

The governing body should ensure the school has proper procedures for dealing with allegations against members of staff and volunteers. Once again, this is equally applicable to early years settings, and once again, it raises a question regarding the thoroughness of such policies. While the national guidance has an eight-page chapter devoted to this, to which schools can refer when required, the model child policy on the Teachernet website referred to earlier has one statement related to this as follows: 'Develop and then follow procedures where an allegation is made against a member of staff or volunteer' (Teachernet, 2007, p. 1). Would it not be logical to provide a summary of these procedures within the child protection policy itself (perhaps as an appendix), or at the very least to cross-reference them, by their full title, to where they can be found within the school? The danger in simply referring to vague procedures in a single sentence is that actually no one is clear what these procedures are, what they are called or where they are held within the school. A time of crisis involving an allegation against a member of staff is not the time to begin looking for procedures, or read for the first time the rather wordy national guidance on this issue, even though a helpful summary of procedures is provided at the end of the chapter.

The role of the designated officer

Schools should have in place a senior member of the school's leadership team to take lead responsibility for child protection. Here there is a direct correlation with the requirement on early years settings to appoint a designated officer. Furthermore, although, in schools, this person need not be a teacher, they 'must have the status and authority within the school management structure to carry out the duties of the post . . . including committing resources to child protection matters, and where appropriate directing other staff' (DfES, 2006e, p. 14). The guidance also specifies that a deputy should always be available to take over in the absence of the designated person, and in large establishments, or where there are a large number of child protection concerns, more than one designated person may be needed.

 Information: Summary of the role of the designated officer in schools

The designated person should:

- take the lead in coordinating child protection activity within the school or setting
- provide advice and support to other staff
- liaise with the local authority and work with other agencies

There may appear to be something of a contradiction in the specification that the designated person must be a senior member of the school leadership team but does not have to be a teacher. While in early years settings it is clear who this might be (a manager, a deputy manager or perhaps a senior officer), within a school it is more difficult to think of someone who might meet these criteria. The obvious candidates – the headteacher, the deputy headteacher or a senior teacher, perhaps the Special Educational Needs Coordinator (SENCO) – are all qualified teachers. (The danger in using the SENCO is the inherent assumption that any child about whom there might be child protection concerns has Special Educational Needs, although more positively the SENCO does have access to a host of knowledge and resources to assist children with a whole variety of needs.) As described in Chapter 1, some schools employ learning mentors, who are non-teaching staff working to try to ensure that children engage more effectively in learning. They may well be on the school leadership team because of the unique knowledge and perspective they can bring to discussions about children, and as they do not have a teaching load, may also be asked to take the lead as designated person. Without for a moment wishing to doubt the competence or suitability of individual learning mentors for this role, there are some inherent dangers if they do act as designated person. Notwithstanding that they may well have enormous respect from colleagues, and a very positive working relationship with them, most learning mentors occupy within the school structure a position at best equivalent to class teachers. Their salary depends on the recognition by authorities of the professionalism of the role: some equate expertise and therefore salary to that of a newly qualified teacher or social worker; others pay a support-role salary (Prospects, 2006). In this context, it would take an exceptional individual to, for example, instruct more senior members of staff (including the headteacher) that they must attend training courses on child protection. It would surely also take an equally exceptional headteacher to send a learning mentor to a child protection conference who is fully able to commit school time and resources to supporting individual children.

In Appendix Three of the national guidance (DfES, 2006e), a full page is devoted to specifying the broad areas of responsibility of the designated person in more detail. This includes, in addition to the three areas outlined above, referring cases to social services, attending multi-agency child protection conferences and other meetings, ensuring that all staff are appropriately trained (including induction for new members of staff), keeping records, liaising with other schools or settings when a pupil leaves or arrives. In fulfilling this extensive role, particularly where there are relatively large numbers of children who may need safeguarding, similar issues regarding the availability of school resources to support the role arise, and it is imperative that the headteacher is unswerving in their support of the designated person. Especially in a climate where schools are chiefly judged on pupil attainment, by the publication of one-dimensional performance tables (characterized as 'league tables') based on Standard Assessment Tests (SATs) and General Certificate of Secondary Education (GCSE) examinations outcomes, there may well be pressure upon schools to focus upon the academic achievement of children at the expense of other areas of their experience. Of course, a counter argument is that in order to maximize a child's potential in every aspect of their life, including the academic, it is necessary to address such matters as child protection, as they are all inseparable. A child, for example, who is sat in a classroom worried about being hit when they get home, or hungry and tired, or concerned that their mother is being hit by their father, is far less likely to be able to concentrate on their schoolwork compared to their peers who have no such concerns. Therefore, in addressing these matters rigorously, schools are indeed assisting in the academic development of the child.

Two chapters of the national guidance are devoted to Recruitment, Selection and Vetting checks and this is clearly an important area for schools and local authorities to get right, particularly in the light of the Bichard inquiry report (HC 653, 2004a). The heartbreaking and dramatic case to which this relates has led to the development of a much tighter recruitment and selection system, described in detail in the national guidance, no doubt because the case remains a powerful reminder of how appalling the consequences can be when systems fail. Nevertheless, it is somewhat curious that the national guidance for schools makes relatively scant mention of some of the detail of the role of the designated person. For example, mention of how to record concerns or disclosures from children is made in an Annex under two separate headings titled, respectively, 'Listening to children' and 'If you have concerns about a child's welfare'. Further very brief mention is also made under a section headed 'Training' where it states that the designated person should be 'able to keep detailed accurate secure written records of referral and or concerns' (DfES, 2006e, p. 83). While these entries are helpful, they do not, perhaps, give enough detail to make them fully accessible.

 Information: The Bichard inquiry report, 2004

This was led by Sir Michael Bichard. It was set up following the conviction of Ian Huntley for the murder of two schoolgirls, Jessica Chapman and Holly Wells, in the village of Soham in Cambridgeshire, England in 2002. Huntley had been employed as a school caretaker, despite, as it transpired, there being eight separate allegations of sexual offences against him. These allegations had been neither fully investigated nor communicated effectively between authorities and agencies, such that he was able to secure the position of caretaker at Soham Village College, a secondary school. Although he did not meet Jessica Chapman and Holly Wells directly as a result of this job (their paths crossed because his girlfriend was employed as a teaching assistant in their class at the nearby primary school) clearly he should never have been employed in this position.

While at one level this is understandable – the intention here is clearly that the designated person should access local training to gain further information and insight – it could be argued that there is a place, in national guidance, for a fuller account of the key issues here. The following are some the matters of which the designated person should be aware, and they apply equally to schools and to early years settings.

Training issues for schools and early years settings

Governing bodies should ensure that the designated person undertakes initial training for their role, and refresher training every 2 years. Furthermore, all school staff, including the headteacher, should have training which is refreshed every 3 years. It is interesting that no such requirements for refresher training appear to be placed upon staff in early years settings. Their training requirements are catered for within *Working Together to Safeguard Children* (DfES, 2006i) in a chapter aimed at all agencies working with children. Here, it is specified that managers have a responsibility to ensure that staff access training according to their level of contact and involvement with children, on a hierarchical basis as follows:

- **Those in 'regular contact'** (ibid., p. 94) with children should have introductory training to enable them to work together to safeguard and promote the welfare of children. The phrase 'regular contact' is not defined but includes, in the list of examples, staff in day care settings. The guidance recognizes one of the major difficulties here – the large numbers of people involved (the list includes staff and volunteers working directly with children, as well as with adults who happen to be parents, including, for instance those within leisure and sport). One solution suggested is the use of 'creative methods' (ibid.) such as open, distance learning or the use of cascade training, where one person from an organization attends a central training event, and then returns to their own setting and cascades this training down to their colleagues. The worry here is that the quality of the training experience is diluted or compromised. With open learning, is it really possible to fully learn how to work together with others while completing paper or electronically based tasks away from a group (although of course it might be possible to set up a virtual group via a web-based resource)? The idea of cascade training, too, is in danger of contradicting one of the central tenets of the guidance on training – that those delivering it should have both appropriate knowledge and training skills. Of course it is perfectly possible for a member of staff to attend central training and share this with colleagues, but to make this a rich, impactful experience for those colleagues takes more than simply sharing information. Training skills, backed by an understanding of how adults learn, are required. Once more, the central danger is that settings are encouraged to take a tick-box approach, marking off training as having been completed irrespective of its value or quality.

- **Those who 'work regularly'** (ibid., p. 95) with children should have a higher minimum level of expertise, including a fuller understanding of how to 'work together to identify and assess concerns, and to plan, undertake and review interventions' (ibid.). Within the list of relevant workers here are family and children's centre staff. So, the first distinction that managers in early years settings need to make, on reading this, is whether they are a day care setting (as identified under those in 'regular contact' with children), or whether they are a family or children's centre (as identified under those who 'work regularly' with children), or whether they could have staff who fit into both descriptions, given that children's centres are also surely day care settings. Furthermore, as the terms are not defined, managers will have to decipher the difference between those staff who have 'regular contact' with children and those who 'work regularly' with them. Use of the same word here may lead to some confusion, even if the emphasis is designed to be on the difference between 'contact' and 'work'. For early years settings, those in 'regular contact' with children or parents might include a receptionist or secretary, cleaners, a caretaker and so on, while those who 'work regularly' with children are likely to include all staff who work directly with the children, including management.

- **Those who have particular responsibility** for child protection should receive more specialist training giving a thorough understanding of the complex issues that can arise. Therefore, the designated person in early years settings should attend this training. There is further mention made of the need for managers to take responsibility to release staff to attend appropriate multi-agency training, and certainly designated persons from early years settings should be able to access such training locally to supplement any single agency training they may have undertaken. What is missing here, though, as from the guidance on training for all staff in 'regular contact' or who 'work regularly' with children, is any mention of refresher training, as there is for school staff. One wonders if this is a further example of the overregulation of school staff compared to others, like early years staff, who have equally, if not more, intense contact with children.

The quality and detail of any training provided is crucial in determining how suspicions or disclosures of abuse are handled, which in turn can have a huge impact on subsequent multi-agency work. If the setting monitors and records incidents related to children effectively, handles disclosures from children correctly, and passes on appropriate referrals and disclosures, this is much more likely to produce and maintain positive working relationships between the agencies involved. If, on the other hand, such concerns are dealt with in a manner which could be criticized, the opposite is more likely to be true. Take one aspect of dealing with a disclosure: the question of whether there should always be two members of staff present when a child divulges abuse. Ideally, this may well be the case: it allows for a witness to be present, for one person to make notes while the other speaks to and supports the child, and for a sharing of the emotional burden. However, if this approach was dogmatically adhered to by a particular setting, it could lead to difficulties. Is it always in the best interests of children to have two adults present? It may be that the child has a particularly positive relationship with one staff member and would feel inhibited if another adult were present. Certainly, the adults concerned may be successful in appropriately 'selling' to the child the reasons why two adults are needed, but it calls into question what the setting is defining as a disclosure. If any expression of concern by a child was interpreted as a disclosure, then a child in a group situation with one adult present may be stopped from speaking until a situation involving two adults can be engineered. This is not only likely to be difficult to achieve (children may well make 'disclosures' which involve blurting out statements while they are in the middle of working or playing) but may also inhibit the child from speaking further once they are placed in the relatively artificial situation involving two adults. Other agencies, principally social services perhaps, would presumably have an opinion that would not be entirely favourable if they discovered that disclosures were being suppressed (albeit unwittingly) as a result of a hard and fast rule preventing a single member of staff ever dealing with a disclosure of abuse from a child.

 Information: The role of headteachers in safeguarding children

Headteachers of schools have specific responsibilities which include:

- ensuring that the child protection policy and procedures are fully implemented
- committing sufficient resources and time to allow staff to fulfil their responsibilities, including attendance at meetings, or contributing to multi-agency assessments
- ensuring that all staff feel able to raise concerns about poor or unsafe practice, and where this happens, to respond appropriately.

Discussion on the role of headteachers in safeguarding children

Headteachers are likely to face some dilemmas in trying to fulfil their responsibility. Allowing staff to attend regular multi-agency meetings can have a serious impact on the school's ability to fulfil its other, core functions. Particularly where the designated person is a teaching member of staff, if they are to attend a meeting (which could take up to half a day, especially where travel is involved) either cover from a supply teacher would be required, or classes would have to be doubled up for that time. The first is expensive and may well prevent the school from spending that money on other resources which some would argue are of equal importance; the second may have an impact of standards of teaching and learning. Even where the designated person is not a full-time teaching member of staff, their absence from school is likely to have an impact at some level – after all, they would be doing something else in the school if they were not attending the meeting. Furthermore, it may be deemed necessary for two members of staff to attend a particular meeting (e.g. the designated person and the class teacher) in which these issues are potentially doubled. For every child subject to a formal child protection plan, there is likely to be a series of fairly regular meetings to which the school will be invited, along with the completion of written reports and assisting with a Core Assessment. If a school has several children in such circumstances, this can amount to a significant amount of work, potentially having an equally significant impact on the school's ability to carry out its fundamental role of teaching children. These comments are not intended as criticism, but as a reflection of some of the real problems faced by school staff as they endeavour to balance their responsibilities to individual children, to all the children, and to the governing body. Tension may arise within a school where a particular designated person feels strongly that they should attend a particular meeting, but where a headteacher feels they cannot spare their absence. Who has the final say over committing resources here – the designated person as per their 'job description' or the headteacher who has overall responsibility? Tension could also arise between school and, say, social services, if the school's absence is interpreted as a lack of commitment where the main focus of social services is the welfare of the individual child and not also the general education of a whole school population, as it is with the school.

The role of early years setting managers

In early years settings, similar responsibilities as headteachers can be taken to apply to managers. They should, therefore, ensure appropriate child protection procedures are in place, cover absences of staff to attend multi-agency meetings and foster a culture which allows all staff to raise concerns. Equally likely to arise is the issue of balancing resources committed to supporting individual children with a general responsibility to provide good quality childcare for all the children – if one member of staff is away attending a meeting, it may mean that the staff–child ratio for that time period is not ideal, unless cover is provided or funded. Clearly, careful planning by managers can ameliorate some of this, although it is possible that some level of tension will remain here.

The role of schools and early years settings in the prevention of harm

So far, the discussion has focused on the protective role of the school or setting; that is, where there are possible or actual concerns about a child. However, it is important to acknowledge that schools and early years settings play a vital part at two other levels: prevention of abuse in the first place, and support for pupils who have experienced abuse.

Prevention features in the national guidance, although the term itself is not used. Under the section titled 'Maintaining a safer culture' mention is made of 'including relevant material from the framework of Personal Social and Health Education in the curriculum' (DfES, 2006e, p. 34). This is then expanded upon in an Annex on additional guidance and advice, under the title of 'Educating children about issues' (ibid., p. 71). Here, reference is made to the importance of raising awareness among children of unacceptable behaviour they may encounter, and of how they can keep themselves safe. The guidance quite rightly points out that Personal Social and Health Education (PSHE) provides opportunities to learn about such matters, as well as other practical issues such as who to ask for help if they feel unsafe. In addition, the guidance states that children should be taught

- how to recognize and manage risks and how to respond responsibly
- how to distinguish acceptable from unacceptable physical contact
- how to recognize unreasonable pressure from others and develop strategies for dealing with this
- how to use assertiveness techniques to resist unhelpful pressure.

Generally speaking, the aim of such work, the guidance tells us, is to give a clear message that any kind of violence or violation is unacceptable, and to let children know that asking for help is encouraged, and to point children to sources of help where appropriate. The importance of listening to children, of providing appropriate spaces within the setting where this can take place, of displaying national children's help line numbers (e.g. Childline, NSPCC), and of peer support schemes are highlighted.

These are all laudable and very positive elements of the preventive role of schools and early years settings, although clearly not all will be appropriate for the latter. However, there are some inherent difficulties and tensions here. Certainly, the manner in which the work under the banner of PSHE is conducted is crucial, as there is the possibility that, in emphasising the personal role of the child in keeping themselves safe, the child may receive the message that, should they be harmed, it is wholly or partly their fault for not being responsible enough in keeping themselves safe. Allied to this work, therefore, should be a very clear message that although there are strategies at hand upon which children can draw if needed, ultimately the responsibility for abuse lies with the abuser and not the child.

> **(?) Reflections: Preventative work with children: possible contradictions and tensions**
>
> In the United Kingdom, there is a structural power imbalance between children and adults which is emphasized both in schools or early settings and society in general. Two examples will illustrate this. First, an expectation that children, generally, will do as they are asked by an adult and that if they question this, they are somehow being cheeky. Second, children often receive firm messages that they should never tell a lie.
>
> **1** Can you think how these messages to children might contradict the aim of carrying out preventative work on abuse with children in schools or early years settings?

A major part of prevention not highlighted in the national guidance is the use of what has been called the informal or hidden curriculum (see McGettrick, 1995). In addition to the formal curriculum (the classroom or room-based teaching or input), schools and early years settings have an informal curriculum (which can include such activities as volunteering, community work or fund-raising) and a hidden curriculum (the whole atmosphere and ethos of the school or setting, including the way it is organized and how adults address children). These three levels of curriculum, McGettrick argues, all have a powerful impact on the children, through the values they extol and reinforce. Therefore, there is a responsibility not only to encourage schools and settings to be explicit about such values (again as McGettrick argues), but also to assist schools and settings in seeing and making the link between the development and acting out of key values which are 'just and caring' (ibid., p. 6), and safeguarding children. In developing children's self-esteem, self-image and confidence, along with appropriate respect for others, schools and settings will, knowingly or not, be feeding into child protection, since a child who is self-assured is likely to be more capable of avoiding the various levels of manipulation by an ill-meaning adult.

The role of schools and early years settings in supporting children who have been abused

The national guidance also makes scant mention of the role of schools or settings in supporting children who have experienced abuse; indeed there appear to be no specific references to this. However, this is an important area, for the figures demonstrate that most children subject to child protection measures remain living at home (Gibbons, Conroy and Bell, 1995) and therefore, stay at the same school or setting. To put it another way, schools and settings have children, and therefore a responsibility to deal with the attendant issues, before, during and after any abuse. With this in mind, the role of schools and settings in supporting children who have experienced abuse could include:

- using existing relationships between children and school and setting staff so that the child knows someone cares about them
- helping the child, if necessary, to put responsibility for the abuse firmly with the abuser
- helping the child with questions they may have about what has happened
- supporting the child in developing protective strategies for the future, including the development of assertiveness skills
- where children display disruptive behaviour, supporting them to manage this. This might include helping them to see the impact of their behaviour on others, or setting and maintaining clear boundaries for what is acceptable while at the same time being sympathetic and supportive towards the child
- the use of the curriculum to address such issues as individual rights and responsibilities or the importance of listening to others. In this way, individual children who have been abused may well feel supported in a way that avoids singling them out as different.

Once again, however, there is the potential for conflict between what individual children might need, and the broader demands of the school curriculum or general setting input. Teachers may well struggle with knowing that children would benefit from time and support away from the detailed coursework, but may also be driven by an outcome focused system. Early years settings, on the other hand, may have the advantage of having, perhaps, more opportunity to take a clear child-centred approach and of affording the child the full support necessary to help them recover and move forward in their lives.

> ### ⑦ Reflections: Case study – Peter (early years child)
>
> Peter is a white British boy aged 3 who attends an early years setting. He lives with both parents in a respectable part of town. His father works as a shop manager, and his mother also works full time as a secretary. Peter is an only child. Since he started, Peter has presented as very timid. His general progress has been limited. He usually plays alone, although sometimes he does spend time with another boy in the setting. He never joins in boisterous games, and prefers craft-type activities. One day a staff member, Jenny, noticed bruising on the back of Peter's legs, but assumed they were the result of play. No record was made of this. A month later, Peter arrived at the setting with a bruise to his temple. His father, who dropped him off, explained to the member of staff, Nicola, that Peter had fallen while playfighting with him and hit his head on a coffee table. Nicola thought this sounded unusual for Peter and asked him about it again quietly and away from the other children. Peter said his father hit him and called him a 'sissy' because he doesn't like rough games.
>
> Nicola wrote all of this down and relayed it to the manager. Initially, the manager was uncertain as to what to do, saying she did not want to fall out with Peter's parents or get the setting a bad name
>
>

by having to make a child protection referral. After consulting with the Designated Officer, however, she decided to contact social services to make a referral.

1 Can you identify mistakes or poor practice in this case study?
2 Can you identify good practice here?
3 How could the setting have helped Peter more prior to the abuse coming to light?
4 How can the setting now ensure they support Peter effectively, both in school and with the multi-agency process?

(?) Reflections: Case study – Patricia (high school child)

Patricia is 13 years old and attends her local high school where she is in Year 8. She is white British. School have had no concerns about her whatsoever. One day, she asks to speak to her Head of Year in confidence. Before she starts, she asks that what she is about to say be kept confidential. The teacher explains she cannot promise this, and says that depending on what it is, she may have to pass it on so the school can help. Patricia goes on to disclose sexual abuse by her stepfather. The teacher stays calm and does not show any emotions. She allows Patricia to tell her story, occasionally reassuring her and encouraging her through the use of phrases such as 'Go on' and 'I can see this is difficult, you are doing really well.' At one point the teacher asks Patricia 'Did your stepfather touch your breasts?' to which she replies 'Yes'. Patricia goes on to say that he also touched her 'front bottom'. The teacher, who has already agreed with Patricia at the beginning of the interview that she will make some notes, records 'Stepfather touched her vagina'. At the end, Patricia suddenly says that actually she was being silly and has just made it all up to get her stepfather into trouble because he was cross with her last night. The teacher thanks Patricia and explains that she will still have to pass on the information. She writes up the discussion fully and gives this to the designated officer, who makes a referral to social services.

1 Can you identify good practice in how the teacher dealt with this disclosure?
2 Can you see any areas which could have been handled better?

(?) Reflections: Case study – Charlie (special school primary aged child)

Charlie is 9 years old, white British and attends a special school. He has moderate learning disabilities, limited speech and communicates chiefly using the Makaton signing system (a simple language based on everyday words, which uses speech, gesture, facial expression, eye contact, body language, signs, symbols and words to aid communication). He also expresses bizarre behaviour at times, such as flapping or biting his hands. His parents receive respite care, involving a home sitter (not always the same person) to allow them time alone, and Charlie staying with the same foster parents one weekend

---

in every eight. School have noticed that recently Charlie's behaviour is deteriorating. He has started wetting and occasionally soiling at school, and has struck out at a fellow pupil and a member of staff, something he has never done before. His class teacher, Jonathan, meets with the Designated Officer to discuss this. Jonathan feels that this behaviour is uncharacteristic of Charlie, and that something must be distressing him. The Designated Officer, however, is more dismissive, arguing that it's probably just part of Charlie's condition that he will go through phases of bad behaviour. He is even wary of contacting Charlie's parents to discuss this, saying that they can be awkward because they know their rights and often take a conflictual stance with the school. In the end, they agree to continue to keep an eye on Charlie without formally monitoring his progress.

1   What do you think are the key issues here?
2   How do you think school could support Charlie more effectively?

(?) **Reflections: Case study – Jasmine (primary school child)**

Jasmine is 7 years old and in Year 2 of primary school. She is black Caribbean, one of only three such children in the school. Her teachers have had some minor concerns regarding her general care (chiefly poor hygiene and late attendance) and are monitoring her. One day, her mother is 15 minutes late in collecting her from school and appears under the influence of drink. She walks Jasmine home. The teacher adds a note to the monitoring records as follows: 'Today, when mum collected Jasmine, she was drunk.'

1   What might be your concerns about Jasmine's care in this scenario?
2   What issues are there in the way the teacher records the incident?

Conclusions

This chapter has considered the national guidance covering the role of schools and early years settings in safeguarding children. This role has three elements to it: prevention, protection and support. Although discussed separately here, they are nevertheless intertwined. For example, a school or setting may be delivering a prevention programme to a whole group on, say, the difference between a 'good touch' (such as cuddles or comfort from a trusted adult) and a 'bad touch' (such as uninvited or unwanted invasions of space). For most of those children, this is likely to be reaching them at the level of prevention; however, if there is a child in the group who is experiencing a 'bad touch' this may well reach them at the level of protection as they realize or have confirmed for them that this is wrong, and that they should tell someone. There are some real tensions likely to be experienced by schools and settings in trying to satisfy the requirement to safeguard children at all three levels, and further tensions between this duty and their core role of educating children according to the National Curriculum.

6 Children in care

Introduction

There were, in March 2007, around 60,000 children in care in England, and this figure has remained fairly constant since 2001 (DfCSF, 2007a). Approximate figures for the other three countries of the United Kingdom are:

Wales: 4,400
Scotland: 13,000
Northern Ireland: 2,400.

The current systems and processes in place to support these children are fundamentally multi-agency in nature. Where children in care have complex social, emotional, psychological or physical needs, adding perhaps to their sense of isolation or vulnerability, this multi-agency network can also be complicated. This chapter explores these structures and processes, the benefits that can and do derive from them, and some of the difficulties that may also arise, with a significant focus on the education of children in care, as this is a key issue.

However, before this can be done, it is useful to provide some background information on the reasons for children being admitted into care, and the different placement types in which they live, so as to illustrate the need for a multi-agency response to meet their varying needs.

 Information: Terminology for children in care

Children in care may also be known as 'looked after children' or 'children in public care'. Government lead on the terminology in the 1990s favoured a change away from the predominant term 'children in care' towards what was felt to be a term which emphasized the supportive and nurturing aspect of being in care – 'looked after'. However, in 2000, with the publication of new guidance for England on enhancing educational outcomes for such children (DfEE and DH, 2000) the term 'children in public care' was introduced. This term stressed the shared responsibilities that any adult working directly or indirectly with or for children in care should undertake. Nevertheless, the term 'looked after children' continues to be used, in guidance for school governors (DfES, 2006g) and official government documentation, such as annual statistical summaries (DfCSF, 2007a). In 2006, the government published a green paper proposing and consulting on new ideas to support what was now called, to revert to original terminology, 'children in care' (DfES, 2006a). No explanation is offered for the change of language, although as the proposals contained within this document, and the white paper which followed shortly afterwards (DfES, 2007a) are chiefly practical and on occasion radical, it may reflect a more business-like approach to the plight of such children. Essentially, though, the terms are all interchangeable.

Reasons why children come into care

Children come into care for a variety of reasons. The figures in each of the categories that follow are taken from the Department for Children, Schools and Families (DfCSF, 2007a):

- **Abuse and neglect** (62 per cent). This is a major reason for children to be in care.
- **Family problems** (32 per cent). This includes parental illness or disability, acute family stress, family dysfunction and absent parenting.
- **Disability** (4 per cent). The severity of the child's disability necessitates them being in care in order for them to have their needs met.
- **Socially unacceptable behaviour** (2 per cent). This includes children coming into care as a result of offending.

These figures indicate that the vast majority of children (98 per cent) are in care through no fault of their own. This is important, as it combats something of a stereotype about children in care, that they are all 'bad' children, bent on defying boundaries and social norms. The figures also illustrate that children in care are likely to have needs related to any combination of mental health issues, emotional and behavioural difficulties, physical disability or sensory impairment. That is not to say that children in care are necessarily disturbed or in great need of physical care; they are a heterogeneous group and of course, many children in care are emotionally stable, settled and capable of fulfilling their potential.

Types of official legal statuses

All children in care have an official legal status, which reflects the above reasons for entering care.

Care Order under Section 31 of the Children Act 1989 (65 per cent)

The figure here clearly reflects the fact that two-thirds of children are in care as a result of abuse or neglect. A Care Order can only be granted by a court, and will only be made if the court is satisfied that a child is suffering or is likely to suffer significant harm, and the making of the order would be better for the child than if no order was made. A Care Order lasts until the child is 18 years old, unless an alternative order is made (e.g. adoption) or the order is revoked. Under a Care Order the local authority (represented by a social worker) shares parental responsibility with the parents. This means that, for some decisions, the social worker can override the wishes of the parents, but for other, perhaps major decisions about the child's life, they would have to consult with the parents and perhaps even return to court to resolve some issues.

Accommodated under Section 20 of the Children Act 1989 (30 per cent)

Accommodation is defined as that which is provided by the local authority on a voluntary basis for a period of more than 24 hours. The local authority must provide accommodation for any child in need as a result of there being no-one with parental responsibility, or because the child is lost or abandoned, or because the person who has been caring for the child is prevented from providing suitable accommodation or care. Parents can request that the local authority accommodate their child, for example, because the child is beyond control of the parent. If the local authority agrees to this, on the basis that it is in the interests of the child, they provide care and accommodation in agreement or in partnership with the parents. Where a child is accommodated, any person with parental responsibility can remove the child from care at any time, without giving notice. This is the main reason why accommodation is described as voluntary – it is voluntary arrangement between the parents and the local authority. Accommodation is the legal status of children receiving respite care (a series of short breaks), perhaps because they have a disability or a behavioural problem which places the family under stress, and respite is seen as a positive part of a support package for the family.

Remand to local authority accommodation (0.3 per cent)

A court can order that a child is remanded to local authority accommodation as an alternative to being given bail or being remanded in secure accommodation or in custody. The child will have been charged with an offence, and will be awaiting sentence or the final hearing. In these circumstances the local authority has a duty to provide accommodation, but they do not acquire parental responsibility. Nevertheless, for the period of the remand, the child is deemed to be in care.

Other legal status (4 per cent)

At any one time, children can be in care under a variety of legal imperatives. These are often temporary orders and include, for example, an Interim Care Order under Section 38 of the Children Act 1989, an Emergency Protection Order under Section 44 of the Children Act 1989, Police Protection under Section 46 of the Children Act 1989 and being freed for adoption. With these, parental responsibility passes to, or remains with, the local authority until a permanent solution also resolves the question of who attains long-term parental responsibility.

Placement types

Children in care live in a variety of placements:

Foster care (70 per cent)

The majority of children in care live with foster carers. Foster carers are recruited and trained by fostering officers who work for social services or for private or independent agencies. These fostering officers also provide ongoing advice and support to foster carers. Children can live in foster homes long-term, short-term or for respite care, and there are a variety of fostering schemes aimed at meeting the needs of specific children, for example, disabled children, or those with challenging behaviour. While foster carers provide day-to-day care on behalf of the local authority, they do not have parental responsibility for the children they foster, unless they formally acquire it through the courts. This can sometimes lead to confusion and difficulty with other professionals. If a teacher at the child's school is unaware that foster carers do not have parental responsibility they may ask the carer to sign consent forms for such things as school trips, where technically, the social worker (perhaps in consultation with parents depending on the circumstances) needs to approve these, unless they have expressly delegated responsibility for this to the foster carer. This issue is especially important if the trip is abroad, since there are strict rules governing children subject to Care Orders leaving the country, even for short periods of time.

Residential care, or children's homes (13 per cent)

These are group homes, owned by the local authority or by private or independent agencies, usually offering places for between three and sixteen children. Children can live there long-term, short-term or for respite care. Some homes specialize in the care of disabled children. In addition to the social worker, each child in a residential home will usually have a key worker from the home, who takes a special responsibility for individual children. Most group homes try to reproduce a family home situation as closely as possible, within the constraints of available resources, the building and the dynamics of group living.

Secure units

The official government figures subsume the figures for children in care living in secure units at any one time with those in residential care, so no separate figures are available. However, as they are fundamentally different from children's homes, they are being treated here as a separate category. The child is held securely, in the sense they are not let off the premises unsupervised (the units usually have high perimeter fences and tight security arrangements). The site will have its own educational and health facilities. Children are placed in secure accommodation on a number of grounds. They may pose a significant risk to the safety of themselves or others. This is called the welfare grounds and comes under Section 25 of the Children Act 1989. They may be on remand to secure accommodation having been charged with a serious offence, or they may have been sentenced to a period in secure accommodation following the establishment of guilt for a serious criminal offence. A child's stay in a secure unit is usually a temporary arrangement, the timescale for which can vary from around a month to a number of years.

Placed for adoption (5 per cent)

Where children have been freed for adoption (a legal process involving the courts), and appropriate adoptive parents have been located and approved, children can be placed with these prospective adoptive parents pending the finalization of the adoption arrangements. Clearly, this is a temporary arrangement, and once formally adopted (again, this is a legal process involving the courts) the adoptive parents gain full parental responsibility for the child, although they may require post-adoptive support.

Placement with parents (9 per cent)

Some children subject to a Care Order may be placed with one or both of their parents. The reasons for this vary – it may be that one parent was not responsible for the harm, and therefore is being given an opportunity to parent their child away from the abusive parent, although the safeguard of an order is deemed necessary. Alternatively, it is possible that the parents' circumstances have changed since the order was made, and it has been decided to return the child to the care of the parents because it is now deemed safe, albeit with the safeguard of the order, at least for a limited time. This arrangement is designed to be a temporary one, and if good progress is made, the case should be referred back to the courts for the Care Order to be revoked, upon which full parental responsibility returns to the parents. This may seem like a contradictory position, for a child to be in care but living with their parents. However the key to them being in care is their legal status, not the placement where they live – in this case while the Care Order remains in place, the child is deemed to be in care. This can be somewhat confusing for professionals working with children in care who may be living at home with parents. Technically, parental responsibility is shared between the local authority and the parent. However, since the parent has the day-to-day care, and is after all the birth parent of the child in question, professionals may be forgiven for omitting to fully consult with the social worker (as a representative of the local authority) over certain matters. This can lead to similar difficulties as those encountered with foster carers. For instance, if a parents approaches a teacher to act as a witness on a passport application form for a child, and the teacher unwittingly signs this, unaware that the social worker should be leading this process (albeit in tandem with the parent), this can lead to the possibility that a child can obtain a passport without knowledge of the social worker, with the ultimate possibility, if the deception by the parent was deliberate, that the child could be taken out of the country without the permission or knowledge of the local authority who have parental responsibility. Technically, the parent would be abducting their own child, and hence the teacher would have unknowingly contributed to a very serious offence.

Family network or kinship carers

It is curious that there is no such category in the government figures, and there is no reference here to it being subsumed within the 'Placed with parents' category, although a government green paper does suggest this is the case by stating '9% of children in care are placed with family and friends' (DfES, 2006a, p. 51). Nevertheless, as children in care live with relatives other than their parents or occasionally with close friends of the family, this is being considered a separate category in its own right. These placements with relatives are referred to using such terms as family network or kinship carers. The children placed with relatives will usually be subject to a Care Order, although some may be accommodated. At some point during proceedings, a suitable relative (or close friend) was identified who could provide care for the child, and it was deemed in the child's best interests to be placed with them. Family network carers, like foster carers, are formally assessed and approved, and they care for the child on a day-to-day basis; however, they do not have parental responsibility (although they could acquire it at a later stage if they applied through the courts and were successful).

As with foster carers, and in circumstances where children are placed with their parents, there needs to be certainty and clarity among the multi-agency team involved with the child as to where parental responsibility lies, in order to avoid poor decisions being made. A further issue regarding family network carers is the possibility that the Children Act 1989 principle of maintaining children within families, or wider families, supported by research quoted by the government (DfES, 2006a) that placements within wider families are more stable, will influence decisions on approval for family network carers. That is not to say that family network carers are inferior to other carers; however, if the dogma of maintaining family ties is strongly adhered to, it may lead to a belief that unless the prospective family network carers are palpably weak, they are a better bet than standard foster carers as a result of them being able to maintain clear links with the child's identity, origins and so on. In other words, their strengths in being who they are might be seen to outweigh any weaknesses they may have in their ability to provide effective and ongoing care for the child. This decision may also be influenced (consciously or otherwise) by the fact that there is a shortage of standard foster carers (British Association for Adoption and Fostering, 2007) such that the perceived advantages of family network carers are seen to trump any concerns regarding the quality of care they may be able to provide.

Other accommodation (4 per cent)

This includes older children living in lodgings or similar accommodation. Usually, this is in preparation for leaving care, and is part of a planned programme, with support, of independence training.

Placements for children in care may not always be in the immediate area from which they originate. There are usually two chief reasons for this: a specialist placement (of any sort) has been located which can meet the complex needs of the child which cannot otherwise be met by the original local authority; or an appropriate relative (including a parent) has been located, but they live in a different area. These placements are termed 'out of authority' placements, since they are outside the boundary of the local authority who originally received the child into care. The regulations governing such placements are complex and convoluted; however, the chief issues are that the original local authority retains overall responsibility for the child, but the receiving local authority has a responsibility to assist them by perhaps taking on a portion of the regular oversight of the child, and certainly by providing education (in other words, admitting them to a local school). It has been recognized (see DfES, 2006a) that such children are among the most vulnerable of those in care, as they are often isolated from known social networks, and least supported by regular contact with the social worker who holds overall responsibility for the direction of the child's life. Social workers in receiving authorities may well resent being asked to provide support to children who they do not perceive as 'theirs', and social workers in the original authority may struggle, in terms of time and distance, to visit the child as regularly as they would wish.

Multi-agency support for children in care

Once a child is in care, irrespective of the reason for this, and of the placement in which the child is living, they are entitled to a minimum level of support from the range of agencies involved. This support should be recorded through two key plans – the Care Plan and the Personal Education Plan (PEP) – which include short- and long-term aims related to the care placement, the health needs of the child, the child's educational progress, and any other relevant matters, for example, leisure or social pursuits. The social worker is responsible for coordinating the completion of both these plans, although responsibility for completion of elements of the work will be shared among the agencies involved.

For all children and young people in public care, there is a requirement for the social worker to visit them on a regular basis. The usual time interval is at least once every 28 days, although if the child or young person is in a settled long-term placement this can be extended. The Care Plans are subject to regular multi-agency reviews, the main purpose of which is to consider the relevance of the overall care plan rather than the details of the particular placement. The time intervals for these reviews should be:

- upon a new placement, or change of placement where this constitutes a significant change to the Care Plan, within 28 days of the placement
- a second review within 3 months of the 28-day review
- further reviews should then take place no longer than every 6 months.

In addition to the carer (which could be a key worker for children in residential care) and the social worker, these reviews should include attendance by a school or early years setting staff member, a relevant health professional, and, where appropriate, the child themselves and their parents. The meetings are chaired by an Independent Reviewing Officer, so called because they are independent from the social work team or line management, although they are employed, like the social worker, by social services.

School and early years setting staff or health professionals may face similar problems in attending children in care reviews as they may in attending child protection meetings: they may have competing priorities, or staff cover may be unavailable or expensive to maintain. Where attendance is not possible, workers are expected to send a written report to the meeting. A further difficulty may be that unless the purpose of the review is clearly shared and understood, there is a danger the meeting is hijacked by one professional who has a particular issue they wish to pursue, which may not be relevant to the core function of the meeting, for instance regarding a narrow aspect of the placement. Furthermore, unless this is carefully managed by the Independent Reviewing Officer, resentment can build such that a complaint may then be made to senior management within the relevant agency responsible, in this example, for the placement. There may also be a perception among professionals other than those employed by social services that although the Reviewing Officer is ostensibly independent, there may be a bias towards the social worker, as they are both employed by the same agency. It is interesting that the government white paper (DfES, 2007a) proposes making Reviewing Officers more independent.

More professionals than those mentioned above may well be involved in the life of a child in care and working towards fulfilling elements of the Care Plan. These might include:

- specialist local authority education staff, where children in care have special educational needs
- an education welfare officer, where there are problems of school attendance
- Youth Offending Service staff, where children in care are at risk of, or are involved in, offending
- careers staff, where children in care are of the appropriate age
- a variety of health staff to meet individual health needs
- a paediatrician based in a hospital clinic, where children in care have particular health needs.

The second major multi-agency tool to support children in care – the PEP will be discussed under the section dealing with the education of children in care. However, all of the staff in the above list, and those already mentioned above – carers, social workers, school and early years setting staff – are expected to prioritize children in care as part of their role as a 'corporate parent' a term introduced by the national guidance for England (DfEE and DH, 2000). This means agencies should go out of their way to support the child in any manner they can, as if the child were their own. This laudable aim is not without its difficulties. Where staff are working in pressured environments, perhaps with limited personnel and resources, prioritizing children in care may involve them making some very hard choices between them and other equally deserving and needy children who may not be in care. If for instance, a child protection conference clashes with a children in care review for two different children, and a worker has to choose between the two, they should, according to the national guidance, attend the latter meeting. However, this is to prioritize a meeting where a child should be safe, and may well be settled and progressing well, over a meeting where a child, albeit living at home, may be at risk of significant harm. Following the expectations of national guidance may not always sit easily with the moral or professional judgements of individual workers.

 Information: What is corporate parenting?

Corporate parenting is the collective responsibility of all agencies involved, directly or indirectly, with children in care to achieve good parenting. The national guidance identified six principles of effective corporate parenting:

1. **Prioritizing education:** valuing and supporting education as a place where children in care can not only achieve academically, but also develop self confidence and skills, receive praise and encouragement and build relationships.

⇨

2. **Having high expectations:** all corporate parents should have high expectations for children in care, which is translated into actions such as ensuring regular school attendance, securing a school place without delay, providing homework and study support, and behaviour support where appropriate.
3. **Challenging and changing attitudes:** corporate parents need to ensure that children in care have equal access to education and other opportunities. This might include ensuring they are not stereotyped into a homogenous group, nor discriminated against or bullied because of their circumstances, which can be compounded by race, disability or gender.
4. **Achieving continuity and stability:** corporate parents need to liaise in order to limit the number of school and placement changes, and the number of exclusions from school.
5. **Early intervention and prioritizing action:** corporate parents are expected to respond immediately to problems, and act upon these. They should avoid delay and drift.
6. **Listening to children:** corporate parents should have structures and systems to ensure children in care are consulted and listened to in order to plan and deliver effective services.

Education and children in care

The relatively poor educational outcomes for children in care compared to their peers not in care have been a key issue now since at least the mid 1980s, and there remains a significant gap in attainment between the two groups. By way of illustration, the figures in Table 6.1 should suffice. The English national guidance on improving educational outcomes for children in care (DfEE and DH, 2000) is supplemented in the other three United Kingdom countries by the following:

- Wales: The National Assembly for Wales (2001) publication *Guidance on the Education of Children Looked After by Local Authorities*.
- Scotland: Guidance titled *Extraordinary Lives* (Social Work Inspection Agency, 2006) promotes good practice in supporting the education of children in care.
- Northern Ireland: The DHSSPS (2007a) guidance *Care Matters in Northern Ireland* contains detailed proposals for supporting the education of children in care.

Table 6.1 Educational outcomes for children in care in England

	Children in care		All children	
Indicator	2000	2006	2000	2006
% achieving Level 2 at the end of Key Stage 1 (7-year-olds)	47	58	82	85
% achieving Level 4 at the end of Key Stage 2 (11-year-olds)	36	47	76	81
% achieving Level 5 at the end of Key Stage 3 (14-year-olds)	19	30	62	74
% achieving at least 5 GCSEs graded A*–C at the end of Key Stage 4 (16-year-olds)	7	12	49	59

Source: DH (2001) and DfES (2007e)

The figures in Table 6.1 show that (with the exception of General Certificate of Secondary Education (GCSE) outcomes) there has been an 11 per cent increase over 7 years in the percentage of children in care achieving the expected target. Nevertheless, there is still a substantial gap between the attainment of children in care and their peers at every stage of educational testing. Indeed, although this gap has narrowed slightly at Key Stages 1 and 2, at Key Stages 3 and 4, the gap has actually increased over the 7 years covered by the table. This is in spite of the various government initiatives and is partly due to the fact that for all children, their rate of improvement has outstripped that of children in care. Two other features of these figures are worthy of note. First, that although there is a reduction in the percentage of children receiving the required outcomes as they get older (for both children in care and all children) there is a dramatic reduction once children in care reach high school. It appears that children in care find the transition to high school very difficult and possibly coupled with the onset of adolescence where identity issues surface, this impacts dramatically on their Key Stage 3 performance. It is interesting that for children in care the dip from Key Stage 2 to 3 is 17 per cent for both 2000 (from 36 to 19) and 2006 (from 47 to 30), and yet for all children the same dip has halved over the same time period (from 14 per cent in 2000 to 7 per cent in 2006). Second, results for children in care obtaining at least 5 good GCSEs have remained obstinately low, rising by only 5 per cent compared to the same figures for all children, which have increased by 10 per cent – the gap between the 2 sets of children has risen by 5 points.

One final statistic is worth mentioning, and that is for the percentage of children in care who are permanently excluded. Children who are permanently excluded cannot return to the school which has excluded them, and either attend an alternative school or some alternative educational provision. Bearing in mind that permanent exclusions are supposed to be used as a last resort (DfES, 2006c) it is therefore interesting that children in care are eight times more likely to be permanently excluded than their peers not in care (0.8 per cent of children in care are permanently excluded compared to 0.1 per cent of all children). The reasons behind this, and indeed behind the relatively poor educational outcomes of children in care in general, are complex and cannot be explained away simply by arguing that children in care are less well behaved or less intelligent than their peers. These reasons will now be explored.

Reason for poor outcomes for children in care

The first major study to highlight the poor outcomes for this group of children was that conducted by Jackson (1987b). In the same year, she began to explore possible reasons for this, and challenged the prevailing view that children in care could not be expected to do well since they had more pressing issues to deal with, such as emotional trauma, separation and loss, or worse, that they were delinquent slow learners. Instead, she reached the conclusion that the poor outcomes resulted from a lack of appropriate support, encouragement and cooperation from those responsible for them (Jackson, 1987a).

Since this seminal work, the possible reasons for the gap in attainment between children in care and their peers are now well documented. By way of summary, some of the key findings are:

- inflexible or unavailable personal support for children at a time of crisis
- poor liaison and collaboration between schools and social services
- a lack of training for teachers on meeting the needs of, and responsibilities for, the children
- insufficient priority given to education by social services staff
- insufficient support in the care setting to help compensate for educational disadvantage
- the lack of a single advocate for the children
- the lack of encouragement to attend or do well at school
- teachers' and carers' low expectations of what children in care can achieve
- learning being disrupted by frequent moves
- not having enough space or resources to complete homework
- being bullied and stigmatized at school.

(Borland, 1998; Social Services Inspectorate and Ofsted, 1995; The Who Cares? Trust, 2003).

What is clear from this list is that these barriers to learning for children in care originate within and between a variety of agencies and settings, and therefore any solutions for improving the plight of such children must also lie across a number of agencies. The reason why it is seen as so critical to address the underachievement of children in care is that there is evidence that poor experiences of education and care can contribute to social exclusion in later life. For instance, between a quarter and a third of adult rough sleepers were in care; young people who have been in care are two and a half times more likely to be teenage parents, and around a quarter of adults in prison spent some time in care as children (Social Exclusion Unit, 2003).

What might lead to better outcomes?

There is, thankfully, research available into what might improve the situation. Borland (1998) argues for collaborative support involving specific education planning. The Who Cares? Trust (1999) articulated this as PEPs, a tool which the national guidance for England (DfEE and DH, 2000) implemented as an essential requirement for every child in public care, and which further research corroborated as crucial (Jackson and Sachdev, 2001). This PEP, which every child in care should have, should contain clear short- and long-term educational targets together with a description of the support on offer from each individual in each agency involved to help achieve these. The plan should be drawn up at a face-to-face meeting involving the school or early years setting, carer, social worker, parent and young person if appropriate. It is the responsibility of the social worker to ensure this plan is in place, and that it is reviewed at the same time as the Care Plan, preferably at the very same meeting, since most of the people attending are likely to have an interest in both plans.

The PEP has the potential to be an extremely useful way of coordinating support to enhance the education of children in care. It can specify in detail what each agency or individual, including the carer and child themselves, will do to support the education of the child in question. In this way, individuals can be held to account at review meetings, and, for example, asked to explain why a particular action they committed to has not been carried out. Whether an agency, however, can *make* another agency conform is another question entirely, but if all concerned are aware that their action (or inaction) is going to be scrutinized in an open meeting, this may act as a catalyst to ensure each party delivers what they promise in the PEP. Attendance at meetings to formulate and review the PEP may be another issue – where professionals have to balance priorities or demands on their time, or where the business of the PEP is not perceived by them to be core to their role, attendance may slip. The impact of this on the ability of those who do attend to then construct a meaningful PEP can be severe. If a face-to-face meeting cannot be set up within a timescale that is meaningful to the child, the PEP may be drawn up as a paper exercise, where each individual completes 'their' section and then passes it on to the next person. The difficulty with this is that it does little to foster understanding and shared ownership of the issues – there is little opportunity to discuss and distil ideas, to question comments made, to clarify jargon or language used. The danger here is that the process of the PEP becomes merely a paper exercise – of course it is not the existence of the completed form which really counts in terms of supporting the child, but the quality of the work involved. Multi-agency work becomes almost meaningless if it is reduced to producing reams of completed forms purporting to provide effective support, no matter how impressively these forms may be filled out. Some of these difficulties have been identified in research by Hayden (2005) who found that practical difficulties predominated, such as trying to make the PEP system focus on meeting the needs of children as well as practitioners and difficulty in meeting specified timescales for the completion of the PEP (which should be completed within 28 days of the child coming into care or moving to a new school).

---

⑦ Reflections: Case study – Carlton

Carlton is 11 years old, black Caribbean and has been in care since the age of 9. He has just moved to high school after finishing his primary education. The social worker is trying to be efficient in setting up a PEP meeting within the first 4 weeks, as she feels under pressure to complete the PEP within the required timescale. However, the designated teacher at the school is reluctant to go along with this, arguing that they need more time to get to know Carlton and to assess his needs if the school's contribution to the PEP is going to be meaningful.

1 How might the school and social worker compromise in a way that allows both to meet their different requirements?

In addition to PEPs, other possible solutions to the poor educational plight of children in care, centred on the role of the school, include:

- A designated teacher for children in care (now a requirement under the national guidance).
- Increased awareness of all staff of the issues faced by children in care. This involves training for school staff and is a worthy, although huge undertaking. The designated teacher within school could carry out some of this, providing that they had themselves received effective training.
- A caring, supportive non-stigmatizing school where there is access to an adult in confidence.
- Quick transfer of information when children change school.
- Timely assessment of need; and a system for agreeing with children how information about them is handled within school.
- Flexibility within school to enable children to access appropriate support.
- As few exclusions from school as possible. Clearly, if children are not in school, they cannot learn and make progress. Furthermore, exclusions for children in care can have a much more serious impact compared with children living at home because foster carers can argue that unless the child is in school every day they cannot continue to care for them. This can have devastating consequences if the child then has to move placement.
- Structured behaviour management.
- Study support where needed.
- Celebrating success for children in care within school. One tension here is between lauding the success of children in care and maintaining confidentiality and sensitivity about children's circumstances.
- Peer support coupled with anti-bullying strategies.
- Being treated as any young person. Children in care share common needs with all children, and it could be argued that they should not be singled out for special or preferential treatment. They need boundaries and guidance as all children do; however, the difference may be that at times these need to be applied with more sensitivity and thought.

(Borland, 1998; Ofsted, 2001; The Who Cares? Trust, 1999)

Wider factors consistent with more successful outcomes identified by Hunt (2000) and Ofsted (2001) include the following:

- Learning to read before the age of 8. This is associated with building resilience to withstand later setbacks, so the impact of coming into care is lessened.
- Having a carer or parent who values education. If a key adult is enthusiastic and supportive about the child's education, this should benefit the child.
- Having friends outside care who do well at school. The peer group the child chooses can be significant. If they are good attendees at school and value school, then this should encourage the child in care to do well.
- Developing out of school interests. Where children in care can follow leisure pursuits or develop other interests this can have a positive impact upon their education, not only because they may be able to use the knowledge or skills acquired, but also because their general level of confidence may be boosted.
- Having a significant adult who offers consistent encouragement as a mentor, role model or champion. If children in care connect with someone who provides credible assistance this can maintain and increase their engagement with education.

- Access to resources of study. Clearly, where children in care can readily get hold of books, access to the internet and so on, they are likely to be at an advantage compared to those children in care without such access.
- A consistent social worker who is interested in education; commitment and support from carers.

The importance of stability and continuity of care and school placements has also been identified (Hunt, 2000; Ofsted, 2001). Berridge (2000) also discusses this, concluding that changes of school outside normal transfer 'can be highly stressful, and should be avoided wherever possible' (p. 7).

Jackson and Sachdev (2001) consulted directly with children, and they discovered the 'huge gap between well-meaning policies ... and the day to day experiences of young people' (p. 11). They also found that the young people were articulate about the difficulties, and about what did or could help them. This included:

- direct support to young people
- education training for foster carers
- appropriate resources in care homes
- leisure opportunities
- advocacy for children excluded from school. The aim here would be to try to ensure the child is provided with an alternative and appropriate education as soon as possible.

Government proposals for action to support children in care

Many of the ideas and findings discussed above appear to have found their way into proposals within the government white paper (DfES, 2007a) whose explicit aim is to 'transform once and for all the experiences and prospects of children in care' (p. 4). The proposals within this are ambitious and far-reaching, and deal with ideas not only for improving the educational outcomes for children in care, but all aspects of their lives. They relate to the responsibilities of central government, local authorities as a whole, schools, social workers and other agencies. This chapter cannot deal in detail with all of the proposals, but will highlight some examples for discussion. The reader is encouraged to refer to the full document.

Under the heading of *Corporate Parenting: Getting It Right*, the document sets out a number of proposals which are strategic, relating to:

- the development of children in care councils at local level
- issuing a pledge to children in care setting out the services and support they can expect to receive

- setting out responsibilities of senior managers
- inspection of outcomes.

It seems appropriate here to be reminded of the warning issued by Jackson and Sachdev (2001) that children in care experience a gap between policy and practice – the key to the success of these new ideas will be ensuring that these high-level actions translate into palpable improvements for individual children.

A second heading is *Family and Parenting Support* where proposals include reducing the numbers of children entering or remaining in care. The latter is to be achieved by enabling relatives to apply for a residence order for children in care (and thereby give the relative parental responsibility), and producing guidance on more effective care planning to enable the child to return home to parents, where it is safe for them to do so. While this may seem a good idea, there is a danger here as previously discussed in relation to the use of family network carers. Should there develop a dogma around always supporting relatives to apply for residence orders or assuming that the default position is that agencies should work towards returning children home, this dogma could interfere with, and influence, clear decision making around what is truly in the best interests of the child. This could be a recipe for multi-agency disagreements. Where there may be pressure on, say, social services to reduce the numbers of children in care, this could lead them to supporting plans for a child to live with relatives or return to the care of their parents, while other agencies believe the child needs to be cared for in a traditional foster family, as neither the relative or parent can fully meet the child's needs.

Proposals integrated within a third heading titled *Care Placements: A Better Experience for Everyone* include introducing a skills standards framework for foster carers which includes training, revising and enforcing minimum standards for foster and residential care, and introducing the use of social pedagogy in residential care. These proposals appear to be drilling down into the day-to-day experiences of children in care, but clarification is still needed on a number of elements. For instance, the standards of care would need to include such attributes as supporting education and homework, adequate space and resources for homework, encouraging leisure interests and so on.

 Information: What is social pedagogy?

Social pedagogy is a holistic approach to social care which focuses on the whole child. It uses the relationship between the child and the worker, which is developed through practical activities as well as discussions, to understand and support the child. Within this model, workers are reflective and use theoretical knowledge to inform their actions. There is an emphasis on children's rights and the place of the child as part of a group (Petrie *et al.*, 2005).

A fourth area is related to *Delivering a First Class Education*. Proposals here are designed to ensure that children in care have full support, stability and continuity in their education, and include:

- Children in care under 5 should have a place in an appropriate high-quality early years provision.
- Older children in care should not have their education disrupted by care planning which involves a move of school, unless this is demonstrably in their interests.
- During GCSE years in particular, children in care should not move school unless in exceptional circumstances.
- The role of the designated teacher is to be placed on a statutory footing. The key question here is, with no extra resources apparently being made available, how schools will balance this requirement with other imperatives placed upon them. In other words, what will teachers not do that they are currently doing in order to carry out this role, and which of these competing tasks will be seen as a priority?
- Funding will be made available to support children at risk of not reaching the expected academic standards. It is envisaged that the designated teacher, social worker and carer, in consultation with the child, will decide how to spend this money. This could afford an opportunity for multi-agency arguments and disagreements as each of these individuals may have very different ideas as to what would support the child's learning.
- The PEPs are still seen as vital tools by which the workers concerned coordinate effective learning and teaching strategies, ensure access to services and minimize disruption to the child's education. In order to maximize their effectiveness, the designated teacher, social worker and carer would not only need to have it specified as a clear part of their role, but would require time and support to complete this task; otherwise competing priorities will inevitably impact on their ability to meet together and reach a common understanding, with the child, of how best to support their education.

The remaining areas of the white paper proposals relate to health and well-being, transitions to adulthood, and the role of the practitioner. A common element among all the areas, if not all the proposals, is that to be successful, they demand a truly multi-agency response. Much of the white paper uses such terminology as 'expecting' or 'requiring' the different agencies to work together more effectively. However, merely expecting or making people work together does not, of course, ensure that it will happen, or if it does happen, that it will happen well. The traditional barriers to multi-agency work, discussed in Chapter 2, will remain to varying degrees, and might even be intensified where there is a resource (such as the allowance to support a child's learning) available.

Conclusions

Children in care are not a homogenous group: they enter care for a wide variety of reasons, live in varied placements and have widely differing needs. This makes the multi-agency system, designed to support the individual circumstances of children, so crucial to implement.

Nevertheless, there are inherent difficulties in achieving positive outcomes. Chief among the poor outcomes, perhaps, is the low educational attainment of children in care compared to their peers not in care. There is a wealth of research identifying some of the complex reasons for this, and signalling possible ways to improve the life chances of children in care. The latest government initiative aimed at achieving better outcomes is to be welcomed. However, if children in care truly are to receive the very best in care and education, then not only are significant resources going to have to be committed, but the very real difficulties involved in bringing a range of workers together to implement the varied and complex measures need to be fully understood and overcome.

Information sharing

Introduction

Information sharing, in relation to multi-agency working, is subject to a series of complex rules. These rules often have sound aims or purposes behind them, relating to the protection of privacy, or respect for the confidential and sensitive nature of the material under consideration. However, the very complexity of the regulations also has the potential to cause confusion and uncertainty for professionals. This chapter explores the key legislation and guidance which governs information sharing, including the Data Protection Act 1998, the Human Rights Act 1998 and specific government guidance in relation to sharing information and safeguarding children. The first two of these are huge and wide-ranging pieces of legislation which cover every aspect of information storing and sharing. This chapter will focus on those aspects of this legislation that are relevant to multi-agency working. The third element to be discussed – government guidance on information sharing – is concerned with circumstances where professionals need to share information in order to support children who have additional needs, or to protect children from harm. This guidance therefore forms the bulk of this chapter.

The Data Protection Act 1998

This Act, which came into effect in the year 2000, converts the European Data Protection Directive into United Kingdom law. As such it is applicable to all four constituent countries – England, Wales, Scotland and Northern Ireland. Within the scope of the Act is a wide range of personal data, which includes anything that can identify a living person, such as a name. Furthermore, the Act specifically identifies certain categories of data as 'sensitive', such as the state of a person's physical and mental health, their racial or ethnic origin, sexual orientation and political beliefs. There are clear restrictions on those who hold personal information (which could be a private business or a local authority) as to what they may do with it and with whom they may share it. Generally, the Act requires organizations to seek explicit consent from individuals before collecting, processing or passing on 'sensitive' information about them. Both computerized and manual records are covered by the Act.

The starting point for understanding the implications of the Act for multi-agency working for children is the eight principles which underpin it, and which should be adhered to at all times. Individual employees can be prosecuted for unlawful action. In these circumstances, these individuals could be liable for fines of up to £5,000, which can be imposed for such misdemeanours as disclosing information about a person without their consent. This could include, for example, giving personal details to a fellow employee who does not need those details to carry out their legitimate duties. Of course, special care must be taken with sensitive data as described above.

 Information: The eight principles of the Data Protection Act 1998

Data must be:

- fairly and lawfully processed
- processed for limited purposes
- adequate, relevant and not excessive
- accurate
- not kept longer than necessary
- processed in accordance with the data subject's rights
- secure
- not transferred to other countries without adequate protection.

The implications of this are that all staff within an organization have to be cognizant of the need to observe the requirements of the Act. They need to make sure, for example, that inadvertent unauthorized disclosure of data does not occur by passing information over the telephone, or by allowing others within the office to read a computer screen. More specifically, workers should:

- not leave people's information on their desk when not in use
- make sure filing cabinets are kept locked
- not leave data displayed on computer screens, and they should make sure that computers are not left logged on and unattended
- not give their computer password to anyone else

- not select a computer password that is easy to guess
- think carefully before sending faxes or emails containing personal data.

It is not difficult to see how these detailed and precise expectations, coupled with the large potential fines for breach of them (for which individuals rather than organizations are liable) can lead to a culture of fear and paralysis when it comes to sharing personal information. If, say a teacher in a school was unsure whether they should share personal data with social services about a child for whom they were concerned (where parental consent to share information is not forthcoming), they may, in the spirit of conforming to the Data Protection Act 1998, choose not to do so, being fearful that they could be committing an offence for which they will personally be liable. However, it may have been appropriate to share this personal information with social services in the specific circumstances of the case, and indeed could have been just the piece of a jigsaw of information which enabled swift protective action to take place for that child. Ironically, in observing what they understood to be the requirements of the Data Protection Act, the teacher may have inadvertently caused unnecessary suffering to the child by not sharing information which might have invoked a child protection response. As we shall see later, although there are guidelines regarding sharing information for professionals who are worried about children, doubts and uncertainties will remain, at least partly fuelled by a fear of the consequences of sharing information inappropriately.

The Human Rights Act 1998

Similar concerns and confusions may also potentially dog the interpretation of the second major piece of legislation which impinges upon information sharing. The Human Rights Act 1998, which like the Data Protection Act 1998 came into force in 2000, is a particularly extensive statute which covers rights and freedoms which everyone should enjoy. These rights are defined as absolute, limited or qualified, depending which one is being described. The rights and freedoms contained within the Act, which applies to the whole of the United Kingdom, are as follows:

- The right to life (Article 2 – a qualified right as there are some very limited circumstances under which the state can take away someone's life).
- Freedom from torture and inhuman or degrading treatment or punishment (Article 3 – an absolute right).
- Freedom from slavery and forced or compulsory labour (Article 4 – an absolute right).
- Personal freedom (Article 5 – a limited right as there are circumstances under which someone can be lawfully detained).
- The right to a fair trial (Article 6 – an absolute right).
- The right to protection from retrospective criminal offences; in other words, someone cannot be found guilty of an offence which at the time of the action, was not unlawful (Article 7 – an absolute right).
- The right to respect for a private and family life (Article 8 – a qualified right as interference with this right is allowed in certain circumstances).

- The right to freedom of thought, conscience and religion (Article 9 – a qualified right as the state can intervene in certain circumstances).
- The right to freedom of expression (Article 10 – a qualified right as the state can intervene in certain circumstances).
- The right to freedom of association and assembly (Article 11 – a qualified right as the state can intervene in certain circumstances).
- The right to marry and found a family (Article 12 – an absolute right, although the state can regulate matters related to marriage and starting a family, which includes adoption).
- Freedom from discrimination (Article 13 – a qualified right, as the state can make a distinction in treatment in some circumstances).
- The right to property (Article 1 of the first protocol – a qualified right, as the state can intervene in certain circumstances).
- The right to education (Article 2 of the first protocol – a qualified right, as the state can intervene in certain circumstances).
- The right to free and fair elections (Article 3 of the first protocol – an absolute right, although the state can regulate matters related to elections).
- The abolition of the death penalty in peacetime (Articles 1 and 2 of the sixth protocol).

Of these, the Article most relevant to multi-agency working for children is Article 8 – the right for people to enjoy a private and family life. As we have seen, this is a qualified right, meaning that interference is acceptable in circumstances that must be justified. Closer scrutiny of some of the concepts contained within this article is useful here, and for this the document *A Guide to the Human Rights Act 1998* (Department for Constitutional Affairs, 2006) has been invaluable. A 'private life' includes the right to live one's own life as is reasonable in a democratic society, as balanced against the rights and freedom of others. This includes the right to choose one's own sexual identity, how one looks and dresses, and freedom from intrusion by the media. Furthermore, in a direct correlation with the Data Protection Act 1998, a private life includes the right of an individual to have information about them kept private and confidential. Article 8 also limits what a public authority can do which invades one's personal body privacy, and this could include such activities as taking blood samples or performing body searches.

The second part of Article 8 deals with the right to a family life. This includes the right to have family relationships recognized by law, and the rights for families to live together and to enjoy each other's company. Interestingly, unmarried mothers are always covered by family life, while foster families may be, depending on the particular circumstances. These rights, and those relating to a private life, can only be breached if the interference with them has a legal basis, and has a clear aim in line with one of the following:

- To uphold the laws of an individual nation.
- To safeguard national security.
- To safeguard public safety or the economic well-being of the country.
- To prevent a crime.

- To uphold public health or morals.
- To protect the freedom and rights of others.

Furthermore, and here another important concept is introduced, any interference must be proportionate; in other words, the action must go only as far as is required to meet the aim specified under any of the list above. Breaches of the right to a private and family life, therefore, must be justifiable and must not exceed any powers or actions that are necessary to execute the requirements of the breach.

 Information: The Human Rights Act 1998 – balancing the rights of parents and children

Where the state has concerns that there is a need to protect the freedom and rights of a child in a family, then the state, in the form of social workers, the police and other professionals who may be involved, can interfere with the parents' right to a private and family life and intervene to protect the child from significant harm, even if this results in the removal of the child from that family. The rights of the parents to a family life do not trump the rights of the child to enjoy protection from harm.

Government guidance on information sharing for practitioners

In relation to professionals responding to concerns about children, the government has issued guidance which includes comprehensive coverage of issues related to the sharing of information (DfES, 2006d) and the bulk of this is reproduced in a more general guide for practitioners worried about children who may be being abused (DfES, 2006h). It is not coincidental that such full guidance was issued after the publication of the report by Laming (2003) into the death of Victoria Climbié which concluded, in relation to information sharing, that exchange of information was inhibited by the legislation, and that workers had genuine concerns that unless it was clearly demonstrated a child was in need of protection, such information sharing would be unlawful. The effect of this is either that information may not be shared when it should be (as in the example involving the teacher given earlier), or that concerns about children are artificially heightened. Neither of these, as Laming points out, are compatible with serving the needs of children and families. He went on to recommend that clear guidance be produced to clarify these matters.

The guidance that followed (DfES, 2006d) begins by setting out six key points on information sharing:

- At the beginning of any work, practitioners should set out clearly and openly the ground rules for information sharing. Consent to share information with other agencies should be sought unless to do so would put a child or adult at risk of serious harm, or would undermine the prevention, detection or prosecution of a serious crime.

- The safety and welfare of the child must be the main consideration when a worker is deciding whether or not to share information about them.
- Where possible, practitioners should respect the wishes of children and parents who may not consent to information about themselves being shared. This consent can be overridden, however, if the worker judges, on the facts of that particular case, that this is justified.
- Workers should seek advice if they are in doubt whether or not to share information or to override consent of the child or parent.
- Practitioners must ensure that information that is shared is accurate, up-to-date, relevant and necessary, and is shared securely and only with those who need to know. This is a reference to the rule of proportionality mentioned earlier. For example, a health visitor concerned that a child may be suffering significant harm from neglect can share information relating to the health and welfare of the child, their development, the condition of the house and so on, but should refrain from telling the social worker receiving the telephone call that the mother is having an affair with the milkman (if it were true), unless this is in some way directly relevant to the neglect of the child.
- Reasons for a decision to share information or not should be recorded.

These six key points serve to emphasize that the decision to share information or not involves a judgement not only about whether to share, but if information is shared, how much to share. To summarize, workers can share information if:

- there is consent by the child or parents
- the child's welfare overrides the withholding of consent by the child or parent or the confidentiality of the information
- disclosure of the information is required by a court or legal order.

Confidentiality and information sharing

The underlying principle throughout this guidance is that the sharing of information between professionals is essential in order to both enable early intervention to help children who need additional services or to safeguard and promote the welfare of children. One of the key concepts here is that of confidentiality, and the guidance contains further information on this. Once again, there is a complex set of rules governing confidentiality which professionals need to negotiate if they are to confidently interpret and implement them.

 Information: Confidentiality

In deciding whether there is a need to share information, practitioners need to consider:

- Is the information confidential? Information is not confidential if it is not of a sensitive nature, is already lawfully in the public domain, is available from a public source or has been shared in circumstances where the person giving the information understood that it might be shared with others.

Information—Cont'd

- If so, is there a public interest which would justify sharing the information? This includes the protection of children from harm, and the practitioner would need to make a judgement, if there were concerns about a child and consent to share information was not given by the parents, or it was inappropriate to seek consent, whether to override confidentiality and share the information.

Confidentiality is breached if the sharing of confidential information is not authorized by the person who either provided it, or to whom it relates. Where the person concerned gave consent to that information being shared, then sharing it is clearly not a breach of confidentiality. However, there are circumstances in which workers can lawfully breach confidentiality – if it is in the public interest – although the worker concerned should seek consent to share the information, unless the very act of seeking consent is likely to undermine the detection, prevention or prosecution of a crime. Public interest includes such matters as protecting children (or adults) from harm, promoting the welfare of children and preventing crime. One of the key considerations once a decision has been made to share information is proportionality – whether the sharing of information in the public interest is a proportionate response to the need to protect the public in the particular way dictated by the circumstances. The guidance goes on to say that the individual practitioner must weigh up the consequences of sharing the information against the consequences of not sharing the information, and make a decision based on a 'reasonable judgement' (DfES, 2006d, p. 9). The term 'reasonable' is not defined in law, and therefore the key questions that remain here are who decides what is reasonable, and whose definition of reasonable should provide the standard against which to judge the action of individuals?

The document goes on to provide yet more complex guidance on this matter. It sets out some circumstances in which the sharing of confidential information will 'normally' (ibid., p. 10) be justified. These are:

- where there is evidence that a child is suffering, or at risk of suffering, significant harm
- where there is reasonable cause to believe that a child may be suffering, or at risk of, significant harm
- to prevent significant harm to children or serious harm to adults.

Now, there are two important elements here. The first is that the word 'normally' is crucial, as it suggests these are not absolute circumstances, and that there could well be circumstances in which a worker believes they are doing the right thing in sharing information because of, say, concerns about a child, but actually they have breached confidentiality. This is unavoidable, since, as the guidance recognizes, it is impossible to describe every possible circumstance in which the sharing of confidential information may be justified or not; however, the effect of this is that there is likely to remain a certain level of anxiety among workers regarding any decision to share confidential information where they do not have consent. If they have not received very clear guidance and training on this, the consequence of this is that children may be left unprotected because workers are rightly concerned they will be disciplined or even prosecuted for breaching confidentiality.

This issue relates to the second important element of the circumstances in which the sharing of confidential information would 'normally' be justified. This is that a practitioner requires either evidence or reasonable cause to believe that a child needs protecting from significant harm. There is a distinction to be made between these two – evidence requires some level of physical proof. Reasonable cause, on the other hand, is a lower level of proof and might cover, for example, a worker receiving information via a telephone call from another professional outlining their concerns about a child. As long as the source of the information is credible, this is likely to be classed as reasonable cause. Once again, the worker should seek consent to share information, unless this places the child at increased risk of significant harm or lead to interference with any investigation which might follow. The decision whether or not to seek consent must be driven by what is best for the child. Furthermore, the guidance acknowledges that there may be uncertainty as to what constitutes 'reasonable cause' and if this is the case, the individual concerned should seek advice, and then record the decision that is made. This is yet another layer of understanding that professionals need to absorb and understand if they are to make effective decisions with regard to information sharing: that they only require reasonable cause and not hard evidence in order to lawfully breach confidentiality, that they need to be clear what they are interpreting as 'reasonable cause', and that they then need to make a judgement as to whether to share information or not.

Sharing information and preventative services

Having dealt with confidentiality as such, the guidance goes on to consider the sharing of information related to the provision of preventative services. The dilemma here is that as services become more integrated and involve practitioners from different disciplines or agencies working together to support children and families who have additional needs but who are not at risk of significant harm, these services are likely to have concerns about their ability to share information among themselves, particularly in the light of the complex legislation surrounding it. The suggested solution is that agencies involved seek explicit consent, at the point of the family accessing the service, to share information with those other agencies involved in supporting the family. This process of seeking consent should involve the service explaining their policy on information sharing, and should be open and honest. Of course, non-confidential information can be shared to support any preventative work; but if consent is refused to share confidential information, this should be respected unless any of the circumstances described above justify the overriding of this withholding of consent. The difficulty here is that inherent in this process is the real possibility that parents, suspicious of the motives of agencies in providing services, and equally mistrusting of any service with authority, may withhold their consent to share information. Indeed, once they are approached regarding giving their consent to share information, some parents may elect to withdraw from the receipt of support for themselves and their children. In other words, merely integrating services and setting them up as preventative does not guarantee a seamless transition of support and information across and between agencies and for children and families. There remains a potential clash between the desire to work with families preventatively and provide early intervention, and legislation on information sharing.

The potential for clashes and contradictions, however, is not limited to the relationship between professionals and parents. As the guidance recognizes, different agencies are likely to have different standards for sharing information, covered by individual agency policies and protocols, or local area information sharing protocols, or even by the professional code of particular agencies. This serves to illustrate how complex is the maze of information sharing which workers have to negotiate: not only do they have to be aware of, and understand the implications of, national legislation, but they also need to fully comprehend their own local or single agency guidelines.

 Information: National Health Service Caldicott guardians

In 1997, a report by Dame Fiona Caldicott on the transfer of patient-identifiable information concluded that each NHS organisation should have a senior manager to oversee arrangements for the use and sharing of patient information. This person was known as the Caldicott guardian. Subsequently, similar guardians were also appointed to councils with social service responsibilities. A key part of the role of the Caldicott guardian is to ensure that information sharing adheres to six principles set out in the Caldicott report: justification of the purpose for using confidential information, only using it when necessary, using the minimum required, allowing access on a strict need-to-know basis, ensuring everyone understands their responsibilities and ensuring compliance with the law. Since 1997, the requirements and remit of the role of the Caldicott guardian have expanded to take into account the Data Protection Act 1998 and the Human Rights Act 1998 (DH, 2006).

The issue of consent

A further concept which professionals need to fully appreciate is that of 'consent', a word which has so far been used without further elaboration. It would be a mistake, however, to assume that everyone understands equally what consent means or involves. The guidance acknowledges this, and provides further information about it. In securing consent, it should go without saying that the agency or individual concerned should take a transparent and respectful approach, and should avoid coercion or worse still, a refusal to provide a service unless consent to share information with other agencies is given. Furthermore, consent cannot be taken as having been granted if a parent is asked to provide consent but does not respond to this request. In addition, parents have the right to withdraw consent once they have given it.

Information: What is consent?

Consent must be informed. This means that the person giving consent understands why the information needs to be shared, who will see it, to what purpose it will be put, and what the implications are of sharing information. Consent can be explicit or implicit. The former can be obtained verbally or in writing (although written consent is preferable). Implicit consent is valid where information sharing is intrinsic to the activity, especially where this has been explained. An example would be where a common assessment is being undertaken, and the parents have given consent for this.

Children, too, have the right to give or refuse consent. Children aged 16 and 17, and children under the age of 16 with the capacity to understand and make their decisions, are able to do so. This capacity is generally taken to be present in children aged 12 or over, although children younger than this may also have sufficient understanding to make a decision regarding consent. For children under the age of 16, then, this clearly involves a judgement by the worker as to whether or not the child is mature enough to:

- understand what they are being asked
- understand what information will be shared, the reasons for this, and the implications of sharing or not sharing it
- appreciate or consider any alternatives open to them
- weigh up one aspect of the situation against another
- express a clear personal view on the issue (rather than repeat what someone else has said)
- be consistent in their view.

Where a child is not able to give informed consent then a parent or other person with parental responsibility should be asked to consent on behalf of the child. Only the consent of one parent is required, which could be problematic for a worker concerned if two parents are in conflict and hold opposing views on the matter. In these circumstances, the worker would have to consider whose consent to seek. Where parents are separated, the solution is relatively straightforward, in that the worker should seek consent from the parent with whom the child resides most of the time. If parents are still together, however, and yet disagree, this decision is very difficult. Furthermore, where a competent child's consent (or refusal to consent) clashes with the view of the parent, the child's view overrides the wishes of the parent.

Clearly, and as the guidance readily acknowledges, the above issues raise complex dilemmas. The guiding force should be a worker's own professional code, together with what they believe is in the best interests of the child. Nevertheless, it is possible that conflict between the worker and parents could arise if the worker has upheld the right of a child (particularly aged 12 or under) to consent against the wishes of the parent.

> **Information: The 'Gillick' principle for children giving consent**
>
> This principle relates to the ability of children to make decisions for themselves without the consent of their parents. It stems from a case in the 1980s where a mother – Victoria Gillick – challenged the idea that a doctor could prescribe contraception to her daughter under the age of 16 without the consent of the mother. The case was eventually settled in the House of Lords (the highest court in the land) and the decision was that a child under the age of 16 could make certain decisions for themselves if they have sufficient understanding and intelligence to understand fully what is proposed. Such children are also referred to as being 'Gillick competent'. The underlying principle was subsequently extended to a wide range of decisions, not just the administering of contraception, although competent children cannot refuse medical treatment.

Further issues related to sharing information

To complicate matters further, there are circumstances under which professionals have no choice but to share confidential information. They must do so if they are required to by law. This could include, as the guidance states, situations where a person has a disease about which environmental health must be notified, or where a court has ordered that certain information be made available to them. There is no issue here of gaining consent from the person about whom the information relates – simply, the information must be shared. However, the worker concerned should inform that person that they are sharing the information, the reasons for this, and with whom they are sharing it.

Once a decision is made to share information, whether by gaining consent, or by invoking public interest and overriding consent, or by order of the law, there remain further considerations for professionals. The information should be shared properly, by which it is meant that:

- proportionality should be observed (only information necessary should be shared)
- information should only be shared with the people who need to know
- before sharing it, information should be checked to make sure that it is accurate and up-to-date
- information should be shared securely
- it should be established with the recipient whether they intend to pass the information on to anyone else, and that they understand the limits of any consent which has been given
- the person about whom the information relates, and, if different, the person who provided the information, should be informed, where it is appropriate to do so.

Furthermore, the decision to share (or indeed not to share) information should be recorded, along with details of what information was shared and with whom.

Here we see the coming together of the three key pieces of legislation and guidance – the Data Protection Act 1998 principles of data processing, the Human Rights Act 1998 imperative to respect private and family life, and the underpinning features of the national guidance which emphasize good practice in gaining appropriate, informed consent. These strands are inseparable, and practitioners need to be cognizant of all them. As we have seen, they are complicated, and contain several uncertainties, dilemmas and occasions when the individual (even in consultation with colleagues) are called upon to make a judgement. In doing so, perhaps the best summary that can be provided is the following:

- where consent is gained from the parent or a competent child, the worker can share information
- where consent is not forthcoming, or it is inappropriate to seek it, the worker, if concerned about a child, should act in good faith with the best interests of the child at the heart of what they do, and share information if they believe that it is necessary to do so to either protect or promote the welfare of the child. Clear reasons for this decision should be recorded.

By way of illustrating the variety of contexts within which information might be shared, and some of the resulting issues, readers are invited to consider the scenarios, and the questions that follow them, in each of the reflective boxes.

(?) Reflections: Case Study – Sarah (primary school child)

Sarah is 8 years old and white British. She lives with her parents and younger sister aged 4 in local authority housing. Sarah attends the local primary school, and her sister attends the local children's centre. School have had no concerns about Sarah, although they have noticed that recently she appears tired in class. Today, Sarah tells her class teacher that last night her father came into her bedroom which she shares with her sister, and stroked her thighs under her nightdress, saying how beautiful she was, and that she was his special girl. He went on to say that she should not tell Mummy he had visited her in her room as it was to be their little secret. In saying this, Sarah is matter-of-fact and does not appear to be distressed.

1 In terms of information sharing, what do you think the correct course of action should be?
2 Do you think the school should seek consent from parents before contacting other agencies? Try and think of specific reasons for your answer.

(?) Reflections: Case study – Anisha (early years child)

A health visitor supporting an Asian Pakistani mother and her 3-year-old daughter, Anisha, has some concerns that the mother's depression is impacting both on her relationship with her daughter, and on Anisha's development. Anisha's father works long hours. The health visitor seeks and gains the

---

(?) Reflections—Cont'd

mother's verbal consent to contact the local day nursery to explain the circumstances and to arrange a place for Anisha there.

1 Do you think the health visitor can contact the nursery?
2 If so, can she share information regarding the mother's mental health with the nursery?
3 Do you think the health visitor would also need consent from Anisha's father before she contacted the nursery?

(?) Reflections: Case study – Connor (primary school child)

Connor is 6, of Irish descent, and attends the primary school near where he lives with his parents on a private housing estate. He has a sister aged 2. School staff have some concerns that Connor seems emotionally distant and disengaged. The quality of his schoolwork has begun to suffer. He is often late for school and in a dishevelled state, sometimes saying he has not had breakfast. The teacher speaks to his mother who plays down the concerns, saying that she is trying her best. The teacher discusses Connor with her designated teacher and they decide to speak informally with the school nurse, who confirms she has no concerns that would justify a referral to social services. However, they agree the concerns warrant a discussion with the health visitor, who is monitoring the progress of Connor's sister. The health visitor confirms there are some low-level concerns, and that the parents are working with her to try to improve matters. The health visitor decides not to reveal that the parents are receiving marriage guidance counselling. School agrees to monitor Connor's progress and report any future serious concerns.

1 In terms of sharing information, do you think the school acted appropriately here? Try to think of some reasons for your answer.
2 What issues should the school and school nurse have considered before contacting the health visitor?
3 Do you think the health visitor was correct in withholding the information regarding the parents' relationship? Try to think of some reasons for your answer.

(?) Reflections: Case study – Alison (high school child)

Alison is 14 years old and attends the high school near her home where she lives with her parents. She is an only child and is white British. Her parents struggle to control her and are receiving support from social services over this. Alison is verbally abusive to her parents and sometimes loses her temper, lashing out at them, and then leaving the house in the evening, returning late at night or the following day. Her parents are well-meaning but ineffective and are at a loss to know how to handle her. The social worker, with the consent of the parents, contacts the school to gather their perspective. School staff are surprised to hear the situation at home is so bad, and tell the social worker that Alison's attendance at school is around 60 per cent and that she is struggling to keep up with the work, which is a worry as she is in Year 9 and will be taking SATs soon. However, they fail to tell the social worker that Alison has told a teacher in confidence that when she is out she meets up with older youths and has experimented with drugs, and has been under pressure to have sex, which she has resisted so far.

1   Do you think the school has acted appropriately here? Try to think of some reasons for your answer.

Conclusions

Legislation and guidance on information sharing is complex. While workers need to be mindful of the law, in order to serve the interests of children, they also need to be able to cut through this labyrinth with clarity and keenness of purpose. If professionals are worried about a child, they should speak (appropriately) to that child, they should share information where necessary and they should be confident in defending these decisions if challenged, on the basis of serving what they perceived to be the best interests of the child. If this conviction is lacking, the danger is that professional paralysis or confusion, fuelled by fear of the consequences or uncertainty over the law, could lead to a lack of information sharing which ultimately could leave vulnerable children at serious risk of harm.

8 Working with parents

Introduction

As was mentioned in Chapter 1 of this book, the role of parents or those with day-to-day care of children has a vital bearing on multi-agency work to support or protect children. The Children Act 1989 emphasized the importance of the role of parents not only in circumstances where children might be 'in need' but also where they might require protection from harm. This chapter explores the government policy and guidance on effective engagement with parents along with some of the resultant issues. Although this guidance was produced in England, the generic nature of it makes it applicable to the whole United Kingdom. Throughout the chapter, the term 'parents' is taken to mean either single adults or couples who are either the biological parents of the child, or who may not be the biological parent, but who have daily care for children. This is to avoid the clumsy use of 'parents or carers'.

 Information: The relationship between agencies and parents

The quality of multi-agency relationships, and therefore ultimately the success or otherwise of the work, can depend upon such factors as

- the manner in which parents are engaged with by different agencies
- the extent to which parents are enabled to be involved by different agencies
- the way in which the different agencies involved view the importance of linking in parents with the work.

Working with parents where children are 'in need'

As was seen in Chapter 2, the Children Act 1989 cemented the concept of 'parental responsibility' such that children were effectively perceived to be the private property of parents, and parents could choose to parent them how they wished, so long as this did not amount to significant harm. The role of the state was to respond positively where parents did ask for help, but otherwise to leave well alone unless a crisis loomed. Although this stance has softened somewhat with the change to the Labour government in 1997, strong elements of this philosophy remain. For instance, as was seen in Chapter 4, the government refused to outlaw the smacking of children by retaining in the Children Act 2004 the right of parents to use 'reasonable chastisement'. One of the arguments put forward in defence of this position was that this 'common sense decision balances the essential need for children to be protected with the right of parents not to have the government interfering in family life' (BBC News, 2004).

 Information: Reasons for working in partnership with parents

The national guidance on partnership with parents (DH, 1995) sets out four reasons why involving parents is expected and encouraged:

- **It is effective:** by engaging parents, a cooperative relationship between services and families is fostered, thus securing better outcomes for the child.
- **It contributes to knowledge about the child:** parents are a source of information and can have unique knowledge and understanding of the child's circumstances.
- **It supports citizen's rights:** parents have the right to know what is being said about them, and to contribute to decisions that affect them.
- **It empowers parents:** where parents are involved, they experience this as beneficial.

This idea that parents have inalienable rights over their children permeates down into the published principles of partnerships issued in government guidance which was discussed in Chapter 2 (DH, 1995). Although this document focuses on child protection work, these principles are not only applicable to, but are expected to be put into practice for, work with parents who have children 'in need' of services. In a similar fashion, they are also equally valid for agencies working with parents as they are for agencies working with one another. Certainly, where agencies are carrying out entirely voluntary support work with parents, and where parents are in full control of which service, and the level of service they or their child can access, then the agencies should aim for full partnership with parents. It would be an inefficient, poorly trained or conniving practitioner who did not aim to work in such a manner where children 'in need' are concerned. The assumption of professionals should be that the parent wishes the best for their child, and the role of the professional is to help the parent achieve this. Nevertheless, it would also be naive, perhaps, to believe that such full partnership can always be achieved even when workers are involved in supporting parents of children 'in need'.

Principles of full partnership

Further discussion on each of the principles of full partnership will highlight some relevant issues here.

Shared values

The hope here is that parents and professionals alike share basic beliefs on such matters as the best interests of the child being paramount, or that child safety comes first. However, this may not always be the case. Parents may in fact value their own 'interests' above those of their child, especially if they are exhausted from lack of sleep or exertion in caring for a disabled or stressed child. Their motivation for seeking respite care, for example, may not therefore be primarily to offer the child new and interesting experiences, but to afford themselves the rare luxury of a full night's sleep. The child, indeed, may be resistant to the idea of going away for respite care. Of course the counter argument to this is that if the parents' needs are met, then this is feeding into the child's interests, since a refreshed and well-supported parent is more able to meet the child's enduring needs. The chief point, however, is that the underlying value, of putting what is best for the child first, may be difficult to detect or separate from the interests of the parents. Another manifestation of how this principle may be obscured is that a worker may be restrained by available resources, and may therefore put more value on what is actually available and possible to achieve rather than on purely what the child really needs, which could require more resources than those that are obtainable. The worker could be placed in a difficult position here: on the one hand being expected to adhere to the principle of always putting children first, and on the other hand having to work within limited resources while not being seen to publicly criticize their own employer.

A shared task or goal

This principle should certainly apply to work with parents of children 'in need' – even if resources are thin, or a parent's real motivation clashes with the wishes of their child, the two parties should share an ultimate task or goal of improving the quality of life for the child and the parents. If this is absent, it is likely that the work will be unsuccessful, since the people involved will be working at odds with one another.

All parties contributing resources and/or skills

This refers to respecting what parents can bring to the process, in terms of knowledge or skills. While this is a laudable aim, there is a danger that parents may be expecting the professionals, as the 'experts', to solve the problem by applying their knowledge, skills and resources. If this does not happen, and especially if workers instead encourage the parents to seek solutions within their own resources, this may lead to disillusionment and disappointment on the part of the parents, who may decide the agency has little to offer them, and may then withdraw from the partnership. It is also important that this value does not become one that parents come to see and experience as a 'get-out clause' for hard-pressed professionals working with limited resources, who may tell stressed, exhausted parents at their wits end that the solution lies within themselves, if only they could harness their own resources. This is likely to lead to a contribution of a profane nature by the parents!

Trust between the partners

Trust is not automatic and needs to be built up over time, and gained. It will flow from such things as workers being reliable, doing what they say are going to do, explaining quickly, honestly and clearly if intended aims have not been met, and being seen to put the parent's and child's needs first. From the perspective of the worker, trust will also result from parents being consistent in what they do and say. Once trust is diminished or broken, it could take a long time to recover it, and in the meantime, of course, the child may well not be having their needs met.

Negotiation of plans

It would be a bizarre form of partnership indeed if a worker, in supporting a parent of a child 'in need', went away and formulated a series of plans without consulting the parent (or the child) and then returned with a *fait accompli* of how the family is going to be supported. Certainly, the worker should consult and negotiate with the parents as to what would be appropriate, what pattern any anticipated packages of support might take and so on. If they do not, they cannot expect parents to respond positively to whatever plans they present to them. The parents, on the other hand, may suddenly change their mind about wanting a service or an aspect of it with no discussion or negotiation with the worker. While the worker who finds themselves in this situation should be professional enough to handle this, it may affect their willingness to respond rapidly or enthusiastically should the same parent come back later saying they have changed their mind again and now wish to pursue some support.

Decisions made together

This is closely allied to joint negotiation of plans, but includes such things as workers ensuring that parents are invited to, and supported and encouraged to take part in, planning and review meetings, and that these meetings do not contain any surprises or shocks. Similar issues arise, too, in that if workers or parents make unilateral decisions this will undoubtedly affect the quality of the partnership between them.

Mutual confidence that each partner can and will 'deliver'

Certainly parents need to feel confident that workers will champion their cause, work on their behalf and do their utmost to help them and their child. However, equally important here is the point mentioned earlier, under 'shared values' that should the worker be unable to deliver a resource or an outcome, they should explain openly the reasons for this. Should a worker promise to deliver a particular service, and then be unable to do so, this too is very likely to undermine trust and full partnership working. Similarly, should parents repeatedly fail to 'deliver' in the sense, perhaps, of not attending meetings or not advancing plans of support, then the worker surely has to question their commitment to the work and to the partnership.

Equality or near equality between parties

This is perhaps the most complex of the partnership values to unpack. It is surely very difficult to achieve equality or even near equality between parents and workers even where the latter is supporting a parent of a child 'in need'. Even if ostensibly there is equality – for instance, where the parent, like the worker is well educated, articulate and confident – it is likely that the worker will have certain inherent structural advantages. This could include the fact that there is an intrinsic power imbalance in the relationship. The worker not only usually has a superior understanding of the available services, but ultimately has the power to broker or facilitate access to these various services. This places the parent in the position of being reliant on the worker to work effectively on their behalf. Certainly, a well-educated and articulate parent may be able to self advocate to a manager if they feel they are receiving a raw deal, but the inherent power imbalance is likely to remain – the service has the resource, or access to it, and the parent has to work with the professional in order to access it. What is crucial here is that parents do not receive a deceptive message, that they are equal partners in the process, and that they are as powerful as the worker, when in fact, if power is inseparable from resources or knowledge, they are not. This power imbalance is likely to be exaggerated further where the level of education or confidence or general social functioning is higher in the worker than it is in the parent. Here, workers have a particular responsibility to behave ethically and not take advantage of a parent who may be less able to argue their corner, or complain if they do not receive what they believe they are entitled to.

Choice in entering the partnership

Where children 'in need' are concerned, there should surely be choice on behalf of the parents in entering the partnership. This needs to be a fully informed choice, so parents can make proper decisions about whether they really do wish to pursue particular options, and if so, about how and when these plans might be implemented.

A formalized framework of agreed working arrangements

This refers to the fact that any work should be governed by formal agreements outlining the process under which all parties will operate. Where possible, this should be written down and a copy given to parents. This is to bring clarity to the work and also to facilitate parents to be able to question something that has not happened but should have happened, or indeed something that has happened, which should not have happened. One difficulty here, in a direct link back to the issue of the power imbalance, is that should parents be minded to 'complain' they may perceive that they are at risk of losing a service or a resource. Even if this is not actually true, the fact they have thought it a possibility undermines claims that there is a true and full partnership between workers and parents.

Open sharing of information

Professionals should share appropriate information with parents honestly and openly. For example, if they are aware that a particular resource is scarce, or has a long waiting list, they should tell the parents this, and give them further information about this, or about any available alternatives. Of course, open sharing does not mean that confidentiality is not maintained – respecting privacy is crucial if trust is to be maintained, and as was discussed in Chapter 7, there are legal imperatives for maintaining due respect for confidentiality.

Mechanisms for monitoring, reviewing and ending of the partnership

This is allied to the existence of formal working arrangements, and is designed to ensure that support work with parents is properly reviewed and does not merely drift along. Where support packages are appraised, and where this fully involves the parents, this is surely likely to result in the parents feeling valued and well supported. Where a piece of work comes to a conclusion, it is also important that this is properly recognized and marked so it is clear to all parties involved.

Dealing with power issues

If it is accepted that there is a natural imbalance between professionals and parents, then acknowledging this, and dealing with it is the next step. Particularly where there is a dispute between a worker or service and a parent, especially perhaps involving the lack of provision of a service, then the worker should not only explain clearly the reasons for the decision, but perhaps encourage the parents to seek legal or similar advice or support to challenge the decision. This is a complex ethical issue. The worker may well be persuading parents to seek support to contest a decision made by their employer who may not be best pleased that they are placed in the uncomfortable position of having to explain to, say a solicitor, why the family cannot have a particular resource. The worker here may be trying to satisfy two conflicting loyalties – first to implement good practice with parents and second to protect their employer, who after all pays their wages. Where workers acknowledge and discuss with parents more general power issues, care should be taken that this does not become tokenistic or merely lip-service. For instance, should they on the one hand encourage parental contributions and involvement but on the other hand forge ahead with their own plans without full consultation with them, this is likely to be spotted by parents who may react unfavourably.

National guidance on working with parents in child protection

The full title of the national guidance on working with parents in child protection gives a clue as to the level of difficulty involved in this activity. It is called *The Challenge of Partnership in Child Protection: Practice Guide* (DH, 1995). The major challenge is that it may at first glance seem like a contradiction in terms to argue that it is possible to work in partnership with parents when there is statutory intervention by agencies to protect a child. Those agencies have potentially significant powers, including immediate removal of a child (in the case of the police) or the seeking of a court order to remove a child from the care of the parents (in the case of social care services). Furthermore, talk of a partnership may seem rather hollow when parents do not really have a choice regarding the intervention of agencies to protect their child. Nevertheless, the guidance argues that the underpinning reasons for engaging parents in any work as discussed above are equally valid when considering child protection work.

Partnership themes

To begin exploring this, it is worth revisiting the partnership list to see which elements might apply to child protection work, and if so, how they might be applicable. They have been grouped into themes to avoid repetition of similar issues.

Shared values and a shared task or goal
While one would hope that all parents share the same values and goals of professionals in terms of putting the needs and interests of the child above all else and aiming to achieve this,

this is palpably not the case if one accepts that professionals work to exhaust the possibility of a child remaining with their parents before considering other alternatives. Some parents appear unable to put their children's needs before their own; others, in spite of being provided with support, may not possess adequate parenting skills to make a viable option of them being the long-term carers for the child. Nevertheless, it is incumbent upon professionals to be clear with parents what their driving and underpinning values and aims are at all times, and that the safety and welfare of the child is the first and utmost priority. If this occurs, parents cannot, at least with justification, argue that they did not understand the consequences of any actions, inactions or shortcomings on their part.

All parties contributing resources and/or skills

It may be difficult for parents to feel able to contribute resources or skills to the child protection process if they receive the message, as a result of child protection work, that they have effectively 'failed' as parents. If their confidence or self-esteem if low, or if they are feeling defensive, it may then appear disingenuous for professionals to seek out their help and support in protecting their child. This, therefore, requires careful thought and sensitive handling if the resources that parents can offer are to be effectively harnessed and utilized as part of a plan of protection and support.

Trust between the partners and mutual confidence that each partner can and will 'deliver'

With regard to child protection, trust is likely to involve the professionals giving clear, consistent information and advice, maintaining a consistent position on the direction of the case, and delivering on promises relating to support or resources available. Trust does not of course mean that the professionals and parents always have to agree on matters concerning the child. On the parents' side, if the final direction of the work is to move towards the parents maintaining long-term care of the child, then trust between the professionals and parents is vital: it would be a foolhardy decision to allow a child deemed to be at risk of significant harm to remain with their parents if the professionals were mistrusting of the parents' ability to provide adequate care.

Negotiation of plans, decisions made together and open sharing of information

Even in child protection work, there would be little excuse for professionals not encouraging parental involvement or participation in meetings or other planning forums regarding their child. Ideally, no decision should be made 'behind the parents backs' and there should be no surprises sprung upon parents in meetings or elsewhere. Occasionally, it is necessary for social workers, for example, to seek an Emergency Protection Order to protect a child urgently without consulting with or informing the parents, perhaps because the parents cannot be contacted or because if they were alerted, there is a strong possibility they might flee with the child, increasing the risk to that child. However, these are exceptional circumstances and certainly the general principle is that parents should be fully aware of what plans professionals have in place. Similarly, there should be appropriate open sharing of information between professionals and parents while still maintaining the confidentiality of the parents, or, exceptionally, of a third party such as a member of the public who may have made an initial referral regarding risk to a child.

Equality or near equality between parties and choice in entering the partnership

These are perhaps the most difficult principles of partnership to either achieve or demonstrate in child protection work. Where agencies are statutorily involved with a family where a child is in need of protection, the notions of equality between the professionals and parents, or of parents having a choice in the work taking place appear tenuous. Certainly, parents can in theory choose not to engage with the work, and effectively hand over the care of their child to the state. However, even this idea is fraught with complexities. What is choice? Who decides what level of choice is acceptable? Where parents lack confidence or advocacy or relevant skills, can they really be said to be exercising a choice? In terms of equality, professionals hold a good deal of power, supported by the laws and institutions that guide and frame their work. For instance, although it is correct to state that a social worker does not have the power to remove a child, and that they have to attend court to convince the magistrates or judge that the child is at risk of significant harm before they can do so, it is also correct to acknowledge that what the social worker tells the court is hugely influential upon the decision made by the court. It would be quite wrong, therefore, for a social worker to state they are equal to the parents before the court, and to argue that the social worker's input is somehow insignificant. The social worker is attending court not as an individual, but as a representative of a local authority, with a powerful and generally respected legacy behind it. In contrast, parents may have the services of a solicitor (as will the social worker of course) but essentially they are on their own. One of the key ways, however, in which professionals can attempt to meet these principles in part, is to be explicit with parents about what they intend to do, and why, and to spell out not only the possible consequences of various 'choices' parents may make, but also to urge parents to seek legal representation or other independent advice or support. If a social worker failed to do this, on the basis that they want to make sure they 'win' the case with as little challenge as possible from parents, they would rightly be open to criticism that they were acting against the principles of good partnership with parents.

A formalized framework of agreed working arrangements and mechanisms for monitoring, reviewing and ending of the partnership

In child protection work, there already exist formal mechanisms such as Initial Child Protection Conferences, Child Protection Review Conferences, or even very formal court hearings, all of which contribute (or should do) to a framework providing clarity of decision making. It is particularly important, where child protection work with a family comes to a conclusion, that such clarity is apparent to parents – they have the right to understand precisely why the decision was taken not to proceed with further child protection activity, or indeed, at the other end of the spectrum, why a court order to protect the child was sought and obtained.

Dealing with power issues

Where agencies are responding to concerns about abuse, there is no doubt that the bulk of the institutional power lies with them as opposed to the parents. There is a whole system in place designed to allow the agencies to make whatever enquiries are necessary to determine what needs to be done to safeguard the child. This includes, where necessary, visits with the police in order to gain access to homes. Nevertheless, workers can strive to work in partnership with parents by acknowledging this power differential, and by providing very clear information regarding their responsibilities, and the rights parents have (for instance to seek the support of a solicitor to challenge decisions). Furthermore, where parents are being uncooperative with agencies in the latter's attempts to protect a child, the potential consequences of this should be pointed out to the parents by the workers involved. In these ways, although there is inherent power with the professionals, backed up by law, parents can be offered means of challenging or responding to this power which enhance their rights and status in the process.

Principles of working in partnership

Some of these issues are referred to in an additional list from the guidance of 15 essential principles of working in partnership with parents. It is worth looking at them in full. In the guidance they are written as though they are directly addressed to workers, and they are reproduced here verbatim:

- Treat all family members as you would wish to be treated, with dignity and respect.
- Ensure that family members know that the child's safety and welfare must be given first priority, but that each of them has a right to a courteous, caring and professionally competent service.
- Take care not to infringe privacy any more than is necessary to safeguard the welfare of the child.
- Be clear with yourself and with family members about your power to intervene, and the purpose of your professional involvement at each stage.
- Be aware of the effects on family members of the power you have as a professional, and the impact and implications of what you say and do.
- Respect confidentiality of family members and your observations about them, unless they give permission for information to be passed to others or it is essential to do to protect the child.
- Listen to the concerns of the children and their families, and take care to learn about their understanding, fears and wishes before arriving at your own explanations and plans.
- Learn about and consider children within their family relationships and communities, including their cultural and religious contexts, and their place within their own families.

- Consider the strengths and potential of family members, as well as their weaknesses, problems and limitations.
- Ensure that children, families and other carers know their responsibilities and rights, including the right to services, and their right to refuse services and any consequences of doing so.
- Use plain, jargon-free language appropriate to the age and culture of each person. Explain unavoidable technical and professional terms.
- Be open and honest about your concerns and responsibilities, plans and limitations, without being defensive.
- Allow children and families time to take in and understand concerns and processes. A balance needs to be found between appropriate speed and the needs of people who may need extra time in which to communicate.
- Take care to distinguish between personal feelings, values, prejudices and beliefs, and professional roles and responsibilities, and ensure that you have good supervision to check that you are doing so.
- If a mistake or misinterpretation has been made, or you are unable to keep to an agreement, provide an explanation. Always acknowledge the distress experienced by adults and children and do all you can to keep it to a minimum.

These 15 principles are laudable, and offer professionals a clear blueprint for how to conduct themselves. Some of them are obvious and should be relatively easy to implement, such as maintaining respect and confidentiality – this is tantamount to saying to workers they should not 'gossip' about families inappropriately in staffrooms or corridors. The issues regarding power are complex and have already been discussed to some extent. The expectation that staff should be constantly self aware, of themselves as role models to parents and children, and of the potential impact of their own beliefs and attitudes upon their decisions, is an interesting and highly complex one. This will require effective training and high-quality supervision from managers, which for various reasons may not always be available. In the heat of the moment, at a time of crisis responding to a serious allegation of abuse, it would take a very experienced, self-assured worker to automatically set aside all preconceptions and constantly monitor their own words and deeds while dealing with the mechanics and emotions of a child protection enquiry. The requirement here for workers to ensure they receive good quality supervision raises interesting questions about what happens if this is not happening. First of all, whose view of 'good quality' should be considered as having precedent – the worker's or the manager's? To whom does the worker complain – the same manager who is supposed to be providing the supervision? Will workers feel empowered to do this? Will they be supported by more senior managers? What might be the impact on relationships within the workplace if such a complaint is made?

Following on from the introduction of these underpinning principles of working in partnership with parents, the guidance goes on to detail how child protection processes might be handled effectively. This includes referrals to social services, the enquiry stage and Initial Assessment, the Initial Child Protection Conference, the Core Assessment, Child Protection Review Conferences, and ending the intervention. Interestingly, scant mention is made of working with parents where professionals approach the court for an order to protect the child, and this only includes immediate protection such as an Emergency Protection Order, rather than a longer term process such as applying for a full Care Order after a child has been removed from the care of parents on, say, an Interim Care Order. With the latter, the issues and complexities associated with working in partnership with parents are amplified. From the parents' point of view, the authorities already 'have' their child, and they may feel powerless as a result. There could be two opposing responses here – either they negotiate whatever course the professionals suggest in an attempt to regain the care of their children, or they resign themselves to having 'lost'. If this latter response is adopted, parents may well then either give up trying to prove their competence as parents, or expend their efforts and energy arguing against the authorities in an attempt to prove that an injustice has been committed. Either way, the power clearly rests with the professionals (including the courts) as they have full control over the destiny of the child.

The key concept and standpoint being promoted within legislation and guidance is that parents have a right to be involved in decisions which affect their children, and this clearly has to be right – they should not be excluded from such decision-making processes unless absolutely necessary. The national guidance *Working Together* (DfES, 2006i) contains a section on involving children and family members in the Initial Child Protection Conference which illustrates this neatly. The default position is that parents should not only be invited to attend the conference, but should be properly prepared for it, with the provision of information about the proceedings, the agenda and so on. Children, by the way, should also be invited (where appropriate) and where they do not wish to attend, or it is inappropriate for them to do so, their ascertainable wishes should be sought and put to the conference. Parents should only be excluded if they present a 'strong risk of violence or intimidation' (ibid., p. 125) or if they may be prosecuted for an offence and their presence at the conference is deemed to be inappropriate. Even where parents are excluded, alternative means of allowing them to express their views should be put in place, for instance, by encouraging them to write a statement which is read out by the chairperson of the conference. Of course, it is necessary that professionals can share information openly without fear of violence or intimidation, and parental exclusion from meetings is therefore sometimes unavoidable. Nevertheless, it does raise an interesting philosophical issue. Where parents feel powerless, experiencing all the impetus and control as lying with the professionals, and where they may be alienated by a child protection process which to them is culturally unfamiliar, dominant, accusatory and adversarial, their only recourse, with limited personal resources, may be to rail against this process using threats of, or actual, violence, in an attempt to wrestle back some element of power. The irony, and the tragedy, is that this response is only likely to further alienate them as the professionals are likely to respond by excluding them from meetings, thus further adding to the parents' sense of powerlessness, and possibly setting up a vicious cycle of aggression.

As this example shows, working with parents, particularly in child protection is difficult for all professionals. Aside from dealing with threats of violence, the day-to-day work of supporting parents, explaining processes and decisions, and working through difficult issues, including past life experiences of parents, raises serious issues for the workers concerned. There is every chance that professionals will have an emotional response to the parents with whom they are working. This could include overidentifying with them such that the focus of the work becomes the parents' needs rather than the child. Workers can come to 'feel sorry' for particular parents who may have had traumatic life experiences, and workers may therefore attempt to treat them leniently. The key point here is that parents, and professionals, are real people who operate at an emotional level as well as a rational, reflective and reasoned one. This emphasizes the need for professionals to receive high-quality supervision to help them process these issues and to ensure the focus correctly remains the welfare of the child rather than the needs of the adults concerned.

Multi-agency approaches to working with parents

Much of the discussion so far has focused on the responsibilities of a single agency working with parents. However, the situation becomes significantly more complicated when one considers that several agencies may well be involved with one family, and that each may have a different approach or attitude towards the parents concerned. It is useful here to revisit the framework as set out by Morrison (1991) in Chapter 2: that different agencies have varying orientations towards engaging in multi-agency work depending on their perceptions and attitudes. If we consider the four possible positions in terms of working with parents, the complexities of having more than one agency involved with a single family begin to clearly emerge.

A paternalistic approach would see an agency perceiving themselves as 'experts' choosing to share their expertise with parents, for which the latter should be grateful. The agency is likely to find it hard to see parents as having equal rights or status as themselves, and may not see the need to work in partnership with parents.

If an agency had a strategic adversarial approach, collaboration with parents may be approached with wariness as they may see it involving more losses than gains. They may believe that parents will exploit the partnership for their own ends, and thus invest unwieldy amounts of time and energy negotiating the terms of the partnership.

An agency that adopts a play fair approach will attempt to ensure that parents receive an effective service. They are likely to try to ensure that parents are clear about the roles and responsibilities of all concerned, and will respect what parents can bring to the process and planning. Parents will be involved in the work as much as possible.

An agency with a developmental approach is likely to see partnership with parents as not only necessary in itself, but as part of the whole process of change for families – they may argue that change is not possible unless true partnership is inherent in the process. Work with parents is likely to be seen as organic and changing, and the agency may be willing to take risks with parents which other agencies may find unacceptable.

Here, we begin to see the potential impact on multi-agency relationships of different agencies holding, and then acting upon, differing attitudes towards collaboration with parents. Where, within a range of agencies, all four of these approaches is present, the possibility for inter-agency conflict, misunderstanding or confusion is high. Furthermore, parents themselves may become confused, receiving conflicting messages from different agencies regarding what they can or should bring to the process. This could seriously undermine attempts by a particular agency to engage parents constructively.

(?) Reflections: Case study – Christa

Social services receive a referral from Christa's school regarding an injury to the side of her head. Christa is 5 years old, white British, and lives with her mother and stepfather. Social work enquiries reveal that both parents admit struggling with Christa's care – they are both unemployed, and have been caring for their own mothers who live nearby and who need support due to mild dementia. The stepfather admits losing his temper and hitting Christa. Both parents say they would welcome some help. An Initial Child Protection Conference is set up. The social worker strives to involve the parents in this process, explaining the purpose and format of the conference. The Health Visitor also wants to work constructively with the parents, but is wary of them as they have been verbally abusive towards her in the past, frightening her, and she is struggling to see why she should go out of her way to support them now when they rejected her offers of help so vehemently in the past. The school argue that they have tried to talk to the parents about how to improve their parenting to no avail, that the school doesn't have time to attend the meeting, and that it is clear that what Christa needs is to be taken into care. They feel the parents will never listen to their advice so there is little point in them being involved in the process, and they argue strongly that in any case they have no duty to work with the stepfather as he does not have parental responsibility in the eyes of the law.

1 Which elements of the 'partnership list' do you think are present or might apply to the work with parents here?
2 Which of the four different approaches described by Morrison do you think are being adopted by each of the agencies involved?

Conclusions

It is important that professionals understand what partnership means in the two different contexts of a child 'in need' and a child 'in need of protection'. For the former, professionals have a requirement to work in partnership with parents who are engaged in voluntary support work for the benefit of their child. The final decision regarding what should happen for the child rests with the parents. Where children need protecting, however, there is an expectation that workers adhere to the principles of partnership working with parents. This means that although efforts should be made to engage parents in the process, professionals have the right to override the wishes of parents if they believe this to be in the best interests of the child. Furthermore, the various positions which agencies may hold in relation to how they perceive and understand their work with parents is a crucial factor in how that work is carried out. To try to acknowledge and work through these differences may well be a complex and time-consuming business, but unless some level of working agreement is reached, the impact upon families of multiple approaches to partnership with parents is likely to be both positive and negative.

Part Three
LOOKING TO THE FUTURE

The *Every Child Matters* agenda 9

Introduction

In line with the book as a whole, this chapter will focus on the *Every Child Matters* programme in England. In the other countries of the United Kingdom, similar initiatives have been introduced as follows:

Wales: The Welsh Assembly Government (2004) publication *Children and Young People: Rights to Action*.

Scotland: The Scottish Executive (2005a) document *Getting It Right for Every Child: Proposals for Action*.

Northern Ireland: The OFMDFM (2006) publication *Our Children and Young People – Our Pledge*.

Important distinctions between them will be discussed within the chapter as appropriate.

This chapter will outline the origins of the *Every Child Matters* programme before going on to describe the key elements of the vision. The implications for education and multi-agency working will then be discussed. Finally, some key questions and issues related to the vision will be explored, including tensions in social policy towards young people, potential difficulties in achieving integrated multi-agency working and the persistence of structural barriers to the success of the *Every Child Matters* strategy.

The origins of *Every Child Matters*

On 24 February 2000, a taxi containing a woman called Marie-Therese Kouao and an 8-year-old girl left from a London church, having been instructed by the woman to take the girl to hospital. However, the taxi driver was so concerned about the girl's condition that he took them instead to a nearby ambulance station. From there the girl was taken by ambulance to a local hospital where she was treated for hypothermia. In the early hours of the next morning, she was transferred to a different hospital which it was felt could offer her more specialist care. She remained in a critical condition with severe hypothermia and multi-system failure. At 3.15 p.m. on 25 February 2000, having suffered a cardiac arrest, she was declared dead. The post-mortem found the cause of death to be hypothermia, which had arisen in the context of malnourishment, a damp environment and restricted movement. It also found 128 separate injuries on her body showing she had been beaten with a range of sharp and blunt instruments. Her name was Victoria Climbié. On 12 January 2001, Marie-Therese Kouao, Victoria's great aunt, and Carl Manning were convicted of her murder. At the trial, it conspired that in the final weeks of her life Victoria had been kept tied up in a bath, eating like a dog from a plate. She was tied inside a black bag with her own excrement. She was regularly beaten. It also turned out that various agencies had been involved with the family, and as a result the government ordered an inquiry, led by Lord Laming.

It is necessary for readers to experience the sense of revulsion and horror at the details of Victoria's unimaginable suffering in order to recognize the public outcry that followed her death. Using this momentum, the government appeared determined to do its utmost to try to end once and for all such cases of abuse. While acknowledging that no absolute guarantees can be given, the then Prime Minister Tony Blair stated in the foreword to *Every Child Matters* (DfES, 2003) that 'we all desperately want to see people, practices and policies in place to make sure that the risk is as small as is humanly possible' (p. 2). While every civilized government would want to achieve this aim, there is a sense that the government harnessed the media and public response to Victoria's death in order to push through far-reaching reforms not only relating to the protection of children, but to the whole system governing the way agencies work together to support families. A key point to note here is that one of Lord Laming's key conclusions (Laming, 2003) was that the legislative framework for protecting children was sound and that it was the implementation of it that was found wanting in the case of Victoria Climbié. Nevertheless, the government changed the law, choosing instead to focus on another of Laming's comments, that the protection of children cannot be separated from wider support to families. This chapter will not dwell on the full details of Laming's report and findings concerning the actions (or inactions) of the various agencies involved; rather it will focus on the implications of the government's response to the report for multi-agency working.

What followed, then, from Lord Laming's report in January 2003 was the government publication of a consultative green paper titled *Every Child Matters*, in September 2003. Following the consultation, the government then published *Every Child Matters: The Next Steps* (DfES, 2004c), and passed the Children Act 2004, providing the legislative underpinning for the changes to occur. *Every Child Matters: Change for Children* (DfES, 2004a) was then published in November 2004 as the final document outlining the programme in detail, and a dedicated website was launched soon afterwards (www.everychildmatters.gov.uk). While this may seem like impressive haste by the government to put in place systems and processes to benefit children, it must be remembered that Lord Laming made 108 recommendations, 46 of which he stated should be implemented with 3 months, and a further 36 within 6 months. This did not happen. For instance, Laming made specific recommendations that a Children and Families Board, chaired by a minister, and a National Agency for Children and Families, reporting to the Children and Families Board to ensure two-way accountability from local to government level, be established. These did not appear in the *Every Child Matters* programme. This is perhaps further testimony to the selective nature of the government's response to Laming's report as they sought to pursue their own implementation agenda.

What is *Every Child Matters*?

Essentially, *Every Child Matters* has three aspects to it:

- It is a programme of whole system change to improve outcomes for all children.
- It takes forward the Government's vision of radical reform for children and families.
- The new Children Act 2004 provides the legal framework for the programme of reform.

The five outcomes – what are they?

At the heart of the *Every Child Matters* programme are the five outcomes, which has become a kind of shorthand for what the government believes should be the five desirable outcomes for all children, and towards which all work from agencies involved with children and families should be directed. These outcomes were devised in consultation with children, although the green paper *Every Child Matters* (DfES, 2003) does not give details of which, or how many, children were consulted. For each outcome a specified role for parents is considered essential if the outcome is to be achieved. The five outcomes, which as Stepney (2005) points out 'resonate with the aspirations any reasonable parent or caring society would want for their children' (p. 5) are that all children should:

- Be healthy. This means:
  - physically healthy
  - mentally and emotional healthy
  - sexually healthy
  - leading healthy lifestyles
  - choosing not to take illegal drugs.

The role of the parents here is to promote healthy choices.

- Stay safe. This means:
  - safe from maltreatment, neglect, violence and sexual exploitation
  - safe from accidental injury and death
  - safe from bullying and discrimination
  - safe from crime and anti-social behaviour in and out of school
  - having security, stability and being cared for.

The role of the parents here is to provide safe homes and stability.

- Enjoy and achieve. This means:
  - being ready for school
  - attending and enjoying school
  - achieving stretching national educational standards at primary school
  - achieving personal and social development and enjoying recreation
  - achieving stretching national educational standards at secondary school.

The role of the parents here is to support learning.

- Make a positive contribution. This means:
  - engaging in decision making and supporting the community and the environment
  - engaging in law-abiding and positive behaviour in and out of school
  - developing positive relationships and choosing not to bully and discriminate
  - developing self-confidence and successfully dealing with significant life changes and challenges
  - developing enterprising behaviour.

The role of the parents here is to promote positive behaviour.

- Achieve economic well-being. This means:
  - engaging in further education, employment or training on leaving school
  - being ready for employment
  - living in decent homes and sustainable communities
  - having access to transport and material goods
  - living in households free from low income.

Here, parents are to be supported to become economically active.

It is interesting to compare these with the outcomes contained within the documents from the other three countries in the United Kingdom mentioned in the introduction to this chapter.

Wales has seven 'core aims' for all children, which are summarized here, that they should:

- have a flying start in life and best possible basis for their future growth and development
- have access to a comprehensive range of education
- enjoy the best possible health, including freedom from abuse, victimization and exploitation
- have access to play, leisure, sporting and cultural activities
- be listened to, treated with respect, and have their race and cultural identity recognized

- have a safe home and a community which supports physical and emotional well-being
- not be disadvantaged by child poverty.

Scotland's proposals identify four broad desirable outcomes for children as being:

- confident individuals
- effective contributors
- successful learners
- responsible citizens

For these to be achieved, children will need to be:

- o safe
- o nurtured
- o healthy
- o achieving
- o active
- o respected and responsible
- o included.

Northern Ireland's outcomes framework is based on six aims for children, that they should be:

- healthy
- enjoying, learning and achieving
- living in safety and with stability
- experiencing economic and environmental well-being
- contributing positively to community and society
- living in a society which respects their rights.

The differences between the four nations raise interesting questions, such as whether these differences suggest that children in the four nations have varying needs, or whether the differences expose how children's needs are perceived and configured differently by adults across the four nations.

The five outcomes – how might they be achieved?

Every Child Matters proposes that the five outcomes will be fulfilled if the following plans, described across four areas, are acted upon:

Area 1: Supporting parents and carers

- Universal services such as schools, health and social services providing information and advice and engaging parents to support their child's development.
- Targeted and specialist support where needed.
- The use of compulsory Parenting Orders as a last resort where necessary.
- Extended schools or Children's Centres offering on-site childcare from 8.00 a.m. to 6.00 p.m.

Area 2: Early intervention and effective protection
- Improving information sharing, including the possibility of a national database of all children.
- Developing a Common Assessment Framework.
- Developing multi-professional teams based in and around schools and children's centres.
- Establishing a lead professional where children are known to more than one agency.

Area 3: Local, regional and national integration
- The development of Children's Trusts to integrate key services.
- The creation of a Director of Children's Services to lead local action.
- Requiring agencies to work closely with one another to improve outcomes for children and young people.
- The development of Local Safeguarding Children's Boards to replace the current Area Child Protection Committees.
- The establishment of a Children's Commissioner to act as an independent champion for children and report to Parliament.

Area 4: Workforce reform
- Implementing a strategy to improve the skills and effectiveness of the workforce.
- Improved training, and the development of common occupational standards for children's practice.

 Information: What are children's trusts and directors of children's services?

The document *Every Child Matters: The Next Steps* (DfES, 2004c) states that Children's Trusts will be formed through the pooling of budgets and resources across the local education authority, children's social services, Connexions (a careers-type service for young people), certain health services, and where agreed locally, youth offending teams. A Children's Trust will not necessitate structural change or staff transfers. Children's Trusts will be based in local government but engage a wide range of partners, including voluntary and community sector organizations. The primary purpose of a Children's Trust is to secure integrated commissioning of services leading to more integrated service delivery and therefore better outcomes for children and young people. Directors of Children's Services will head up the Children's Trust, providing strategic oversight of the work and leading the transformational change across local services.

The proposed timeline for *Every Child Matters*

Timelines were specified for nine key statutory obligations placed upon local authorities and services (DfES, 2004c). Thus, the duty for services to cooperate with each other was introduced in April 2005, the integrated inspection framework in May 2005, and the duty to promote the education of children in care in June 2005. The duty to safeguard children came into effect in October 2005, and following on from this, the Local Safeguarding Children

Boards (LSCB) had to be in place by April 2006. In the same month, all local authorities were expected to have a single Children and Young People's Plan. By 2008 (the month is not specified) all local authorities must have in place Children's Trusts, a Director of Children's Services, and a Lead Member (an elected member of the local council) for Children's Services.

The staged introduction of this vast programme is not only practical, given the significant changes and developments expected of local authorities, but also serves to emphasize the amorphous and all-encompassing nature of it. The fact that its full implementation is not intended to be complete until at least 4 years after its introduction serves to keep the *Every Child Matters* agenda at the forefront of the thinking and planning of local authorities.

Implications for education

One of the keystones of the *Every Child Matters* programme is that support for children and parents is centred around the place where children are to be found for significant periods of the day, and where parents (especially during the child's primary years) might visit regularly: the school or early years centre. This requirement led to the creation of extended services based in and around schools which have huge implications for education. Put simply, this means that the buildings or grounds of primary or secondary schools will be the base for:

- a core range of support and advice services
- breakfast and after-school clubs
- guaranteed childcare from 8.00 a.m. to 6.00 p.m.

Furthermore, schools will be encouraged to be involved in planning and delivering support services for children and families, in partnership with other agencies.

For the early years, the aim is that:

- parents will be able to choose from a range of accessible, affordable, high-quality options for day care
- payment for this will be according to means
- more early years childcare will be located within school grounds
- these new developments will happen in partnership with the voluntary and private sectors.

 Information: Extended schools: The core range of services on offer

All extended schools will be expected to offer:

- a varied range of activities including study support, sport and music clubs, combined with childcare in primary schools
- parenting and family support
- swift and easy access to targeted and specialist services

Information—Cont'd

- community access to facilities including adult and family learning, Information and Communications Technology (ICT) and sports grounds.

The targets are that by 2008, 50 per cent of primary and 33 per cent of secondary schools, including special schools, will be extended schools, and by 2010, all schools will be extended schools.

For schools and early years centres, therefore, the implications are significant. Even where teachers or early years staff are not expected to offer extended services directly, they will not only need to be aware of what is on offer within their premises, but will be expected to work closely with the various services operating therein. The educator of the future, to caricature them for a moment, will no longer only stand in a classroom and teach, or supervise and facilitate children's play, but will also liaise with a range of other workers offering adult learning or services to children. They will be expected to support parents to solve a wide range of problems and issues, acting as a support mechanism and signpost, encouraging parents to link up with appropriate services, of which the educator will need to have at least a working knowledge.

Implications for multi-agency working

For all staff, in whatever profession, there are clear implications of the *Every Child Matters* programme. The development of more multidisciplinary teams, led by one professional, will undoubtedly mean that workers will be shoehorned together into teams consisting of professionals from a range of disciplines. The full implementation of the Common Assessment Framework (see Chapter 3) will serve to emphasize that professionals are perceived to be interchangeable in that a trained worker from any discipline will be expected to conduct an assessment.

At senior management level, the introduction of Children's Trusts, of a Director of Children's Services, of the development of a single Children and Young People's Plan, and of the pooling of budgets and resources will present a huge challenge to those individual services that previously had very clear identities, cultures, histories, priorities and ways of working. These tensions may well be exacerbated by the development of the integrated common inspection framework which will judge a local area on its performance overall. In effect this will mean that one service which in previous inspections might have been well regarded, will no longer be able to 'blame' another service which might have received less favourable reviews, for failing to adequately support children. The new system will mean that all services, good and poor, will be judged together. The question will no longer be 'How good is education, or the social care service, or health, in supporting the children in, say, Bigtown?', but 'How good is Bigtown in supporting children?' The duty on all agencies to cooperate with one another will further cement the notion that services are all in the work together, in the same boat, and should therefore row in the same direction.

Questions and issues regarding *Every Child Matters*

Tensions within and between the five outcomes

Be healthy

The outcome 'Be healthy' seems to assume that there is a standard, agreed notion among adults of what constitutes good physical and emotional health. However, one might argue that the notion of health is complex and varied, according to the culture and imperatives of different groups of people within society. For instance, the lifestyle of Travellers may appear to some to be unhealthy, living as they might see it in apparently cramped conditions with basic sanitation, and lacking stability and roots. However, to the Travellers themselves, and to others with a different perspective, the lifestyle may well be liberating, supportive due to the close-knit community, and ultimately 'healthier' than any viable alternatives. Furthermore, do adults always know what is best for children's health, and whose advice should be listened to in relation to children's health? Which particular 'expert' should be held up as knowing best? The fact that there is no single definition of good physical, emotional or sexual health means that this outcome becomes complex in its interpretation.

Stay safe

The outcome 'Stay safe' contains some elements that are, or at least should be, universals in a civilized society. Of course, children should be safe from maltreatment, neglect, violence and sexual exploitation. The question is how this can be achieved, especially in the context of children having fewer rights to protection in law than adults. A key issue here is that while on the one hand we are told children should 'stay safe', on other hand parents continue to have the legal right to smack their children. The government argues that to outlaw smacking is to interfere intolerably in family life, but we also have to consider that the same level of violence from an adult towards another adult could constitute assault and lead to a conviction. This contradiction must undermine the credibility of a government purporting to end harm to children.

Another goal related to staying safe refers to children having security, stability and being cared for. Here, the rather woolly terms used are unhelpful. Once more there appears to be an assumption that we all know and agree what these terms mean. The danger here is that these notions are brought into the policy arena without a shared understanding of what level

Reflections: Staying safe

Three subheadings of the aim for children of staying safe are that children should be safe from

- Accidental injury and death
- Bullying and discrimination
- Crime and anti-social behaviour

1 What is your initial response to these targets?
2 How do you think parents might try to make sure their children are safe from these things?
3 Can you see any tensions between these aims and other desired outcomes for children?

or form of security, stability or care is acceptable or desired. By default, the 'norm' for acceptability might become an unspoken white, middle-class world view which may well clash with the experiences and norms of other groups of children and parents. If this occurs, those holding the 'dominant' world-view might bring pressure to bear on these other groups to conform to the 'normal' expectations in order for any intervention to be hailed a success.

Enjoy and achieve

The outcome 'Enjoy and achieve' is interesting in that although the word 'enjoy' appears first, only one of the subheadings in this outcome relates directly to recreation and leisure, although one other aim is that children attend and enjoy school. The 'achieving' half of the outcome seems much more dominant, relating as it does to all subheadings of the outcome in one way or another. Achieving here means that children are prepared for school, attend school, and achieve national targets throughout their school career. This gives rise to a number of questions. Is school a wholly good place for children to be? Is it unquestionably in the interests of all children to pursue the national curriculum? Should good exam results be the ultimate goal for children? If so, what does this say about children who are not able to achieve this, such as those with learning disabilities? Are they lesser achievers?

There is a further issue here. The Education Act 1996 states that it is the duty of parents to secure education for their children of compulsory school age which is efficient, full time and suitable to his or her age, ability, aptitude and any special educational needs. This means that children do not actually have to attend school but may be educated at home, as long as the local authority is satisfied that the education is suitable. With this in mind, the emphasis in this outcome upon schooling, and indeed the whole emphasis on schools as the centre of local service provision, seems to serve to marginalize those children (and their parents) involved in home education. If every child really does matter, surely some reference to this within the outcome might have been made?

Make a positive contribution

The language of the subheadings of the outcome 'Make a positive contribution' also requires further investigation. In particular, the two references to it being desirable for children to engage in 'positive' behaviour and develop 'positive' relationships beg the question: what is meant by 'positive'? Who decides what this means and involves? Whose world-view is seen to be the acceptable standard for behaviour and relationships? The concern here is that if these matters go unchallenged, then a potentially narrow and one-dimensional version of what is acceptable may become foisted upon children and families, with any deviation from this possibly being viewed with hostility.

In addition, the drive to try to ensure that children 'support the community' suggests we are aiming to produce children who do not challenge the status quo. This seems a functionalist view of society, where it is assumed the community is sound and not in need of changing, and citizens are expected to fit into and accept the given community as inherently 'good'. However, if certain children and families do not experience their community as good, if they experience instead poverty, or racism, or social exclusion, then is it reasonable to expect them to accept and support this? Would we not want them, and others, to challenge the status quo and try to develop a different kind of community?

Achieve economic well-being

A similar problem may exist with the outcome that children should 'Achieve economic well-being'. While no-one would want to see children growing up to be impoverished, there does appear to be a certain implicit assumption in this outcome that to be a 'good' citizen means merely becoming ready for employment via education or training. Once more, this seems a functionalist approach, where citizens are expected to fit into the existing structure of how society works, rather than challenge it.

The second difficulty is that this outcome (and this could be said of all the outcomes) assumes that children are malleable; that if only we tweak their world and offer support, then they will do as 'we' (in other words those who decide what is desirable) want them to do. This approach seems to ignore the individual agency of children and parents to plot their own course, according to what they see as important and relevant. To suggest that these personal choices may be somehow 'wrong' or 'misguided' if they do not fit neatly into the framework created by the dominant policy makers who, it could be argued, have a vested interest in maintaining society as it is, with all its inequalities, is a questionable approach.

Measuring success of the five outcomes

A significant problem with all of the outcomes is how to measure whether they are being achieved or not. *Every Child Matters: Change for Children* (DfES, 2004a) contains a densely printed page outlining the outcomes framework which links the five outcomes with targets and indicators, and then with inspection criteria. This is an attempt to make tangible how the success of these outcomes is to be measured. However, some problems exist with this initial framework. The first layer of measurement – targets and indicators – could be said to be reductionist, focusing as it does on percentages of children doing, or not doing, certain things rather than the qualitative and varied experiences of children. This ignores the complexity of children's lives. On the other hand, some of these indicators, interestingly, seem extremely vague. Take, for example, one under the outcome for 'Make a positive contribution', which states that one indicator of success is the percentage of 10- to 19-year-olds who admit to bullying another pupil in the past 12 months, or to attacking, threatening or being rude due to skin colour, race or religion. An obvious criticism here is the difficulty of measuring or defining rudeness. To be fair, this particular indicator seems to be absent from the document produced by Ofsted following consultation with partners on how to firm up measurement of the outcomes (Ofsted, 2007a). This document contains a rather bewildering one hundred and seventy nine indicators upon which inspections will report, and seven more regarding health appear to have been added soon after (Ofsted, 2007b). While on the one hand this could be said to provide a comprehensive range of factors relating to agencies' work with children, it seems suggestive of a surveillance and reductionist approach to childhood, in which the child's lived experience appears largely ignored within an approach that focuses on how children perform across the specified areas. As a report from the Education and Skills Committee points out in quoting Peter Moss, an eminent academic on childhood

> Targets and outcomes can be treated as purely managerial tools, without appreciating that these are necessarily contestable in a democratic and pluralist society because they raise important ethical and political questions. For example, why is the outcome 'being healthy' described [. . .] in terms of avoiding negative behaviours? Or why is 'enjoying and achieving' reduced to school achievement? (HC 40-I, 2005, pp. 43–44)

The report concludes that inspections of children's services, if they are truly to improve children's lives, must contribute to the improvement of services for children. Currently, the mechanism for this appears unclear.

The role of the children's commissioners

All four countries of the United Kingdom now have a Children's Commissioner; England, however, was the last to create the role. The Commissioners for Wales, Scotland and Northern Ireland all have a clear remit to safeguard and protect children's rights. In contrast, the role and remit of the Commissioner for England is to promote the needs and views of children. Hence, the Commissioner for England can be said to have less power than the Commissioners in the other United Kingdom countries. Certainly, the House of Commons Education and Skills Committee remain to be convinced that the role of the Commissioner for England can be 'as effective in practice as one focused on promoting and protecting children's rights' (HC 40-I, 2005, p. 26). Here we see another potential clash between the aim of achieving improved outcomes for children, and the structure put in place to accomplish this. One has to wonder why England, the country with the largest number of children of the four nations of the United Kingdom, has a Children's Commissioner with the least power to effect lasting change for children. Are we to conclude that the rights of English children matter less than their Welsh, Scottish or Northern Irish counterparts?

The national database of children

The proposal to develop a national database of every child, perhaps with certain children flagged as 'at risk' or 'vulnerable' or 'receiving a range of services', raises many serious ethical questions. These include:

- How would the database overcome data protection issues, particularly if some services did not want to be identified as being involved with the child?
- Who should have access to input data?
- Who should ensure the data is accurate?
- Who should decide whether the quality of the information inputted is sufficiently robust to merit entry onto the database?
- Should parents have the right to see what is recorded?
- Should children have the right to see what is recorded?
- If children are going to be tagged, is this labelling them in a simplistic fashion?
- How can it be guaranteed that the database will be fully secure? If children are labelled as 'vulnerable' might they, ironically, be made even more vulnerable by this should paedophiles or other adults with ill intent towards children – possibly including professionals working in children's services – have access to the database?

The nature and number of such significant concerns and issues could be said to call into question the whole proposal for a national database of all children. It might be argued that the money used to create such a database would be better spent on targeting those children who are known to be at risk, and creating a well trained workforce to support those children effectively. As Munro states, cited in the House of Commons Education and Skills Committee report (ibid.), information itself does not rescue or help children; it is seeing and understanding the significance of that information which is the key. In other words, training for the staff that hold and share information is more important than slavishly recording facts without reflecting upon what they mean.

Extended schools

The plan to allow every child in England to access extended services based in or around their school by 2010 requires further scrutiny. With guaranteed childcare from 8.00 a.m. to 6.00 p.m., does this mean that children are going to be cared for, in a school setting, for 10 hours a day, 5 days a week? If so, is this in their interests? What choices will children have about this? Will they want to remain at school (albeit, perhaps, within a separate building on the grounds) in their uniforms, after completing a full day's work? What if a child is being bullied and the bully also attends the after-school club? For the child being bullied, there would be no relief.

The whole proposal for extended schools seems to be predicated on two key concepts: a deficit model of childhood and parenting, and supporting parents to work full time. The deficit model suggests that children from poor or deprived backgrounds need some compensatory input in order to raise them to the same level as other children (see Smith, Cowie and Blades, 2003). Hence, the extended schools model seems to be arguing that children should experience up to 10 hours a day of 'positive' experiences. But who decides, or should decide, what is 'positive'? The inherent assumption here seems to be that the parents of these children are incapable or providing 'appropriate' experiences for their children. The model assumes that there is one uniform way in which children should be brought up, and that it is the one upon which the government itself has decided. There is a further question as to exactly what activities might take place in the before- and after-school clubs. If they become 'homework' clubs, focused upon raising test or exam results, then children could be placed in a highly narrow, competitive and stressful environment for even longer than they are currently. While it is difficult to argue that education, in its broadest sense, is unimportant, an emphasis on narrow achievement, at the expense of other enriching childhood experiences, may well serve to militate against the interests of children, and ultimately the whole of society.

The second underpinning motivation for developing extended schools may well be to allow parents to work full time. If this occurs, then the government gains not only through increased tax revenue, but also because fewer welfare benefits will need to be paid to those parents, particularly perhaps single parents, who previously claimed benefits. Evidence of this may be found in government suggestions that in future, single parents may only be able to claim Income Support benefit without having to seek work until their youngest child is 12, compared to the current age of 16 (BBC News, 2007b). This raises even more questions. If this does happen, how long before the age is then reduced to 5, as these children could in principle attend extended school provision? One could also ask what image of single parents this is reinforcing. That they are generally reluctant to work? Is this the most effective means to support poor families: to pressurize parents to work, and place their children in extended school provision, which they are told is good for them, even in the absence of research-based evidence to support this claim?

Every Child Matters and young people

Perhaps the area which exposes most the contradictions between policies is the interplay between what *Every Child Matters* purports to value, and other approaches to young people. Use of tough sanctions to curb what is seen as anti-social behaviour through the use of the Anti-social Behaviour Order (ASBO) suggests that the government may wish to send a message to young people that if they do not 'fit in' with the vision of society that the government has decided is the 'correct' one, that if young people do not 'make a positive contribution', then they may be dealt with harshly.

 ### Information: Anti-social Behaviour Orders (ASBOs) in the four countries of the UK

The ASBOs were introduced by the New Labour government from 1 April 1999 as part of the Crime and Disorder Act 1998, which is applicable to England and Wales. In Northern Ireland, the Anti-social Behaviour (Northern Ireland) Order 2004 was introduced with very similar powers. These ASBOs were ostensibly devised to tackle behaviour which 'caused or was likely to cause harassment, alarm or distress'. The local authority or the police may make an application for an ASBO with respect to any person aged 10 or over. If approved, the Order prohibits the named person from doing anything prescribed in the order. While being subject to an ASBO itself is not a criminal offence, breach of it is. ASBOs last for a minimum of 2 years and breaching it can lead to a fine or imprisonment. For young people aged 12 to 14, the latter can mean a secure training order which means being locked up in a secure setting; for 15- to 18-year-olds it could lead to a 6-month custodial sentence. In Scotland, the Antisocial Behaviour etc. (Scotland) Act 2004 allows ASBOs to be made for children under the age of 16 but only as low as 12, and only after a full children's hearing. If an order is made, although breach of it is a criminal offence, custody is not an option for those under 16.

A key difficultly appears to be in the wording of the Act regarding the circumstances in which ASBOs can be issued. The language is so broad – *behaviour which caused, or was likely to cause harassment, alarm or distress* – as to allow for some questionable interpretations of it. Foot (2004, p. 2) reveals that under the 'frightening vagueness' of the definition there have been orders banning children from playing football. This seems to contradict the apparently child-centred vision contained within *Every Child Matters*. If every child really does matter, can it be right that a child as young as 12 could effectively receive a custodial sentence for continuing to play football if it has been decided that this activity 'alarms' a neighbour? And if this is so, what does this say about the value our society places upon children?

Furthermore, the fact that ASBOs can be issued without giving people the right to have a jury hear evidence and decide on guilt or innocence, and after hearing only unsubstantiated hearsay evidence, exposes further contradictions in the policies towards young people. In contrast to the aim stated in *Every Child Matters: Change for Children in the Criminal Justice System* (DfES, 2004b), which is to 'minimise the use of custody' (p. 3), there is evidence to suggest that ten young people a week are being jailed as a result of ASBOs (Foot, 2005). This seems to run counter to the message in *Every Child Matters* which stresses the importance of 'services and agencies continuing to move towards prevention and early intervention' (DfES, 2004b, p. 4). There is evidence of a softening of approach to young offenders, with a planned greater emphasis on a restorative approach described in a government *Children's Plan* published late in 2007 (DfCSF, 2007b). Nevertheless, if the use of ASBOs continues unchanged, one conclusion that could be reached is that certain children – those who, without engaging in criminal activity, are perceived to be a nuisance – matter less than others.

The Crime and Disorder Act 1998 made two changes to the way children who do actually offend are dealt with in criminal law. First, where before the prosecution had to prove that a child aged between 10 and 14 knew that what they were doing was wrong, this is now no longer the case. The presumption now is that the child did know it was wrong, that a 10-year-old is capable of making such a distinction. Second, where before a child under 14 years was exempt from the clause that it would be permissible for a court or jury to possibly assume guilt from them remaining silent, this is now not the case. In other words, children aged 10 and over can now lead themselves to have guilt inferred upon them by not giving evidence in court. What this fails to take into account, surely, is the potential stress and trauma to a child of giving evidence in open court, and being subject to cross-examination. We see in both of these changes, the removal of the distinction between children and adults in terms of responsibility and actions, which further undermines the claim of the *Every Child Matters* programme to be child-centred.

Tensions related to multi-agency working and teams

The duty upon agencies to cooperate with one another was, and of course still is, present under Section 27 of the Children Act 1989. What the Children Act 2004 does is to strengthen the wording. The emphasis has shifted away from agencies having to respond if approached by another agency, to having a duty to actively make arrangements to promote cooperation. This suggests that the government does not trust agencies to cooperate without specific requirements being placed upon them to do so. One could therefore legitimately ask whether 'making' agencies work together necessarily means that they will work well together.

The plan to create more multi-agency teams, led by one professional, raises similar questions. Just by locating agencies, and individuals, in one place, does this mean they will work more effectively together than they might have done previously? There seems to be little recognition of the inherent barriers to working together that were discussed in Chapter 2. Since some of these – for instance, a history of different values, of core functions, of using different pieces of legislation – are structural barriers, it seems unlikely they will be overcome merely by shoehorning professionals into one building. Where multi-agency teams have members on different rates of pay and conditions of service (e.g. entitlement to annual leave or progression) but where all are expected to do very similar jobs, this has the potential to lead to discord and disharmony, rather than to closer joint working.

Furthermore, if any member of a team is now expected to carry out general duties that were once the domain of a particular agency, this too could cause resentment, or role confusion. For instance, assessment was historically the key skill of social workers, and they led on the completion of multi-agency assessments. Under the Common Assessment Framework, unless there is evidence of risk of significant harm, any professional could, if trained, conduct an assessment. This could leave the social worker feeling undervalued, deskilled and unclear as to what distinctive skills they can bring to the process of supporting families. A further danger is that several professionals are trained to complete a task to a mediocre standard as opposed to having a few professionals trained to complete it to a high standard. Professional distinctiveness may be lost in the attempt to offer a generic service to families. Further implications for multi-agency working of other issues raised in this chapter about *Every Child Matters* will be discussed in the Conclusion.

Structural barriers to the success of *Every Child Matters*

One of the chief underpinning messages of *Every Child Matters* seems to be that if only services can work more effectively together, then outcomes for children will improve; unless this vast programme of change is put into place, children will continue to be at risk and lead unfulfilling lives which result in society counting the cost. In taking such an approach, it could be argued that the government is seeking to shift responsibility to services and away from themselves. A number of fundamental questions remain as to what the government is doing to tackle some of the more intransigent structural barriers to children successfully negotiating their way to adulthood.

Child poverty is one such enormous barrier. The government have pledged to halve child poverty by 2010, and to eradicate it by 2020, an ambitious target. After some initial success up to 2004, where the consensus seemed to be that the government were on target to reduce child poverty by a quarter, progress has stalled (Hirsch, 2006). There remains a substantial group of families in poverty. To end child poverty by 2020 would cost £28 billion pounds a year for each year up to that date (ibid.). While this is less than 1 year's worth of economic growth in 14, it would require huge payments to families with children, which could be perceived by those out of poverty as unjust. No government is likely to either pay that amount of money or risk alienating the electorate. To truly end child poverty, Hirsch concludes, would take not only a substantial increase in benefits and tax credits, but also measures to improve parents' and future parents' incomes. These measures include a decisive effort to improve educational outcomes for disadvantaged groups, and renewing efforts to improve women's pay and access to childcare. Here, the notion of extended schools to support these endeavours takes on a new dimension – as part of a campaign to end poverty and improve the life experience of those children affected by it. Whether the government will, however, substantially increase benefits to poor families and truly tackle unequal pay between men and women remains to be seen, and will perhaps be a real measure of the extent to which every child really does matter more than political or financial considerations.

 Information: Child poverty in the United Kingdom

Figures for 2006 show that 3.8 million children in the United Kingdom – or 30 per cent – were living in poverty (Palmer, MacInnes and Kenway, 2007). While poverty rates in England, Wales and Scotland are similar, in Northern Ireland the child poverty rate is higher as 32 per cent of children live in households totally dependent on benefits, compared to 19 per cent of children in the other three countries (Horgan, 2005). The measure used in calculating this poverty rate is households with less than 60 per cent of the median (midpoint) national income after housing costs. The government prefers the measure to be 60 per cent of the median (midpoint) national income *before* housing costs (HC 04/23, 2004b). The exclusion of housing costs from the measure of child poverty allows more children to be lifted out of official poverty, and therefore allows the government to claim more success in eradicating child poverty. For instance, under this measure, 2.8 million children – 22 per cent – live in poverty. In reality, housing costs account for a substantial proportion of poorer families' budgets and therefore the potentially hidden group of one million children (the difference between the two ways of measuring poverty) will continue to experience poverty (Lohde, 2004).

Further structural barriers to successful outcomes for children include racism, disability discrimination and poor housing. While there is not sufficient space here to discuss these in any depth, the key point is that no amount of working together by services, no amount of cooperation and co-location and joint planning will remove these structural barriers. They remain major obstacles: insidious, invidious and pernicious, permeating children's lives, and thus undermining the efforts of professionals to create successful outcomes for children.

Conclusions

This chapter has charted the journey from an individual girl's unimaginable agony arising from abuse, to the government's implementation of a system of wholesale change. This new system is designed to ensure, as far as possible, that such individual tragedies do not occur again, but also that every child reaches their full potential. At the heart of this programme is integrated multi-agency work. Of course, such work can be a very positive and life-enhancing experience for children and families, and indeed for the professionals involved. Most professionals are fully committed to supporting children and parents to very high standards. However, the talents and energies of these workers are likely to be compromised by structural obstacles to improvements for children which individual professionals cannot be expected to overcome: poverty, discrimination and social divisions. Furthermore, conflicts between different social policies serve to undermine some of the key messages emanating from central government, and the work of agencies working for children. One has to question whether in fact every child really does matter, when young people who are perceived as 'anti-social' are dealt with as harshly as they are, when very young children at the mercy of parents who choose to use physical punishments are not afforded the same rights in law as adults, and when more has not been done by central government to eradicate child poverty. A final question therefore remains: whether, despite the mantra of *Every Child Matters*, certain groups of children in fact matter less than others.

Conclusion

The starting point of this book, when considering the origins of multi-agency work, was the assertion that it is impossible to separate structured work with families, and the legislation that guides it, from poverty. The New Poor Law cemented, in nineteenth-century England, the notion of the deserving versus the non-deserving poor. This appears to have entered deep into the collective psyche, for it remains with us today, influencing government policy towards the poor, which in turn directly impinges upon patterns and outcomes of multi-agency work with families from all social backgrounds.

Modern child protection systems, and subsequent developments in multi-agency work, have been shown to have been triggered by tragic deaths of individual children where agencies were involved with the family. Furthermore, there is evidence that successive governments use these events – and the energy created by the media and public response to their horror – to push through and justify new polices which go far beyond the issues raised by any review into the death of an individual child. This is no different for perhaps the most radical and far-reaching reforms to multi-agency working yet, certainly in England: the *Every Child Matters* programme.

Multi-agency work is relatively easy to define and recognize, and a wide range of agencies and individual professionals can be involved. They labour within a complex and at times contradictory framework of legislation and guidance, which has the potential to cause uncertainty, confusion or conflict. Furthermore, inherent structural barriers to effective multi-agency work transcend the individual, and can militate against effective outcomes for children and families. While some of these can be overcome by implementing sound principles of local cooperation and camaraderie, there is no doubt that some potentially harmful barriers stubbornly remain. Those closely associated with professional identity, deep cultural practices within and between agencies, and perceptions by agencies of how they see their relationships with others, feature highly among these.

These barriers are perhaps no more clearly apparent than when one considers the complex task of undertaking a multi-agency assessment of a family. Assessments for children who may be 'in need' or 'in need of protection' are led by social workers who coordinate a broad process involving several agencies, all of whom have to understand their multi-agency responsibilities and roles, together with detailed guidance on information sharing. The Common Assessment Framework on the other hand – to be used where children may have 'additional needs' – can be undertaken by a competent professional from any agency. While there are undoubtedly clear benefits of identifying obstacles to optimum development as early as possible, there is the potential for the process to undermine the professional identity of the social worker and cause anxiety for those with lead professional status.

Such changes in emphasis and expectation can be more fundamental than merely at the level of the individual. The shift in how protecting children has been conceptualized – and then operationalized – is a good example of this. Between 1989 and 1997, a strong principle of the then Conservative government was that agencies could and should only breach the sanctity of family life, and cut across the right of parents to bring up their children as they thought fit, if a child was at clear risk of significant harm. This had a direct impact upon the work of all agencies with families, who tended to stand off from families unless it was absolutely necessary for them to intervene. Then from 1997 onwards a clear move away from this philosophy took place under the New Labour government. It was accepted that parenting is a difficult task, that parents have a right to timely and high-quality support, and that the intervention of agencies can be welcome if it is of the right kind. Agencies were thus expected – at the same time as the legislation encouraging an essentially *laissez faire* approach to families remains in place – to assess, support and meet the needs of as many families as they could identify as having 'additional needs'. The potential here is not only for some good preventative work to take place, but also for confusion, resentment or conflict between agencies struggling to interpret, implement and integrate the changes into existing practice and philosophies.

Prevention of harm to children is also a key role for schools and early years centres to undertake, alongside the other two levels of protecting children thought to be at risk, and supporting those known to have experienced abuse. The systems and guidance in place to enable schools and settings to do this work are undoubtedly of great benefit to children; nevertheless individual schools or settings are likely to experience internal tensions between their commitment to these expectations and other demands upon them to achieve good outcomes under the National Curriculum. Furthermore, decisions that schools and settings may make in trying to balance, say, support for an individual child subject to a child protection plan and their duty to provide quality education for all the children in their charge, may lead to tension between themselves and other agencies. If a school is unable to send a teacher to a crucial multi-agency meeting, the other agencies may well have little sympathy with the school's argument that the teacher's attendance would compromise the education of 20 or so other children in the same class.

Similar inter-agency tensions can arise where staff from different services try to support children in care. If key personnel are absent from a Personal Education Planning meeting, this can seriously undermine the quality of, and multi-agency commitment to, the plan. New government proposals for England to transform the life chances of children in care, again underpinned by an expectation of close multi-agency working between agencies, are to be welcomed. However, unless they can be shown to have truly improved, in a meaningful and tangible manner, the life chances of children in care, then they will have failed in their key objective.

The law relating to information sharing is a good example of the discrepancy between intended and actual outcomes. Clearly the Data Protection Act 1998 and Human Rights Act 1998 were both forged with a clear intention of respecting privacy, of protecting individuals from unnecessary intrusion, and of achieving fairness for individuals. Nevertheless, the intrinsic complexities of both of these pieces of legislation, coupled with a fear that individuals can be prosecuted for breaching them, can lead to uncertainty, and a defensive approach to sharing information such that information that should be shared may not be. The impact on this upon children is potentially catastrophic, if the information relates to risk of harm. The question of when professionals should seek or obtain parental consent to share information with another agency is a further source of possible tension between agencies, and between agencies and parents. To combat these difficulties, professionals need clear, unequivocal guidance on the distinction between occasions when they have to share information without seeking or obtaining parenting consent, when they have to seek or obtain consent, and when they should, but do not have to, seek consent. Without this, misunderstandings leading to conflict between agencies, or between agencies and parents, are likely to be a regular occurrence.

Where agencies work with parents, in both family support and safeguarding children, their perception of their relationship with those parents is a critical factor in determining the level of partnership they may aim to achieve. Clearly, where various agencies are involved with a family, there is the potential for a variety of attitudes towards parents to exist within agencies. This can lead to tension and conflict between agencies as each tries to assert their own position or understand that of others. Parents, too, may get caught in the crossfire and become confused as to what is expected of them.

This potential for confusion could also be extended to professionals expected to work closely with other agencies, and to lose clear professional identities, as part of integration within multi-agency teams under the *Every Child Matters* programme. This programme offers exciting opportunities for creative work with families, harnessing an array of talents from a centralized source. However, there remains a concern that by glibly joining agencies together without taking full account of the implications for the individuals and teams concerned, the consequences could be conflict and disorientation rather than improved services for children.

This book has examined multi-agency work with children from a variety of perspectives. It has offered a critique of current and emerging systems and processes in the sincere belief that unless the full extent of the complexities, difficulties and tensions associated with them are explored and understood, then the quality of any multi-agency work is likely to be compromised. The clear benefits of multi-agency work, and of some of the possibilities offered by the *Every Child Matters* vision, should not blind professionals to the real problems that persist, problems that are inherent in the very nature of multi-agency work. Professionals should be cautious about being marched bright-eyed into the future, yoked to colleagues from other agencies, with the promise of better outcomes for children through what appears to be a preoccupation with the close surveillance, monitoring and measuring of a vast array of factors related to children's lives. The government's plan to 'make England the best place in the world for children and young people to grow up' (DfCSF, 2007b, p. 5) by 2020 contains some interesting ideas but is nevertheless heavily reliant on a target and outcomes based approach for children.

Professionals can, and should, pause and question whether the promise of a brighter future for children is fully achievable without the full extent of the intricacies involved in multi-agency work being fully unravelled, processed and commonly distilled and understood. Only then, and in spite of the structural barriers that persist, will professionals be able to engage in multi-agency work which really does have the potential to benefit children and families by improving their life chances in varying fields such as health, social care and education.

Appendix

Points to consider and suggestions for the Reflective box exercises.

Chapter 1

Child death trends

1 What reasons can you think of for the number of child deaths at the hands of parents or carers being constant in spite of a series of improvements to the child surveillance and child protection system?

It has been argued that the position of children in society – their relative lack of power and rights – and what Hanvey (2003) calls the 'deep ambiguity about children, seeing them as angels or villains' (p. 1) coupled with a 'lack of collective and individual responsibility for the safety of vulnerable children within communities' (ibid.) appear to contribute to this state of affairs. You might also want to consider how most legislation regarding children emphasizes that children are effectively the private property of parents, and that others should only interfere with parenting if the child is at risk of serious harm.

Case study – Amy

1 Based on Section 27 of the Children Act 1989, which of the assessment elements do you think the school is obliged to provide?

The school would have a duty to provide information related to the school's core function of education. This would include Amy's performance and progress at school, her social relationships, and any observations the school may have about Amy's relationships with her parents.

2 Which do you think they would have a right to question or refuse to do?

The school could not be expected to provide information regarding the family's financial circumstances as this does not relate to their core function.

> **3** If the school does refuse to carry out any of these requests, how might they go about doing this without harming the relationship with the social worker?

The school would need to balance their assertiveness in explaining that it is not appropriate for them to investigate the family's financial circumstances against maintaining a positive relationship with the social worker. The school should be clear and firm but not aggressive, and should emphasize the elements that they are happy to support the social worker in completing. They should not, however, agree to carry out an inappropriate task merely to placate the social worker.

Case study – Jenny

> **1** How do you think school should respond to this scenario?

While school has a responsibility to maintain a positive relationship with other agencies, this is overridden by their duty to act in Jenny's best interests. They should therefore do what they think is best for Jenny. In this case, this means clearly stating their disagreement with the proposal, along with their reasons for this.

> **2** What arguments could the school bring to bear if they decided to challenge social services on this decision?

School could cite the fact that Jenny is settled in school, and would have a natural move to an appropriate high school at the beginning of Year 7. Furthermore, she is due to sit her SATs test in May, so to move her to a new primary school in April could be disastrous, unsettling her and forcing her to negotiate the whole passage of joining a new school, forming new friends and so on just before these tests. The impact upon her results could be catastrophic.

> **3** How can school act as an advocate for Jenny, and maintain a positive relationship with social services?

The school should consider how they raise their objections. Their focus should be the best interests of Jenny. They should state their case clearly and fully. They should emphasize the positive reasons for keeping Jenny at the school. They should avoid becoming aggressive with the social worker, stressing that this is not a personal issue, but what they see as Jenny's best interests. If necessary, school should be prepared to take the matter up with the social worker's management, again maintaining an assertive but non-aggressive stance.

Chapter 2

Case study – Jack

1 Look at the section of this chapter titled 'The language of partnership'. At what level of partnership do you think the agencies involved in this work are operating? Remember that different agencies can be at different levels. Try to give reasons to support your answer.

Generally, the agencies appear to be around Level 3. There is active involvement via the conference, where all parties are contributing to discussions and decision making. The headteacher, however, appears to have a separate agenda and is not interacting with the other agencies at this level.

2 Can you identify any elements from the list for Level 4 – full partnership – in this scenario?

It could be argued that the following are present:

- Shared values – Jack's safety.
- A shared task or goal – the meeting itself.
- All parties contribute resources or skills – information is shared in the meeting.
- Decisions are made together – there was generally good attendance at the meeting.
- Choice in entering the partnership – there seems to be, considering the good attendance.
- A formalized arrangement for agreed working – the way is meeting is set up and works supports this.

3 From the list of 'barriers to effective multi-agency work' discussed in this chapter choose those you think are present in this scenario. Try to be as specific as you can.

The following barriers could be said to be present in the case study:

- Different values, cultures and practices between agencies – the headteacher keeping separate notes not shared with others.
- A lack of clarity in boundaries – it is not the school's role to keep a log and then use in the way described. There should be open sharing of information.
- Poor communication between the school and other agencies.
- A lack of information sharing between the school and other agencies.
- Conflicting professional and agency cultures – the GP did not attend but sent a letter expressing powerful positive views of the parents which have the potential to sway the meeting.

Chapter 3

Case study – the McLoughlin family

1 Which assessment framework do you think the social worker used here – the *Framework for Assessment* or the Common Assessment Framework?

As the case concerned child protection and significant harm, the social work conducted a full assessment under the *Framework for Assessment* guidance.

2 How were the children's needs addressed?

The children were initially protected and placed in care. Soon afterwards the positive relationship with their father was encouraged and the children were kept within the family as they went to stay with him. Nursery places were secured for Stella and Christopher, and a place was found for Mark at the after-school club. The social worker undertook direct work with, and observations of, the children to determine their wishes and feelings. Practical assistance was provided for the children to attend health appointments.

3 How was Laura's parenting capacity assessed?

The social worker got alongside Laura and engaged her in discussion regarding her parenting. The social worker also gathered information from their own observations and from other agencies regarding Laura's parenting. Her ability to change, restore the flat to a good state and demonstrate commitment to her children was also being assessed throughout this process.

4 What were the significant wider family and environmental factors that impinged on this case? How were they addressed, and how did this contribute to the successful outcome?

Laura was a single parent living with three young children in an overcrowded flat with no safe area for the children to play outside. The family was isolated from services and from wider family support. Income was low. They were addressed by the social worker advocating for Laura in respect of an application for rehousing, ensuring she received all her benefits she was entitled to, and facilitating a placement for the children with their father. This contributed to the successful outcome by providing Laura with practical support and a long-term aim of living in superior accommodation; in other words it helped to lift her out of her depression. By staying with their father, the children were protected from a deep fracturing of their family relationships and were more readily able to adapt to life back with their mother. The success of the housing application helped to contribute to the longer term success.

Chapter 4

When is harm significant?

1 Which of the scenarios do you think amounts to 'significant harm', rather than just 'harm'? Try to give at least one reason for your decision.

In trying to reach a decision, you might consider such factors as:

- the actual or potential impact on the child. This might include thinking about the age of the child, their ability to 'escape' or tell someone and so on
- the duration and frequency of the harm – is it a one off or does it happens many times
- how severe is the act of harm
- the overall atmosphere within which the child lives.

Remember, the focus should be on the impact upon the child, and you should not be distracted by factors such as the motivation of the abusers, whether they meant to deliberately harm the child or whether the abuser is trying their best (but failing) to parent adequately.

Chapter 5

Preventative work with children: possible contradictions and tensions

1 Can you think how these messages to children might contradict the aim of carrying out preventative work on abuse with children in schools or early years settings?

If children have imbibed the messages described, should they find themselves being asked to do something about which they feel uncomfortable, they may be torn between the general message that they should always obey adults, and a specific message given to them that they should resist undue pressure with firmness. It is possible that some children may find it very difficult, for instance, to push the adult away with a firm 'No!' and remove themselves from the situation. Furthermore, there may be circumstances where it would be not only acceptable, but also creative and inventive for children to tell a lie in order to extricate themselves from a tight corner. If they found themselves alone in a house or room with an adult and realized they were in danger, they might be applauded for saying something like 'My parents are due home any minute, so you had better leave' or 'I need the toilet' when this might not but be strictly true but assists an escape.

Case study – Peter

1 Can you identify mistakes or poor practice in this case study?

The first member of staff mentioned, Jenny, made assumptions about the origin of the bruises without following it up. If they had used their knowledge of Peter they would know he was not boisterous, so the injuries were unlikely to have resulted from play. The initial reaction of the manager was more concerned about the relationship with parents and image of the setting than Peter's welfare. Clearly, the needs of the child should come first.

    2 Can you identify good practice here?

The second member of staff, Nicola, used her knowledge of Peter to question the reason given for the injury. She followed this up and spoke to Peter, recorded it and passed it on to the manager. Although there is no information about how she spoke to Peter, we can assume she acted appropriately, asking open questions. She could possibly be criticized for not ensuring a second staff member was present, although it could also be argued she acted in good faith and with Peter's best interests at heart, and that having two staff members present may have inhibited him. The manager did discuss the matter with the trained Designated Officer and a referral to social services was made.

    3 How could the setting have helped Peter more prior to the abuse coming to light?

They could have encouraged Peter to take part in more social play and helped to boost his confidence and self-esteem, perhaps by ensuring his work was displayed, shared enthusiastically with his parents and so on. Setting staff could have maintained careful records of injuries and behaviour. The lack of an appropriate response by Jenny suggests they may not have received relevant training.

    4 How can the setting now ensure they support Peter effectively, both in the setting and with the multi-agency process?

They could implement the measures identified under the previous question. They could cooperate fully with the multi-agency process of making further enquiries, the Initial and Core Assessment, attendance at Initial Child Protection Conference, Core Groups and Review conferences. If they cannot attend, they should send a written report. They should continue their liaison with Peter's parents and support them where necessary. They should continue to monitor and record Peter.

Case study – Patricia

    1 Can you identify good practice in how the teacher dealt with this disclosure?

The teacher was correct in not entering into a pact of secrecy with Patricia and in how she responded. Had Patricia declined to speak further, the teacher should not have pursued this, but should let the child know they are there for them whenever they need support. The staff member should assure the child they will try to help, but that this may involve having to tell other people. The teacher was also correct in remaining calm. The chief reason for this is that, if strong emotions are expressed, the child may well think that it is they, and not the abuse, that has made the adult shocked or angry and so on. The staff member may need to express strong feelings appropriately to colleagues or a supervisor after the event and receive appropriate support for this; however, doing so in front of the child would be wholly inappropriate.

The teacher appropriately reassured Patricia and facilitated her in telling her story in the main by making open and generalized comments. The teacher was also correct in negotiating with Patricia at the beginning that notes would be taken. However, if this is not possible, as soon as possible after the disclosure, the adult should make a detailed and accurate record of the conversation, recording any questions asked. The response to Patricia's retraction of the disclosure was good. Even if the child, having made a clear disclosure, then retracts what they have said, it is essential for the adult to report all that they have heard. A child may, on making the disclosure, feel they are betraying the abuser, or they may have been told that if they tell someone, terrible things will happen to all concerned. This may cause the child to panic once the disclosure is made, and to retract it. Having let the cat out of the bag, they may try to put it back in. However, a child cannot 'unmake' a disclosure, and it should be passed on for others to make a decision as to its validity. The fact that the disclosure was passed on correctly within school, and then on to social services was another positive feature. Any disclosure of abuse from a child should then also be passed on to social services as soon as possible. The reason for this is that a distinction is drawn between a child telling an adult they are being abused (a disclosure) and an adult suspecting a child may be being harmed (staff concerns). Imagine the reaction of other agencies if a disclosure was not passed on, the child continued to be abused, and it later emerged that the school or early years setting knew about this. It would certainly not engender positive feelings of effective multi-agency working.

2 Can you see any areas which could have been handled better?

The point where the teacher asks Patricia 'Did your stepfather touch your breasts?' is a direct, closed question which had the potential to close down the conversation. The adult should encourage the child to talk but avoid asking them leading questions. By contrast, open or indirect questions invite the child to give a statement. Open questions could include 'What happened next?', 'Can you say more about that?', 'How did that come about?' and so on. In this case study, the teacher could have asked, if it were necessary 'Where did he touch you?'

In and among these open questions, it is also acceptable, even advisable, for the adult to check that they have understood correctly what the child is trying to say. This could involve the adult summarizing the child's words. Where children, for whatever reason (and this may be particularly relevant to staff in special schools or early years settings) do not possess the complexity of language, it is acceptable to use more direct questions in relation to the context of the abuse, but not to the abuse itself. Examples of such appropriate direct questions might be to clarify the time of day, such as 'Was it before lunch or after lunch?' or 'Was it light or dark?' These kinds of questions can be very helpful in assisting the child to locate in their memory and experience the actual abuse while also helping the adult to fully contextualize the situation. In recording Patricia's comments, by changing 'front bottom' to 'vagina' the teacher was potentially undermining aspects of how the disclosure was handled. The main reasons for making verbatim or word for word records are twofold: to maintain clarity and accuracy of recording, and to avoid accusations, that if a staff member has changed a particular phrase, then what else in the recording might they have changed?

Case study – Charlie

1 What do you think are the key issues here?

Charlie clearly has limited communication. This will lessen his ability to express himself or describe events that affect him. It may also limit the ability of adults to communicate effectively with him. His characteristic behaviour may make it more likely that other unusual behaviour is linked (wrongly) to his condition when it could indeed be Charlie's attempt to signal distress. A sudden onset of wetting and soiling, coupled with a change of behaviour (the bouts of aggression) are possible signs of abuse, including sexual abuse. Charlie's vulnerability to abuse is heightened by him having multiple carers, who may target him for abuse partly because of his limited communication skills.

2 How do you think school could support Charlie more effectively?

Charlie's class teacher clearly knows Charlie well, and that his changed behaviour is out of character. However, in dismissing this, the Designated Officer is making an assumption that all unusual behaviour is linked to his condition. This is an example of the kinds of myths and stereotypes to which disabled children are subject. Furthermore, by taking into account the attitude of the parents in deciding on the next step, the school is allowing this to override Charlie's best interests. Furthermore, by deciding not to formally monitor him, they are failing in their duty to oversee his welfare. Therefore, school should really be listening carefully to the views of those who know Charlie best, considering the new problems in their own right rather than setting them against his condition, and starting to address them systematically. This may well include talking to the parents to see if they can throw any light as to the change of behaviour, and formally monitoring Charlie. Further attempts to communicate with him should of course also be made to see if he is able to express any worries.

Case study – Jasmine

1 What might be your concerns about Jasmine's care in this scenario?

You may want to consider such matters as the ongoing low-level neglect, and the impact on Jasmine of this – not only the physical effects but how she might feel arriving at school late, or if other children comment on her poor hygiene. If her mother is indeed a regular heavy drinker, this is also likely to be having an impact upon Jasmine, through the quality of care given. Further information would be needed about the role of the father here. In addition, as a black child, Jasmine is very much in a minority within the school. Her situation may therefore be compounded by this. Even if she is not the subject of direct racism, if all the teachers and most of her peers are white, it is likely Jasmine will be receiving images and messages which value 'whiteness' as superior and 'blackness' as derogatory or ambivalent. There is evidence that even for black children under the age of 5 this is the case (Ahmad, 1989). This is one form of indirect discrimination.

2 What issues are there in the way the teacher records the incident?

The teacher's records appear to be rather thin and vague. Rather than describing factually what occurred, she appears to be expressing an opinion that the mother was drunk. What is drunk? One person's view of this may differ from another's. It does not explain why the staff member was concerned. Records should be factual, describing what was seen, or heard or said. Therefore, it would have been better for the teacher to record something like 'When Mum came to collect Jasmine, her breath smelled of alcohol, her speech was incoherent, and she was staggering about. In my opinion, she was drunk, and I was concerned about her being in charge of Jasmine.' This is factual, describing what was seen, and why the staff member was concerned about it. Although it does express an opinion, it does so in the context of a full factual description. It is also a much more powerful piece of evidence than the first description. As it is a criminal offence to be drunk in charge of a child, if the situation worsened, good quality evidence would be vital to effective protection of Jasmine.

Chapter 6

Case study – Carlton

1 How might the school and social worker compromise in a way that allows both to meet their different requirements?

Both professionals should listen carefully to the reasons being given by the other for their position. Ultimately, the completion of the PEP is a statutory requirement upon social workers. One possible solution is to hold the meeting, with Carlton and his carer present, and agree that the main focus of targets in the PEP will be to facilitate school in assessing his needs (bearing in mind there should be background information from the primary school and the social worker). A further meeting could then be held in, say, 3 months time or sooner if needed, to compile more thorough targets. In this way, the social worker is able to fulfil their obligations, and the school can feel satisfied that their professional judgement has been listened to and acted upon, thus hopefully facilitating positive multi-agency working.

Chapter 7

Case study – Sarah

1 In terms of information sharing, what do you think the correct course of action should be?

The school needs to consider the safety and welfare of Sarah (and her younger sister) as paramount. If they believe the information Sarah has given them amounts to 'reasonable cause' that she is at risk of significant harm, they should make a referral to social services and share appropriate information. Only if Sarah's story was palpably untrue or outrageous should they ignore it and do nothing.

2 Do you think the school should seek consent from parents before contacting other agencies? Try and think of specific reasons for your answer.

Although legislation and guidance is predicated on the notion of seeking and gaining consent from parents to share information, this can be jettisoned if seeking consent would put a child at risk of serious harm, or would undermine the prevention, detection or prosecution of a serious crime. With Sarah, if the parents are contacted and their consent sought, or even if they are merely informed a referral to social services has been made, there is the possibility that the parents will destroy forensic or other evidence at the home, or take Sarah out of school immediately and potentially 'get to her' to change her story before formal enquiries can take place by social services or the police. Therefore, the school would be justified in not seeking consent from the parents, but in going straight to social services with the referral based on Sarah's disclosure.

Case study – Anisha

1 Do you think the health visitor can contact the nursery?

The health visitor has explicit verbal consent to contact the nursery. She should record in her notes the fact that such consent was given.

2 If so, can she share information regarding the mother's mental health with the nursery?

The health visitor appears to have discussed with the mother that she would share with the nursery the 'circumstances'. It would be good practice for the health visitor to be absolutely clear with the mother that this would include sharing the fact of her depression – this would ensure informed consent.

3 Do you think the health visitor would also need consent from Anisha's father before she contacted the nursery?

The health visitor has consent to share information and contact the nursery from the mother who has full parental responsibility for Anisha. Unless the health visitor had evidence that there was a clear difference of opinion between the mother and father on this issue, she would not need to seek approval from Anisha's father.

Case study – Connor

1 In terms of sharing information, do you think the school acted appropriately here? Try to think of some reasons for you answer.

The school had genuine concerns regarding Connor. The teacher spoke to his mother and then used the system within school to seek further advice, including approaching the school nurse. They do not appear to have gone beyond their powers.

2 What issues should the school and school nurse have considered before contacting the health visitor?

The school and school nurse should have thought about whether the concerns amount to a possible public interest, in this case, the welfare of Connor and indeed his sister. They could perhaps have approached the mother directly to seek explicit permission to approach the health visitor. Nevertheless, in light of the previous conversation with the mother, and through acting in good faith, putting Connor's interests first, they could justify speaking to the health visitor without such explicit consent.

3 Do you think the health visitor was correct in withholding the information regarding the parents' relationship? Try to think of some reasons for your answer.

The health visitor is fully engaged with the family and confirmed the parents are working positively with her. In deciding not to share that the parents are receiving marriage guidance counselling, she is respecting the parents' confidentiality as she does not have consent to share this sensitive information. The health visitor made a judgement that there was no public interest in revealing this information, as no real benefit to the children will flow from her sharing it.

Case study – Alison

1 Do you think the school has acted appropriately here? Try to think of some reasons for your answer.

School staff have to balance their duty to respect Alison's confidentiality against a duty to promote her welfare or protect her if necessary. School have information that suggests Alison is at risk, possibly of significant harm. She has taken illegal drugs and appears to be under some coercion to have underage sex with older youths (whose precise ages are unknown). In these circumstances the school would not only be justified in sharing this confidential information about Alison in the public interest but may well be criticized later if it emerges that they knew about her situation but had not shared this information when approached.

Chapter 8

Case study – Christa

1 Which elements of the 'partnership list' do you think are present or might apply to the work with parents here?

There appear to be shared values and a shared goal in that the parents see the need for change and support with their parenting. Parents are encouraged by the social worker to contribute to the process. With the conference, information will be shared, and plans and decisions will be made in the presence of the parents, who appear to be choosing to enter into this work. Furthermore, the conference represents a formal framework for the work. Time will tell whether real trust and mutual confidence develops between the workers and parents – certainly this may be an issue for the Health Visitor and the school. Equity and issues of power will also need to be worked through if they are going to be seriously addressed.

2 Which of the four different approaches described by Morrison do you think are being adopted by each of the agencies involved?

The social worker appears to be operating within a Play fair or Developmental approach, encouraging full participation from the parents, and taking a practical view that the step-father, as a day-to-day carer for Christa has a right to be involved, and should be considered as having equal status as a parent for the purposes of being involved in the work. The Health Visitor may be working within a Strategic Adversarial approach, being wary of them as a result of her past experiences, and weighing up the potential losses and gains of her efforts. The school appears to be taking a Paternalistic approach, seeing themselves as having expert knowledge about parenting, for which the parents should be grateful. Their exasperation at the parents' lack of response to this illustrates that the school believes they know best and that their superior understanding of the situation confirms their belief that Christa should be removed from the care of the parents. The school's position is further demonstrated by them taking a narrow legalistic position about working with the stepfather, which is in contrast with the view of the social worker who sees the stepfather as an important figure in the household.

Chapter 9

Staying safe

Three subheadings of the aim for children of staying safe are that children should be safe from

- Accidental injury and death
- Bullying and discrimination
- Crime and anti-social behaviour.

1 What is your initial response to these targets?

They might be seen as very ambitious. Is it really possible to make absolutely certain that children do not incur any accidents, or are bullied or victims of crime?

Is there a preoccupation here with trying to eradicate all risk from children's lives?

Does the specific aim of keeping children safe from discrimination seem realistic when one considers how complex and intransigent are all forms of discrimination, linked as they are to powerful structural forces within society?

2 How do you think parents might try to make sure their children are safe from these things?

Parents may be overprotective of their children, not allowing them to play outside or walk to school. Parents may insist on chaperoning their children on excursions outside the house.

3 Can you see any tensions between these aims and other desired outcomes for children?

Where children are kept indoors, this might undermine the 'Be healthy' outcome. How does a parent, or society, balance possible risk to children against opportunities for development? Reports in the media express concern about the sedentary lifestyles of children who are not afforded opportunities to play outside because parents are worried about traffic or crime. One BBC report on a conference related to this quoted a Professor Mahdjoubi, of the University of the West of England who argued that a lack of outdoor exercise caused heart problems and diabetes (BBC News, 2007a). Here we see a potentially direct clash between two outcomes – in order to make absolutely certain children are safe, parents might keep them indoors for lengthy periods, thus severely undermining the provision for children of physical exercise, not to mention the emotional stimulation associated with playing creative or cooperative games with peers. Furthermore, if parents insist on driving their children to and from school, the impact on the environment, and global warming in particular, could also serve to undermine the quality of the future, a future which parents are trying to secure for their children by not allowing them to walk to and from school.

Bibliography

Advice Services Alliance. (2005), *What is parental responsibility?* [Internet]. London: Advice Services Alliance. Available from: www.advicenow.org.uk/go/livingtogether/feature_251.html [Accessed 14 January 2007].

Ahmad, B. (1989), 'Child care and ethnic minorities', in Kahan, B. (ed.), *Child Care Research, Policy and Practice*. London: Hodder & Stoughton, pp. 152–168.

Amicus/Community Practitioners' and Health Visitors' Association. (2006), *Health visiting service*. [Internet]. London: Amicus/CPHVA. Available from: www.amicus.org/cphva/Default.aspx?page=4 [Accessed 10 January 2007].

An Introduction to the Children Act 1989. (1989), London: HMSO.

BBC News. (2004), *Smacking ban 'will be unworkable'*. [Internet]. London: BBC News. Available from: http://news.bbc.co.uk/1/hi/health/4023271.stm [Accessed 12 July 2007].

BBC News. (2007a), *Children 'must have outside play'*. [Internet]. London: BBC News. Available from: http://news.bbc.co.uk/1/hi/education/5252746.stm [Accessed 7 October 2007].

BBC News. (2007b), *Lone parent benefits 'may change'*. [Internet]. London: BBC News. Available from: http://news.bbc.co.uk/1/hi/uk_politics/6312127.stm [Accessed 12 October 2007].

BBC News. (2007c), *Ministers rule out smacking ban*. [Internet]. London: BBC News. Available from: http://news.bbc.co.uk/1/hi/uk_politics/7061603.stm [Accessed 14 November 2007].

Berridge, D. (2000), *Placement Stability*. London: Department of Health.

Borland, M. (1998), 'Education for children in residential and foster care'. *Research in Education No. 63* [Internet]. Glasgow: Scottish Council for Research in Education. Available from: www.scre.ac.uk/rie/nl63/nl63borland.html [Accessed 21 June 2007].

Brandon, M., Howe, A., Dagley, V., Salter, C., Warren, C., and Black, J. (2006), *Evaluating the Common Assessment Framework and Lead Professional Guidance and Implementation in 2005–6*. London: DfES.

British Association for Adoption and Fostering. (2007), *The cost of foster care*. [Internet]. London: BAAF. Available from: www.baaf.org.uk/gi/campaigns/costfost.shtml [Accessed 20 June 2007].

Bronfenbrenner, U. (1979), *The Ecology of Human Development: Experiments by Nature and Design*. London: Harvard University Press.

Burden, T. (1998), *Social Policy and Welfare*. London: Pluto Press.

Byrne, T., and Padfield, C. (1985), *Social Services Made Simple*. 3rd edn. London: Heinemann.

Cawson, P., Wattam, C., Brooker, S., and Kelly, G. (2000), *Child Maltreatment in the UK: A Study of the Prevalence of Child Abuse and Neglect*. London: NSPCC.

Clark, M., and Waller, T. (eds). (2007), *Early Childhood Education and Care: Policy and Practice*. London: Sage Publications.

Clark, P. (1993), 'A typology of multidisciplinary education in gerontology and geriatrics: are we really doing what we say we are?' *Journal of Interprofessional Care*, 7, (3), 217–227.

Creighton, S., and Tissier, G. (2003), *Child killings in England and Wales*. [Internet]. London: NSPCC. Available from: www.nspcc.org.uk/inform/research/briefings/childkillingsinenglandandwales_ifega45948.html. [Accessed 22 June 2007].

Daines, R., Lyon, K., and Parsloe, P. (1990), *Aiming for Partnership*. Ilford, Essex: Barnardo's.

Daniels, H. (2007), *Patterns of Pay: Results of the Annual Survey of Hours and Earnings 1997–2007*. London: Office for National Statistics.

David, T. (ed.), (1996), *Working Together for Young Children: Multi-Professionalism in Action*. London: Routledge.

Department for Constitutional Affairs. (2006), *A Guide to the Human Rights Act 1998*. 3rd edn. London: Department for Constitutional Affairs.

Department of Education Northern Ireland. (1999), *Pastoral Care in Schools: Child Protection*. Bangor, County Down: Department of Education Northern Ireland.

DfCSF (Department for Children, Schools and Families). (2007a), *Children Looked After in England (Including Adoption and Care Leavers) Year Ending 31 March 2007*. London: DfCSF.

DfCSF (Department for Children, Schools and Families). (2007b), *The Children's Plan: Building Brighter Futures*. Norwich: Stationery Office.

DfCSF (Department for Children, Schools and Families). (2007c), *Referrals, Assessments and Children and Young People Who Are Subject of a Child Protection Plan or Are on Child Protection Registers England, Year Ending 31 March 2007*. London: DfCSF.

DfEE (Department for Education and Employment). (2000), *The National Curriculum Handbook for Primary Teachers in England, Key Stages 1 and 2*. London: Stationery Office.

DfEE and DH (Department for Education and Employment and Department of Health). (2000), *Education of Young People in Public Care: Guidance*. London: DfEE and DH.

DfES (Department for Education and Skills). (2001), *Special Educational Needs Code of Practice*. London: DfES.

DfES (Department for Education and Skills). (2003), *Every Child Matters: The Green Paper*. London: Stationery Office.

DfES (Department for Education and Skills). (2004a), *Every Child Matters: Change for Children*. London: DfES.

DfES (Department for Education and Skills). (2004b), *Every Child Matters: Change for Children in the Criminal Justice System*. London: Stationery Office.

DfES (Department for Education and Skills). (2004c), *Every Child Matters: The Next Steps*. London: DfES.

DfES (Department for Education and Skills). (2005a), *Background on the voluntary and community sector*. [Internet]. London: DfES. Available from: www.everychildmatters.gov.uk/strategy/voluntaryandcommunity [Accessed 11 January 2007].

DfES (Department for Education and Skills). (2005b), *Children's social services*. [Internet]. London: DfES. Available from: www.everychildmatters.gov.uk/socialcare/socialservices [Accessed 11 January 2007].

DfES (Department for Education and Skills). (2005c), *Housing department*. [Internet]. London: DfES. Available from: www.everychildmatters.gov.uk/socialcare/housing [Accessed 11 January 2007].

DfES (Department for Education and Skills). (2005d), *What is a lead professional?* [Internet]. London: DfES. Available from: www.everychildmatters.gov.uk/deliveringservices/leadprofessional/whatisaleadprofessional [Accessed 23 May 2007].

DfES (Department for Education and Skills). (2006a), *Care Matters: Transforming the Lives of Children in Care*. Norwich: Stationery Office.

DfES (Department for Education and Skills). (2006b), *The Common Assessment Framework for children and young people: practitioner's guide*. [Internet]. London: DfES. Available from: www.everychildmatters.gov.uk/_files/F7 1B9C32893BE5D30342A2896043C234.pdf [Accessed 9 May 2007].

DfES (Department for Education and Skills). (2006c), *Improving Behaviour and Attendance: Guidance on Exclusion from Schools and Pupil Referral Units*. Nottingham: DfES Publications.

DfES (Department for Education and Skills). (2006d), *Information Sharing: Practitioner's Guide*. Nottingham: DfES Publications.

DfES (Department for Education and Skills). (2006e), *Safeguarding Children and Safer Recruitment in Education*. Nottingham: DfES Publications.

DfES (Department for Education and Skills). (2006f), *Setting up multi-agency services.* [Internet]. London: DfES. Available from: www.everychildmatters.gov.uk/deliveringservices/multiagencyworking [accessed 6 February 2007].

DfES (Department for Education and Skills). (2006g), *Supporting Looked After Learners: A Practical Guide for School Governors*. Nottingham: DfES Publications.

DfES (Department for Education and Skills). (2006h), *What to Do if You're Worried a Child Is Being Abused*. Nottingham: DfES Publications.

DfES (Department for Education and Skills). (2006i), *Working Together to Safeguard Children: A Guide to Inter-Agency Working to Safeguard and Promote the Welfare of Children*. Norwich: Stationery Office.

DfES (Department for Education and Skills). (2007a), *Care Matters: Time for Change*. Norwich: Stationery Office.

DfES (Department for Education and Skills). (2007b), *Common Assessment Framework*. [Internet]. London: DfES. Available from: www.everychildmatters.gov.uk/deliveringservices/caf [Accessed 22 May 2007].

DfES (Department for Education and Skills). (2007c), *The Early Years Foundation Stage: Setting the Standards for Learning, Development and Care for Children from Birth to Five*. Nottingham: DfES Publications.

DfES (Department for Education and Skills). (2007d), *Learning mentors – removing barriers to learning and supporting achievement.* [Internet]. London: DfES. Available from: www.standards.dfes.gov.uk/learningmentors [Accessed 9 January 2007].

DfES (Department for Education and Skills). (2007e), *Outcome Indicators for Looked After Children: Twelve Months to 30 September 2006, England*. London: DfES.

DfES and QCA (Department for Education and Skills and Qualifications and Curriculum Authority). (2004), *The National Curriculum Handbook for Secondary Teachers in England, Key Stages 3 and 4*. London: DfES and QCA.

DH (Department of Health). (1995), *The Challenge of Partnership in Child Protection: Practice Guide*. London: HMSO.

DH (Department of Health). (2000a), *Assessing Children in Need and Their Families: Practice Guidance*. London: Stationery Office.

DH (Department of Health). (2000b), *The Child's World: Assessing Children in Need*. London: Department of Health.

DH (Department of Health). (2001), *Outcome Indicators for Looked After Children: Year Ending 30 September 2000*. London: Department of Health.

DH (Department of Health). (2002), *Women's Mental Health: Into the Mainstream – Strategic Development of Mental Health Care for Women*. London: Department of Health.

DH (Department of Health). (2006), *The Caldicott Guardian Manual 2006*. London: DH.

DH, DfEE and HO (Department of Health, Department of Education and Employment and Home Office). (2000), *Framework for the Assessment of Children in Need and Their Families*. London: Stationery Office.

DH and DfES (Department of Health and Department for Education and Skills). (2002), *School Nursing*. London: Stationery Office.

DH, HO and DfEE (Department of Health, Home Office and Department for Education and Employment). (1999), *Working Together to Safeguard Children*. London: Stationery Office.

DHSSPS (Department of Health, Social Services and Public Safety). (2003), *Co-operating to Safeguard Children*. Belfast: DHSSPS.

DHSSPS (Department of Health, Social Services and Public Safety). (2007a), *Care Matters in Northern Ireland: A Bridge to a Better Future*. Belfast: DHSSPS.

DHSSPS (Department of Health, Social Services and Public Safety). (2007b), *Protecting children is a shared responsibility – Goggins*. Press Release. [Internet]. Belfast: DHSSPS. Available from: http://archive.nics.gov.uk/hss/070115a-hss.htm [Accessed 14 October 2007].

Foot, M. (2004), 'Asbo absurdities'. *The Guardian* [Internet]. 1 December 2004. Available from: http://society.guardian.co.uk/societyguardian/story/0,,1362899,00.html [Accessed 12 October 2007].

Foot, M. (2005), 'A triumph of hearsay and hysteria'. *The Guardian* [Internet]. 5 April 2005. Available from: www.guardian.co.uk/comment/story/0,,1452197,00.html [Accessed 12 October 2007].

Freeman, M. (2002), 'Children's rights ten years after ratification', in Franklin, B. (ed.), *The New Handbook of Children's Rights*. London: Routledge, pp. 97–117.

Gibbons, J., Conroy, S., and Bell, C. (1995), *Operating the Child Protection System: A Study of Child Protection Practices in English Local Authorities*. London: HMSO.

Greco, V., Sloper, P., Webb, R., and Beecham, J. (2005), *An Exploration of Different Models of Multi-Agency Partnerships in Key Worker Services for Disabled Children: Effectiveness and Costs*. London: DfES.

Green, K. (2006), *Reforming the child support agency*. [Internet]. London: Child Poverty Action Group. Available from:_____www.childpoverty.org.uk/info/briefings_policy/CPAG_Child_Support_Agency_letter_%20for_Henshaw_Review.pdf [Accessed 9 May 2007].

Hagele, D. (2005), 'The impact of maltreatment on the developing child'. *North Carolina Medical Journal*, 66, (5), 356–359.

Hanvey, C. (2003), *The lessons we never learn*. [Internet]. Manchester: Guardian Unlimited. Available from: http://society.guardian.co.uk/climbie/comment/0,,882568,00.html [Accessed 22 June 2007].

Haslam, D. (2006), *So, You Want To Be a GP?* London: Royal College of General Practitioners.

Hayden, C. (2005), 'More than a piece of paper?: personal education plans and 'looked after' children in England'. *Child and Family Social Work*, 10, (4), 343–352.

HC (House of Commons) 653. (2004a), *The Bichard Inquiry Report*. London: Stationery Office.

HC (House of Commons) 04/23. (2004b), *Poverty: Measures and Targets*. London: Stationery Office.

HC (House of Commons) 40-I. (2005), *Every Child Matters Volume 1: Report, Together with Formal Minutes*. London: Stationery Office.

Her Majesty's Inspectorate of Constabulary. (1999), *Child Protection: HMIC Thematic Report*. London: HMIC.

Hirsch, D. (2006), *What Will It Take to End Child Poverty? Firing on All Cylinders*. York: Joseph Rowntree Foundation.

HO and DH (Home Office and Department of Health). (1992), *Memorandum of Good Practice on Video Recorded Interviews with Child Witnesses for Criminal Proceedings*. London: HMSO.

Horgan, G. (2005), 'Child poverty in Northern Ireland: the limits of welfare-to-work policies'. *Social Policy and Administration*, 39, (1), 49–64.

Hunt, R. (2000), *The Educational Performance of Children in Need and Children Looked After*. London: Department of Health.

Jackson, S. (1987a), 'Residential care and education'. *Children & Society* 2, (4), 335–350.

Jackson, S. (1987b), *The Education of Children in Care*. Bristol: University of Bristol.

Jackson, S., and Sachdev, D. (2001), *Better Education, Better Futures: Research, Practice and the Views of Young People in Public Care*. Ilford, Essex: Barnardo's.

Joughin, C., and Law, C. (2005), *Evidence to Inform the National Service Framework for Children, Young People and Maternity Services*. London: Department for Education and Skills and Department of Health.

Kirby, P. (2003), *Child Labour in Britain 1750–1870*. Basingstoke: Palgrave Macmillan.

Laming, L. (2003), *The Victoria Climbié Inquiry*. London: Crown Copyright.

Lohde, L. (2004), 'Will the poor measure up?' *The Guardian* [Internet]. 18 March 2004. Available from: http://society.guardian.co.uk/socialexclusion/comment/0,,1171392,00.html [Accessed 12 October 2007].

Marsh, P., and Crow, G. (1998), *Family Group Conferences in Child Welfare*. Oxford: Blackwell Publishers.

McGettrick, B. (1995), *Values and Educating the Whole Person*. Dundee, Scotland: Scottish Consultative Council on the Curriculum.

McTernan, E., and Godfrey, A. (2006), 'Children's services planning in Northern Ireland: developing a planning model to address rights and needs'. *Child Care in Practice*, 12, (3), 219–240.

Mitchison, R. (2000), *The Old Poor Law in Scotland: The Experience of Poverty, 1574–1845*. Edinburgh: Edinburgh University Press.

Morrison, T. (1991), 'Partnership, collaboration and change under the Children Act', in Adcock, M., and White, R. (eds), *Significant Harm: Its Management and Outcome*. Croydon: Significant Publications, pp. 85–100.

Mullender, A., and Morley, R. (eds). (1994), *Children Living with Domestic Violence: Putting Men's Abuse of Women on the Child Care Agenda*. London: Whiting & Birch.

National Assembly for Wales. (2001), *Guidance on the Education of Children Looked After by Local Authorities*. Cardiff: National Assembly for Wales.

National Assembly for Wales and Home Office. (2001), *Framework for the Assessment of Children in Need and Their Families*. London: Stationery Office.

National Commission of Inquiry into the Prevention of Child Abuse. (1996), *Childhood Matters: Report of the National Commission of Inquiry into the Prevention of Child Abuse, Volume 1: The Report*. London: Stationery Office.

National Probation Service for England and Wales. (2005), *National Probation Service for England and Wales*. London: National Probation Service for England and Wales.

NHS Careers. (2006), *NHS careers*. [Internet]. Available from: www.nhscareers.nhs.uk/index.shtml [Accessed 10 January 2007].

NSPCC (National Society for the Prevention of Cruelty to Children). (2006), *Leaving children at home alone*. [Internet]. London: NSPCC. Available from: www.nspcc.org.uk/helpandadvice/parentsandcarers/homealone/homealone_wda35965.html [Accessed 6 June 2007].

O'Connor, J. (1993), *The Workhouses of Ireland*. Blackrock, County Dublin: Anvil Books.

ODPM (Office of the Deputy Prime Minister). (2004), *Guidance on Arms Length Management of Local Authority Housing*. London: Office of the Deputy Prime Minister.

Office for National Statistics. (2004), *The Health of Children and Young People*. London: Office for National Statistics.

OFMDFM (Office of the First Minister and Deputy First Minister. (2006), *Our Children and Young People – Our Pledge: A Ten Year Strategy for Children and Young People in Northern Ireland 2006–2016*. Belfast: OFMDFM.

Ofsted. (2001), *Raising Achievement of Children in Public Care*. London: Ofsted.

Ofsted. (2007a), *Annual Performance Assessment: Handbook for Procedures for 2007*. London: Ofsted.

Ofsted. (2007b), *Annual Performance Assessment 2007 and Joint Area Reviews: Update on Data Issues: June 2007*. London: Ofsted.

Palmer, G., MacInnes, T., and Kenway, P. (2007), *Monitoring Poverty and Social Exclusion 2007*. York: Joseph Rowntree Foundation.

Parton, N. (1985), *The Politics of Child Abuse*. London: MacMillan Publishers.

Petrie, P., Boddy, J., Cameron, C., Heptinstall, E., McQuail, S., Simon, A., and Wigfall, V. (2005), *Pedagogy – a Holistic, Personal Approach to Work with Children and Young People, Across Services*. London: Thomas Coram Research Institute.

Pragnell, C. (2002), *The Cleveland Child sexual abuse scandal*. [Internet]. Northampton: University of Northampton. Available from: www.childrenuk.co.uk/choct2002/choct2002/pragnell%20cleveland%20abuse.html [Accessed 2 May 2007].

Prospects. (2006), *Learning mentor: salary and conditions*. [Internet]. Manchester: Graduate Prospects Ltd. Available from: www.prospects.ac.uk/cms/ShowPage/Home_page/Explore_types_of_jobs/Types_of_Job/p!eipa L?state=showocc&idno=898&pageno=2 [Accessed 12 June 2007].

Royal College of Midwives. (2006), *What does a midwife do?* [Internet]. London: Royal College of Midwives. Available from: www.rcm.org.uk/career/pages/introduction.php?id=3#what [Accessed 10 January 2007].

Scottish Executive. (2004), *Protecting Children and Young People: Framework for Standards*. Edinburgh: Scottish Executive.

Scottish Executive. (2005a), *Getting It Right for Every Child: Proposals for Action*. Edinburgh: Scottish Executive.

Scottish Executive. (2005b), *Safe and Well: A Handbook for Staff, Schools and Education Authorities*. Edinburgh: Scottish Executive.

Shelter. (2005), *Who gets priority*. [Internet]. London: Shelter. Available from: http://england.shelter.org.uk/advice/advice-3174.cfm#wipLive-9987-2 [Accessed 19 April 2007].

Smith, P, Cowie, H and Blades, M. (2003), *Understanding Children's Development*. 4th edn. Oxford: Blackwell Publishers.

Social Exclusion Unit. (2003), *A Better Education for Children in Care*. London: Social Exclusion Unit/Office of the Deputy Prime Minister.

Social Services Inspectorate and Ofsted. (1995), *The Education of Children Who Are Looked After by Local Authorities*. London: Social Services Inspectorate and Ofsted.

Social Work Inspection Agency. (2006), *Extraordinary Lives: Creating a Positive Future for Looked After Children and Young People in Scotland*. Edinburgh: Social Work Inspection Agency.

Stainton Rogers, W. (1989), 'Effective co-operation in child protection work', in Morgan, S., and Righton, P. (eds), *Child Care: Concerns and Conflicts*. London: Hodder & Stoughton, pp. 82–94. Reproduced by permission of Hodder & Stoughton Ltd.

Stepney, P. (2005), 'Mission impossible? Critical practice in social work'. *British Journal of Social Work*, 36, (8), 1289–1307.

Teachernet. (2007), *Example of a child protection policy*. [Internet]. London: DfES. Available from: www.teacher-net.gov.uk/wholeschool/familyandcommunity/childprotection/schools/examplepolicy/ [Accessed 11 June 2007].

The Concise Oxford Dictionary of Current English. (1976), 6th edn. Oxford: OUP/Clarendon Press.

The Who Cares? Trust. (1999), *Equal Chances: Improving the Education of Looked After Children and Young People*. London: The Who Cares? Trust and Calouste Gulbenkian Foundation.

The Who Cares? Trust. (2003), *Education Matters*. London: The Who Cares? Trust.

Waterhouse, L. (1989), 'In defence of residential care', in Morgan, S., and Righton, P. (eds), *Child Care: Concerns and Conflicts*. London: Hodder & Stoughton, pp. 95–111.

Webb, S., and Webb, B. (1963), *English Poor Law History Part 1: The Old Poor Law*. London: Frank Cass and Company.

Welsh Assembly Government. (2004), *Children and Young People: Rights to Action*. Cardiff: Welsh Assembly Government.

Welsh Assembly Government. (2007a), *Safeguarding Children: Working Together under the Children Act 2004*. Cardiff: Welsh Assembly Government.

Welsh Assembly Government. (2007b), *Safeguarding Children in Education: The Role of Local Authorities and Governing Bodies under the Education Act 2002*. Cardiff: Welsh Assembly Government.

Whitney, B. (1993), *The Children Act and Schools: A Guide to Good Practice*. London: Kogan Page.

Wigfall, V., and Moss, P. (2001), *More Than the Sum of Its Parts? A Study of a Multi-Agency Child Care Network*. London: National Children's Bureau.

Williams, R. (1961), *The Long Revolution*. London: Chatto and Windus.

Wilson, V., and Pirrie, A. (2000), *Multidisciplinary Teamworking: Indicators of Good Practice*. Edinburgh: The Scottish Council for Research in Education.

Youth Justice Board. (2006), *Youth offending teams – who are they? what do they do?* [Internet]. London: Youth Justice Board for England and Wales. Available from: www.yjb.gov.uk/en-gb/yjs/YouthOffendingTeams [Accessed 11 January 2007].

Index